AF755119

VARIOUS INTERPRETATIONS
OF
THE ṚBHU—HYMNS IN THE ṚGVEDA

SRI GARIB DASS ORIENTAL SERIES NO.—130

Various Interpretations of the Ṛbhu—hymns in the Ṛgveda

[*From* Sāyaṇācārya (14th century A.D. To Prof. Louis Renou (1965)]

Translated into English and compiled by

Dr. Miss G.V. Davane

SRI SATGURU PUBLICATIONS
A Division of
INDIAN BOOKS CENTRE
DELHI-INDIA

Published by :
SRI SATGURU PUBLICATIONS
A Division of
INDIAN BOOKS CENTRE
Indological & Oriental Publishers
40/5, Shakti Nagar
Delhi-110007
(INDIA)

All Rights Reserved. No part of this work covered by the copyright hereon may be reproduced or copied in any means—graphics, electronics or mechanical including photocopying, microfiche reading without written permission from the publishers.

First Edition :—Delhi 1991

ISBN-81-7030-292-7

Printed in India:
At Sainion Printary
Delhi-110032.

Respectfully Dedicated
to
my teacher and a renowned Indologist
Dr. R.N. Dandekar,
who inspired me to study the Ṛgveda and initiated me into the comparative and critical method of studying it.

Miss G.V. Davane

Contents

*English Rendering Published by Permission.

Preface

For research on the Ṛbhus I had to study critically the eleven Ṛbhus-hymns in the Ṛgveda first. While studying these hymns I could find in the library of the University of Bombay and in the library of the Bhandarkar Oriental Research Institute, Pune, various German and French translations of the hymns by eminent scholars. For my own purpose I rendered all these translations into English. I had already prepared Sāyaṇa's translation on the basis of his commentary in Sanskrit. To this I added English rendering of Marathi translation given by Pandit Siddheshvarshastri Chitrav.

Then I compiled all these English-renderings together. Now English translations of these hymns by Prof. H.H. Wilson, Prof. R.T.H. Griffith and Prof. S.A. Upadhyay have been published already. English translation of 3 Ṛbhu-hymns by H.D. Velankar has also been published. I have included all these in my present compilation. I feel the whole together can present a thorough and interesting perspective of the Ṛbhu-hymns as understood from 14th century A. D. (Sāyaṇācārya) to 1965 (Prof. Louis Renou). While going through these various interpretations one is struck by the divergence of interpretation in many cases. It is very interesting to note how one and the same quarter, hemistich or stanza has been understood variously by different scholars. e.g. I 161, 8; III 60, 1; IV 33, 2d etc.

Now German and French translations of these hymns are not accessible to many Sanskrit scholars in India. Some of them may be knowing German only, others may be knowing

French only, while many may not be knowing either of the two languages. A very few eminent Indologists, who have mastered both languages are extremely busy and hence they connot find time for translating such material into English. Since I have already rendered this material into English I feel it is my duty to make it available to scholars working in the field of the Vedic literature. By publishing this book I hope to help the research-scholars towards a better understanding of the obscure but interesting myth of the Ṛbhus.

Moreover some of these German and French books are very old and extremely rare. The copies of the books in the library of the University of Bombay, which I have been using are in a precarious condition. Hence by publishing my English rendering of the translations of the Ṛbhu-hymns I shall be helping towards the preservation of at least a little portion from these precious rare books.

All these translations have been arranged in a chronological order. Here I must explain that though Ludwig's German translation has been published earlier (1876) than Grassmann's German translation (1881) I have put Grassmann's earlier. This is so for the simple reason that Ludwig's notes (Volume IV) were published later in 1881 and in these notes Ludwig has often referred to Grassmann.

I must also explain that I have dropped purely metrical details from Prof. Oldenberg's '*Die Ṛgveda Noten*'. These details are not pertinent to my theme. Therefore I have tried to save my labour here.

The edition of Marathi translation by Pandit Siddheshvarshastri Chitrav, which I have used is dated 1969 : but his first edition was published in 1929. Threfore I have put his translation immediately after Prof. Geldner's.

This book is a compilation of useful material from various sources. For convenience of study Sanskrit text of the eleven hymns has been prefixed to this book.

Now it is my pleasant duty to express my sincere sense of gratitude to the following persons and institutions for having allowed me to publish my English rendering of the original material :—

(1) The President and Fellows of the Harvard College, Harvard University Press, Massachusettes, (German translation of the hymns by Prof. Karl Geldner HOS Volumes 33, 34, 1951).

(2) Mrs. Colette Caillat, Director, Institute of Asia, Indian Civilization, 22 Avenue of President Wilson, 75116, PARIS and Mrs. Renou (French translation of the hymns by Prof. Louis Renou - Eludés Védiques et Paniniennés Volume XV—Editions E.De Boccard, 1 Rue De Medicins, 1 Paris 1965).

(3) Prof. S.A. Upadhyay, Bharatiya Vidya Bhavan, Bombay (English translation of the hymns by Prof. S.A. Upadhyay—Bhāratīya Vidyā—Volume 22 Nos 1 to 4, 1962) English translation of VII 48 by Prof. H.D. Velankar—Ṛgveda Maṇḍala VII, Bharatiya Vidya Bhavan, 1963 – English translation of IV 33—Ṛksūktaśatī, Bharatiya Vidya Bhavan, 1972).

(4) Assistant Registrar, Bombay University Press, Bombay (English translation of III 60 by Prof. H.D. Velankar—Ṛgveda Maṇḍala III, University of Bombay, Bombay 1968).

(5) Mr. V.S. Chitrav, Bharatiya Caritra Kośa Maṇḍala, Pune-411004 (Marathi translation of the Ṛgveda by Pandit Siddheshwarshastri Chitrav, Bhāratīya Caritra Kośa Maṇḍala, Pune, 1969).

(6) Ajanta Books International, Delhi (English rendering of Prof. F. Neve's French translation by Dr. Miss G.V. Davane 'An Essay on The Myth of the Ṛbhus'—Chapter V, 1985).

Mr. A.C. Tikekar, Chief Librarian, Library of the University of Bombay, allowed me to have the rare books on my table in the library for a long time and helped me in all ways. It would not have been possible for me to do this work but for the valuable help rendered to me by him and by the entire staff of the library. I am heartily thankful to all of them for this.

I am highly obliged to Mr. V.L. Manjul, Chief Librarian, Library of the Bhandarkar Oriental Research Institute, Pune, for having helped me in all possible ways throughout the progress of this work.

I am indeed short of words in expressing my heartfelt gratitude to Dr. R.V. Paranjpe, Retired Professor of German, University of Bombay and to Dr. Mrs. Mangala Sirdeshpande, Head of the Department of French, Univerity of Bombay. Both these friends of mine are not familiar with the original Sanskrit text. Even then Dr. Paranjpe was kind enough to go through my English renderings of German translations and Dr. Mrs. Sirdeshpande did me a similar favour by going through my English renderings of French translations.

Finally I hope students of Sanskrit and the research-scholars working in the field of the Vedic Literature will find this book useful to them.

June 1991

Dr. Miss G.V. Davane

About the Editions used for the English Renderings

I. Sāyaṇa (14th Century A.D.)—Ṛgveda Saṁhita Published by the Vaidika Saṁśodhana Maṇḍala, Pune 411030, 1951.

II. F. Nève—Original French Translation, Paris, *1847*. English Rendering—'The Myth of the Ṛbhus'—Miss G.V. Davane, Ajanta Publications, Delhi 110007, 1985.

III. S.A. Langlois—'Ṛgveda, Livre de Hymnes', Librarie de Fermin Depot, Freve, *1848*.

IV. H.H. Wilson—First Ed *1856*. Reprint—Cosmo Publications, 24B, Ansari Road, New Delhi, 110002, 1971.

V. H. Grassmann—'Der Ṛgveda' Leipzeig, F.A. Brochhaus, *1876*, *1877*.

VI. A. Ludwig—'Der Ṛgveda' Verlag Von F. Temsky, Prag, Vol. I *1876*; Vol. IV *1881*.

VII. R.T.H. Griffith—First Ed - Banaras 1889; Revised Reprint Motilal Banarasidass, Delhi, 110007, 1976.

VIII. H. Oldenberg—'Ṛgveda Noten', Weidmannsche Buchhandlung, Berlin, Vol. I *1909*; Vol. II *1912*.

IX. A. Hillebrandt—'Lieder des Ṛgveda'—Vandenhoech and Ruprecht, Göttingen, *1923*.

X. K.F. Geldner—'Dev Ṛgveda'—Firt Ed. *1923*; Third Ed—Oxford University Press, HOS Vol. 33, 34, Leipzeig, Cambrige, Massachusetts, 02138, 1951.

XI. S. Chitrav—Morathi Translation of the Ṛgveda, Bhāratiya Caritra Kośa Maṇḍala, Pune 411004, First Ed. *1929*, Revised Ed. 1969.

XII. S.A. Upadhyay—Bhāratīya Vidyā, Vol. 22, Nos. 1 to 4, Bharatiya Vidya Bhavan, Bombay 400007, *1962*.

XIII. H.D. Velankar—Ṛgveda, Maṇḍala VII' Bharatiya Vidya Bhavan, Bombay 400007, *1963*; 'Ṛgveda, Mandola III', University of Bombay, Bombay 400032, *1968*; 'Ṛksūktaśati' Bharaṭiya Vidya Bhavan, Bombay 400007, *1972*.

XIV. L. Renou—'Etudés Védiques et Paniniennés' Vol. XV E.E. Boccard, 1 Rue De Medicins, Paris, *1965*.

A List of Abbreviations

A. B.	Aitareya Brāhmaṇa
As. Gr. Su	Āśvalāyana Gṛhya Sūtra
As S.S.	Aśvalāyana Śrauta Sūtra
AV	Atharva Veda
Br. Dev	Bṛhaddevatā
EVP	Etudés Védiques et Paniniennés
Kat S. S.	Kātyāyana Śrauta Sūtra
Kath	Kāṭhaka Saṁhitā
Lat. S.S.	Lātyāyana Śrauta Sūtra
Nigh	Nighaṇṭu
RV	Ṛgveda
San Br.	Sānkhyāyana Brāhmaṇa
San. Sr. Su	Sānkhyāyana Śrauta Sūtra
S. B.	Śatapatha Brāhmaṇa
Tai. Br. (T.B.)	Taittirīya Brāhmaṇa
Tai Up	Taittirīya Upaniṣad
Tan. Mah. B.	Tāṇḍya Mahābrāhmaṇa
T. S.	Taittirīya Saṁhitā
V. S.	Vājasaneyī Saṁhitā

I

Translation According to Sāyaṇa's Sanskrit Commentary

I 20

(1) *Tr.* This song of praise, bestowing choice-treasures, has been prepared by the priests with their own mouth in order to please the divinity viz : the group of Ṛbhus, being born.

(2) *Tr.* (The Ṛbhus), who, by means of their mind obtained for Indra the two Haris, harnessed by mere word, have pervaded (our) sacrifice by means of their acts.

(3) *Tr.* For the Nāsatyas i.e. the Aśvins they carved a chariot, moving around, comfortable (to sit). They obtained a cow pouring milk.

(4) Tr. The straightforward Ṛbhus, of truthful chants, with neverfailing efficiency, made their old parents young again.

(5) *Tr.* O Ṛbhus, your exhilarating Soma-draughts are united with Indra in company of the Maruts and with the shining Ādityas.

(6) Tr. The carving art of god Tvaṣṭṛ produced that new cup. (His pupils) the Ṛbhus divided it fourfold.

(7) Tr. O Ṛbhus, you (being glorified) by our praises give to our sacrificer the three types i.e. the highest, the mediocre and the lowest of treasures and accomplish our sacrificial works, put in groups of seven each, repeated thrice.

Note : *Agnyādhāna* with others forms one group. *Aupāsana-homa, with* 6 others forms the second group and *Agniṣṭoma, with 6 more forms the* third group.

(8) *Tr.* The accomplishers of sacrifice (i.e. the (Ṛbhus) held up their lives (i.e. they became immortal). By means of good works (of procuring the material which served as a means of sacrifice) they stood amongst the gods and secured a share in the sacrifice.

I 110

(1) *Tr.* O Ṛbhus, the (ritualistic) work, which was often performed by me formerly, the same is being performed again. The sweetest prayer is being recited for the praise-worthy ones. This (surging) Soma-juice has been prepared so as to be sufficient for all gods. Be pleased with (the drinking of) the juice that has been offered, in the fire with the call' svāhā.

(2) Tr. O Ṛbhus, you immature forefathers of mine, who had gone (to the forest for performing penance) as you were desirous of the enjoyable Soma-juice, you Sons of Sudhanvan, by the greatness (of your penance) you came to the house of the sacrificer pressing Soma and making gifts *Or* you came to the house of Savitṛ i.e. to the Third libation.

(3) *Tr.* When you came to the house of Savitṛ, that cannot be hidden, requesting him for the expected (Soma-drink), he gave you immortality, since under orders from the gods you had divided fourfold the cup for drinking Soma, which was prepared by Tvaṣṭṛ.

Note : *The* Ṛbhus made one cup of Tvaṣṭṛ fourfold i.e. they divided it into *Hotṛ-camasa*, *Adhvaryu-casmasa* etc.

(4) *Tr*. The Ṛbhus) having quickly performed (the ritualistic and other) actions along with the priests, though mortal, attained immortality. The Sons of Sudhanvan, possessing the brilliance or the intelligence of the sun, were equipped with i.e. were worthy of the oblations, by means of (Agniṣṭoma and other) seasonal rituals (to be performed) during (the part of) the year i.e. during the spring etc.

(5) *Tr*. The Ṛbhus, asking for the praiseworthy Some-food, desiring for the sacrificial food i.e. the Soma amongst the gods, measured out with a sharp instrument the one single cup, which was trying (to be of use in the work of oblation), so that it could be made fourfold, just as one measures a piece of land. That time they were praised by the sages standing by the side.

(6) *Tr*. With knowledge we offer praise unto the Ṛbhus, connected with the mid-region, leaders of the sacrifice *or* the leaders of the mid-region, just as one offers clarified butter through the ladle (according to the precepts), to the Ṛbhus, who have secured the skill in swimming that is possessed by this (sun), the father (of the world), and have acquired the food of the heaven i.e. the Soma (by means of their work).

(7) *Tr*. Ṛbhu, the more praised one on account of his strength, is our lord *or* Indra is our Ṛbhu. With the help of nourishments and treasures he makes abodes for us. May he be the giver of our nourishments *or* treasures. O Ṛbhu and others, O gods‘ through your favour may we, on an auspicious day, overcome the armies of the enemies who do not press Soma.

(8) *Tr*. Ṛbhus, you glued the hide on the cow and then united the mother with the calf. O Sons of Aṅgiras, leaders of sacrifice, with your desire to do good works, you made the old parents young again.

(9) *Tr*. O Indra, accompanied by the Ṛbhus, give us food at the feast of the food *or* protect us with the horses in the battle. Be pleased to give us choice-treasures. May Mitra,

Varuṇa, Aditi, Sindhu, the Earth and the Heaven honour this wish of ours.

I 111

(1) *Tr.* Accomplishing the work through excellent knowledge, the Ṛbhus fabricated (for the Aśvins) a chariot rolling smoothly or a chariot with good wheels. They fashioned the two Haris, possessed of splendid wealth *or* possessed of splendid strength, the carriers of Indra. They bestowed on their parents a life possessed of youth. They created for the calf its mother, staying by its side.

(2) *Tr.* O Ṛbhus, for the sake of our sacrifice produce bright food in the form of oblation. For our ritual and for our strength fashion food, associated with good progeny. For strength bestow well upon us such a treasure, with which we shall dwell happily with our progeny, all made up of heroes.

(3) *Tr.* O Ṛbhus. O leaders (of sacrifice), fashion for us food *or* wealth, fashion for our progeny, or for our chariot, fashion food *or* wealth (fit) for our horses: May all people always honour our victorious wealth. May we (overpower) in battle the attacking enemy, whether a relative or a foe.

(4) *Tr.* I invoke the great Indra for protection. I invoke the Ṛbhus, the Maruts for a draught of Soma. Both Mitrāvaruṇā and the Aśvins (I invoke for the Soma-drink). May they inspire us to gain wealth (for the sake of ritual) and for winning over the enemies.

(5) Tr. May Ṛbhus sharpen wealth for war. May Vāja, vanquisher of the enemies in battle, protect us. May Mitra, Varuṇa, Aditi, Sindhu, the Earth and the Heaven honour that (demand of ours).

I 161

Introductory note

The Ṛbhus are the three sons of Sudhanvan, Ṛbhu, Vibhvan and Vāja. Though human, they attained godhead through their good work and then began to drink the Soma at the ritual. God Agni, who was sent to them by the gods observed them, who were looking alike. He assumed a similar form and being the fourth amongst them he too started drinking. The Ṛbhus saw him, who had arrived there. Seeing him as having a similar form and hence being unable to distinguish him from themselves, they express doubts amongst themselves as follows :

(1) Tr. "Has the best i.e., the eldest or the youngest of us come here ? Or is the duty of a messenger being performed i.e. Has a messenger of the gods come to us ?" (How to decide this) that we are talking about ?" (Having come to the conclusion that the particular one was the stranger, to him they say,—) "O brother Agni, we are not blaming the cup, which springs from a great family (being produced by Tvaṣṭṛ). We are speaking about the attainment of the wooden (cup)."

(2) Tr. (Agni replies) 'Make one cup into four'. So have the gods said to you. O Sons of Sudhanvan. I have come to tell you of this (as a means of attaining godhead). 'If you do so, you will be worthy of sacrifice along with the gods ?' (so have they said).

(3) *Tr.* (The Ṛbhus speak) O god Agni, the works about which they (i.e. the gods) have said viz.—One horse is to be created (from another). A chariot is to be prepared. A cow is to be fashioned. The two parents, that have become aged are to be rejuvenated.—O brother, having performed all these works, we shall come (to the gods) *Or* The seer says to the Ṛbhus, "A horse is to be made (from another)......rejuvenated. Having performed all these works, we shall come to the gods." So you said.

(4) Tr. O Ṛbhus, when you had done that work you asked, "Where is that messenger, who had come to us ?" When Tvaṣṭṛ saw the four cups prepared, immediately he annointed himself among the women i.e. thought himself to be a woman.

(5) Tr. Tvaṣṭṛ said "Let us kill them who have beguiled the cup which serves for the gods to drink." (i.e. the Ṛbhus, the mortals having accepted the cup of Tvaṣṭṛ, fit for the gods, have divided it into four. Hence I shall kill them). Since then when the Soma is pressed these Ṛbhus address themselves with other names while drinking it (i.e. they address themselves as Hotṛ, Adhvaryu etc.). Formerly the mother pleased them with other names.

(6) Tr. Indra yoked the haris, the Aśvins the chariot. Bṛhaspati approached i.e. accepted the cow Viśvarūpā. (i.e. Indra and others claimed as their own the creations of yours), Ṛbhu, Vibhvan and Vāja went to the gods and they, of excellent works, attained the sacrificial share.

(7) Tr. O Sons of Sudhanvan, from the hide (of a dead cow) you created a new cow. So also the parents, who had become old, you made them young again. From one horse you created another. Yoking your chariot you approached the gods.

(8) *Tr. Explanation* (*i*) The poet is reporting back to the gods what they had said to the (Ṛbhus)—You said to the Ṛbhus – "O Sons of Sudhanvan, drink this water in the form of the draught of Soma. (This refers to the Morning—libation) Or drink this Soma purified with Miñja grass (This refers to the Mid-day libation). If you do not desire either, then take delight in the Third libation." Or. *Explanation* (*ii*) (The poet is addressing the Ṛbhus) O Sons of Sudhanvan, (when you attained godhead and came in a chariot for the Soma-drink, the horses yoked to your chariot were exhausted and you said to them) "Drink this watar......the Third libation."

(9) *Tr*. One said, "Waters are the greatest." The other said, "Fire is the greatest." The other one talking to many said. "The row of clouds that desires the thunderbolt is the greatest." The other one said, "The earth that desires for its own destruction for the sake of many creatures is the greatest." Thus speaking truth you divided the cup fourfold.

(10) *Note* : The Ṛbhus, acting as the officiating priests are accomplishing the sacrifice. *Tr.* One (priest i.e. one of the Ṛbhus) leads the red-coloured water i.e. blood (outside the sacrificial hall for the demons). Another divides the flesh brought (there, after being cut) with the axe. Still another removes the cow-dung from the well-cut flesh. When every thing was done by (the Ṛbhus, who were as good as) the sons, what indeed, did the parents (i.e. the sacrifier and his wife) have to do ? i.e. they had nothing for them to do. *Or* One leads the lame cow to the water. Another cuts the flesh brought by the female flesh-sellor. The third one removes the dung before the sum-set. What more should the parents get from their sons ?

(11) *Note* – The Ṛbhus are being praised as the rays of the sun. *Tr.* O leaders (of light, water etc.), you created grass i.e. harvest on high lands for this (world of the living beings), with the desire of doing good works you created water in low lands, as long as you slept (at night) in the house of the sun, whom none can grasp. Do not repeat it for the same length of time now during the day. *Or* As long as you slept in the house of the sun, whom none can conceal (i.e. you stayed away from showering rains during the summer), at the same time i.e., for the same length of time do not repeat it now. i.e. As long as you stayed away from showering rains in the summer, now in the rainy season you should shower rains for the same length of time.

(12) *Tr.* O Ṛbhus, when you move on showering forth, having enclosed all the living beings (with clouds) that time where, indeed, are staying, (the sun and the moon) the parents i.e. the protectors of the universe when the rain-water is spreading onwards ? *Or* During these rainy seasons where are they staying ? *Or* where then are staying the parents of that period ? You destroy him who holds your hand. Whosoever stops you with a shout, you threaten him well. *Or* whosoever praises you, glorify him.

(13) *Tr.* When you slept in the orb of the sun you asked, "O sun, whom none can hide, who indeed, inspires us (to this act of pouring rain) ?" The sun spoke about the wind as the inspirer. (Having poured rains with the help of the wind) now at the end of the year you have illumined the universe. *Note*—Formerly you had hidden even the sun and the moon with rain-clouds. Now that the rainy season is over, you are making the universe manifest.

(14) *Tr.* O Ṛbhus, O Descendants of strength, *Or* O the Showerers of rain, the gods desiring you i.e., desiring that you should be inclined to shower rains, are coming here. The Maruts came from the heaven, Agni from the earth, wind from the mid-region, Varuṇa from the waters. *Or* these gods, who had come to your help in the act of showering rains have accomplished their work. Now desiring your favour they are again returning to their respective abodes.

III 60

(1) Explanation (i) *Tr.* O Ṛbhus, O Men, O Sons of Sudhanvan, the host of the (ritualistic) works, which you accomplish through knowledge and by means of which you, desirous (of a sacrificial portion), possessing lustre capable of over powering the rivals, obtained a share in the sacrifice viz. the Soma-drink are, known to the minds of all here. Explanation (ii) O Ṛbhus, O Sons of Sudhanvan, O conductors (of sacrifice) the singers desirous (of you) and equipped with the wealth in the form of oblation, here know in a friendly spirit about your deeds (like the creation of four cups) by means of which you obtained a portion in the sacrifice.

(2) *Tr.* O Ṛbhus, the powers with which you divided the cup four-fold, the intelligence by means of which you fashioned a cow with the help of a hide, the mind with which you carved the Haris of Indra, by all that you have attained godhead.

(3) *Tr.* The Ṛbhus, the sons of human Aṅgiras, performers of (ritualistic) works, obtained the friendship of Indra and

held up (their lives). The Sons of Sudhanvan, good workers, having pervaded all over with their many works and by means of good work obtained immortality.

(4) *Tr.* In (the sacrifice) where Soma is pressed, you go in the same chariot with Indra. Being such you are in the glory i.e. you receive the glory (praise and offerings) from the human beings. O Sons of Sudhanvan, bearers of fruit (i.e. immortality) *or* the intelligent ones, your good works are without a match, so also your exploits.

(5) *Sr. O Indra, accompained by the* Ṛbhus along with Vāja or accompanied by the Ṛbhus possessed of food, let the Soma-juice well-sprinkled with water, extracted (by the stones) trickle through both your hands i.e. Hold the cup in both the hands and drink it. Inspired by the action (in the form of prayer) be exhilarated with Soma in the house of the sacrificer, in company of the Ṛbhus, the men.

(6) *Tr.* O Indra, O much-praised one, be exhilarated (with the Soma drink) in this Third libation in our sacrifice, along with the Ṛbhus, along with Vāja, along with Indrāṇi Or along with your action. These days have been fixed for you i.e. for you to drink Soma. The action of gods, along with the ritualistic actions of men have also been destined for you.

(7) Tr. O Indra, accompanied by the Ṛbhus, having Vāja amongst them, come here in this sacrifice to this sacrifice-worthy song of the singer, providing food for him. You, having thousand ways, come here for the sake of the sacrificer at this offering of Soma, along with hundred Maruts and along with speedy horses.

IV 33

(1) Tr. I send my praise like a messenger to the Ṛbhus (to the deities of this name, shining from afar). I ask of the Ṛbhus a cow yielding milk *or* a very white cow, in order to be spread over the Soma, (of the Ṛbhus), swift as wind, performing works beneficial to the world, who pervade the

heaven instantly with (their) agile horses, the helpers in crossing (space).

(2) *Tr.* When the Ṛbhus had done a lot for their parents by serving them and by keeping around them *or* by dressing them up i.e. by rendering the old ones young again, and through other miraculous deeds, then they obtained the friendship of the gods. The intelligent ones bring nourishment of cattle etc. to the sacrificer *or* they bring nourishment of all type to the lofty-mindedness.

(3) *Tr.* Vāja, Vibhvan, Ṛbhu, who rendered their parents that were lying decrepit like two sacrificial pillars, permanently young, (the Ṛbhus) who are enjoyers of sweet Soma or who are of charming appearance, may they, along with Indra, protect our sacrifice *or* may they come to our sacrifice.

(4) *Tr.* They protected the cow for one year *or* along with the calf. They fashioned her flesh i.e., the beauty of her limbs for one year *or* along with the calf. With these acts they obtained godhead.

(5) *Tr.* The eldest i.e. Ṛbhu said, "Let us make the cup into two." The younger Vibhvan said, "Let us make it into three." The youngest said, "Let us make it into four". O Ṛbhus, Tvaṣṭṛ praised i.e., accepted that speech of yours.

(6) Tr. The Ṛbhus, the men spoke truth, since they did likewise i.e. divided the cup fourfold. They received the sacrificial food (in the form of Soma). Then Tvaṣṭṛ saw the cups, shining like a day and desired for them i.e. accepted them.

(7) Tr. The Ṛbhus, staying in the house of the unconcealable one i.e. the sun, for twelve days (i.e. twelve constellations of the ıainy season viz. ārdrā and others) delight in his hospitality. At that time they made the fields fertile, they urged on the rivers. Now plants stood in the desert land and waters stood below in lowlands.

(8) Tr. The Ṛbhus, who fashioned a chariot with good wheels or a chariot rotating smoothy, the chariot moving on the

wheels, they, who created the all inspiring cow of universal form, may these Ṛbhus of good works, possessed of good *or* affording good protection, having skilled hands, create wealth for us.

(9) *Tr.* The gods, who shine with the action (of conferring boons), who have a mind (full of favour), accepted the work of Ṛbhus. Vāja was connected with all gods, Ṛbhu i.e. Ṛbhukṣan with Indra, Vibhvan with Varuṇa.

(10) Tr. The Ṛbhus, who created the two bay-horses, easy to be yoked, for the sake of Indra and who, by means of their intellect delighted the horses with praises, may these Ṛbhus bring to us augmentation of wealth and treasures i.e. the cattle etc. *or* may they bring happiness, desiring our wellbeing like a friend.

(11) *Tr.* Now the gods have given you this draught of the day i.e. the Third libation. The gods do not become friends of a man, unless he exerts himself. O Ṛbhus, great as you are, place treasures for us in this Third libation.

IV 34

(1) Tr. O Ṛbhu, Vibhvan, Vāja, Indra come here to our sacrifice to give us treasures. Now the goddess of Speech has placed for you this Soma-draught of the day (connected with the Somābhiṣava). The exhilarations have joined you or your exhilarations have joined the gods.

Note : the goddess of Speech—i.e. what Prajāpati says in Aitareya Brāhmaṇa III 30.

(2) *Tr.* O Ṛbhus, you who are shining with food (in the form of Soma), you knowing the acquisition of godhead *or* (though human by birth and yet) knowing the acquisition of Soma, be delighted with the Ṛtus. The exhilarations have united with you, so also the praise. Such as you are, urge forth for us wealth accompanied by heroic sons.

(3) *Tr.* O Ṛbhus, this sacrifice has been arranged for you. You, shining brilliantly, hold it (in your belly) like a

human being. For that the Soma-draughts, longing for you, have started towards you. Holding these (in your belly) all of you become enjoyers of precedence.

(4) *Tr.* O leaders, O Ṛbhus, now i.e. in this Third Savana, through your favour, let there be choice-treasures for the mortal sacrificer, who attends upon you (with praise) and pours his libation, i.e. (let there be choice-treasres for me). So O Vājas, drink of it. This ample Third libation (i.e. the Soma poured in it) has been offered to you in order to delight you or gratify you.

(5) Tr. O Vājas, O Ṛbhukṣans, O leaders, you praising high treasures, come to us. At the close of the day i.e. in the Evening libation these draughts are coming to you just as the recently-delivered cows come to the stable.

(6) Tr. O Sons of Strength, *Or* You, who never let the strength fail, i.e. the strong ones, being invoked by means of a hymn, do approach this sacrifice of ours. You intelligent ones, taking delight along with Indra to whom you belong, being accompained by Indra, you donors of choice-treasures, drink of this sweet Soma.

(7) *Tr.* O Indra, worthy of being praised in words, drink Soma, taking delight along with Varuṇa, taking delight along with the Maruts. Drink it delighting with the gods who drink first; with the gods who drink at the particular seasons. Drink with the divinities that protect women. Drink with the Ṛbhus, who give choice-treasures. *Or* Drink with divinities that protect women, donors of choice-treasures.

(8) *Tr.* O Ṛbhus, be delighted with the Ādityas. Be delighted with the particular deities worshipped on specific occasions. Take delight with Savitṛ, favourable to the gods. Take delight with (the deities of) the rivers, the bestrowers of treasures.

(9) Tr. The Ṛbhus, who delighted the Aśvins by the act of fashioning the chariot), who by their acts made their old parents young again, who formed (i.e. renovated) the

(dead) cow, who fashioned the two horses, who fabricated the armours (for the gods), who separated the heaven and the earth, these all pervasive ones, the leaders, who performed the acts (leading to their to their exaltation) may these Ṛbhus (give treasures to us—from stz. 10).

(10) *Tr.* O Ṛbhus, you, who possess wealth (in order to be given to me), (wealth) along with the cattle, along with food, along with good sons, along with property, which is rich in food, those you, O Ṛbhus, the first drinkers, being exhilarated, give treasure to us, you who praise the gift *Or* you who praise the given Soma, *or* you who give treasures to us and to the sacrificers, who praise the gift.

(11) *Tr.* O Ṛbhus, do not go away. (Do not be displeased). We will not leave you thirsty. Hence O Ṛbhus, being blameless be delighted in this sacrifice along with Indra, along with the Maruts, along with other shining gods, in order to give us choice-treasures.

IV 35

(1) *Tr.* O Sons of Strength *or* you not letting strength to fail, O Sons of Sudhanvan, O Ṛbhus, do not go away. In this libation may the exhilarating Soma-draughts go to you after Indra, the donor of charming wealth. *Or* May the Soma-draughts follow Indra and yourselves.

(2) *Tr.* O Ṛbhus, may the gift of choice-treasures come from you to me in this Evening libation. *Or* May the choice-treasures in the form of Soma come to you, O Ṛbhus, since the drinking of well-pressed Soma has been secured (for you by Prajāpati), because you have rendered fourfold the single cup with your skill of hands and with your desire to perform good deeds.

(3) *Tr.* O Ṛbhus, you made the cup fourfold and said, "O friends (Agni), favour us (with the Soma-drink now." Then Agni said to you, "O deft-handed Ṛbhus go to the path of immortality. Go to the host of gods."

(4) Tr. Of which material was the cup made, which you made into four with your skill ? Now (O priests), press Soma for the delight of the Ṛbhus. O Ṛbhus, do drink the sweet mead of Soma.

(5) *Tr.* O Ṛbhus, enjoying excellent food (of Soma), by means of your skill you rejuvenated your parents. With your work, (by dividing the cup four-fold) you made it worthy of being used for drinking by the gods. By your act of carving you procured the two more speedy bay-horses, the carriers of Indra.

(6) *Tr.* O Ṛbhus, possessing food, give to the sacrificer, who presses Soma for your exhilaration at the close of the day (i.e. in the Evening libation), wealth, associated with heroes, you showerers (of fruit), being delighted with Soma.

(7) *Tr.* O Indra with the bay-horses, do drink the Soma pressed in the morning. The Mid-day libation is yours only. Drink of the Third libation along with the Ṛbhus of covetable gifts, whom you have made friends because of good work.

(8) *Tr.* O Ṛbhus, you have become gods on account of your good work. You are seated in the heaven like hawks. O Sons of Strength, give us treasures. O Sons of Sudhanvan, you have become the immortal ones i.e. the gods.

(9) *Tr.* O deft-handed Ṛbhus, Third libation, possessing the gift of Soma, which you have secured through your desire to do good works, drink of it now; since it has been sprinkled. (Drink) with your organs getting fully exhilarated.

IV 36

(1) *Tr.* O Ṛbhus, the chariot (of the Aśvins, fabricated by you), has become one without horses, without reins and is praiseworthy. With three wheels it rotates around the firmament. This act is expressive of your divine nature.

So also that act by which you nourish the heaven and the earth.

(2) Tr. O Vājas, O Ṛbhus, you of noble heart. you who quickly fashioned the non-faltering, smoothy-rolling chariot by means of the thinking of your mind (only), we invite you, who are like that, for drinking (the Soma of) this libation.

(3) Tr. O Vājas, O Ṛbhus, O Vibhvans, this greatness of yours becomes laudable amongst the gods, that you made your old parents, who were ever feebled, once again permanently young so as to be capable of walking.

(4) Tr. O Ṛbhus, you made a single cup into four. With your acts you brought forth a new cow out of a hide. Hence you obtained immortality amongst the gods. Such an act of yours immediately becomes praiseworthy.

(5) *Tr.* May we get from the Ṛbhus, wealth that enjoys fame *or* food of the first order, the wealth, which the Ṛbhus, the leaders renowned for food, have created. The cup *or* the chariot carved by the Vibhvans (i.e. the Ṛbhus) is to be highly lauded in the sacrificial assemblies. The chariot *or* the cup that you protect, O gods, becomes worthy of being seen variously.

(6) *Tr.* He, being strong, becomes skilled in movements. He being a seer becomes equipped with praise. He being brave becomes an overthrower of the enemies. He becomes invincible in battles. He possesses growing wealth. He possesses good bravery, he whom Vāja, Vibhvan, whom the Ṛbhus have taken under their protection.

(7) Tr. Your form has been placed forth as the best one, worthseeing. Hence here is our hymn of praise worthy of it. O Vājas, O Ṛbhus, please find pleasure in it. We invoke you with this holy song, you who are wise, intelligent, possessed of knowledge. Or we invoke you with this holy song, you, whom the wise, intelligent singers possessed of knowledge, are praising.

(8) *Tr.* O Ṛbhus, from our praises you know about all enjoyments, beneficial to human beings or you know about all enjoyments beneficial to human beings more than what we can think of. So please accomplish these for us. Fashion for us a treasure, brilliant, powerful, excellent, which squeezes out the strength of the enemies. Also provide food for us.

(9) *Tr.* O Ṛbhus, taking delight in this sacrifice of ours, create progeny for us and wealth for us. So also fashion here in this sacrifice glory, associated with heroic people. Give us that choice-food, by means of which we shall be known as being superior to all others.

IV 37

(1) *Tr.* O Vājas, O Ṛbhuṣans, come to this sacrifice of ours by the paths, meant for the gods, in order that you, O charming ones, sustain our sacrifice among these mortal sacrificers, descendants of Manu, so as to cause auspicious days.

(2) Tr. May (the Soma-draughts in) the sacrifice, today, be to the gratification of your heart and mind. May these abundant Soma-draughts, having a lustrous form due to the mixed material, go to your heart today. The extracted Soma-juices, filled in the cups, are being carried for your sake *Or* the extracted Soma-juices, filled in the cups, are longing for you. When drunk for the ritual and energy, may they delight your

(3) *Tr.* O Vājas, O Ṛbhukṣans, the Soma-offering in the three libations, beneficial to gods or placed by gods, sustains you. So also the song of praise sustains you. Therefore, I, amongst the devout people, like Manu, offer you the Soma poured in many cups amidst the very respleundent gods.

(4) *Tr.* O Vājas, may you have sturdy horses, brilliant chariot, iron-strong chins and excellent treasure. O Sons of Indra i.e. who are to be protected like sons by Indra, O Sons of

Strength, this last (i.e. the Third) libation has been ordained among the gods in order to exhilarate you.

(5) Tr. O Ṛbhukṣans, we invoke your group, that shines afar, which is of the form of wealth (i.e. generates wealth), which is mightly in battle, which is mutually associated with one another, which possesses strength of the organs, which is always most liberal and possesses horses.

(6) Tr. O Ṛbhus, the mortal, whom you and Indra take under protection may he alone be supreme. May he alone be the enjoyer (of pleasures) by means of his ritualistic actions. In the sacrifice may he alone be possessed of a speedy horse.

(7) *Tr.* O Vāja, O Ṛbhukṣans, instruct us about the ways of performing sacrifice. O intelligent ones, when praised, give us the capacity to cross all quarters.

(8) *Tr.* O Vājas, O Ṛbhukṣans, O Indra, O Nāsatyas, bless us well, the mortal singers, with such abundant treasures, plentiful horses, that we shall be capable of making gifts.

VII 48

(1) Tr. O Ṛbhukṣans, O Vājas, O leaders, O bountiful ones, be gratified with the pressed Soma, kept here, amidst us. Now as you have started, may your active capable horses, facing towards us, lead your chariot here, the chariot, which is beneficial to human beings.

(2) *Tr.* O Ṛbhus, becoming vast with you, the Ṛbhus, becoming capable with you, the Vibhus, with the help of your strength, may we overpower the inimical forces. May Vāja protect us in war. May we smash down the enemy, with Indra as our companion.

(3) *Tr.* They i.e. Indra and the Ṛbhus, through their command *or* through their weapon overpower many inimical forces. They destroy all foes in the battle. May

Indra, Vibhvan, Ṛbhukṣan, Vāja attack the enemies and eradicate the vigour of the enemy, by means of violence.

(4) *Tr.* O brilliant (Ṛbhus), give us wealth today. May you, all Ṛbhus, finding delight together, be for our protection. May the praiseworthy Ṛbhus bestow food on us. O Ṛbhus, you protect us ever with (your) blessings.

II

Félix Nève

HYMNS TO THE ṚBHUS[1]

I—20

(1) *Tr.* Addressed to a divine generation this hymn, dispenser of richest treasures, has come out of the mouth of the singers.

(2) *Tr.* (The Ṛbhus), who have produced by thought for Indra the tawny horses, yoking themselves at the sound of the voice, have obtained the sacrifice by their meritorious[2] works.

(3) *Tr.* They have fashioned for the truthful (Aśvins) a chariot, rapid in its march and bearing happiness.[3] They have formed a cow, abundant in milk.[4]

(4) *Tr.* Faithful to the prayers,[5] friends of the just, the Ṛbhus have rendered, by efficacy of their works,[6] their parents, gifted anew with youth.

(5) *Tr.* The libations have gone towards you,[7] at the same time, as towards Indra, accompanied by Maruts, and towards the luminous Ādityas.

(6) *Tr.* The new bowl, production of god Tvaṣṭṛ, you have divided it yet again into four[8] parts.

(7) Tr. Dispense for us to the one, who sacrifices, because of excellent praises, the diverse riches attaining the number of three times seven, coming one after the other.[9]

(8) *Tr.* Bearers of the offerings,[10] the Ṛbhus have lived this life.[11] By their good actions, they have obtained among the Devas, a felicity, honoured by the sacrifices.

I—110

(2) *Tr.* This[12] work, accomplished not long before, by myself has been accomploshed anew. The sweetest invocation is pronounced as a sign of praise.[13] This liquor is placed here for all the Devas.[14] Quench your thirst, O Ṛbhus, with the well-poured libations.

(2) *Tr.* When the ancient sages, men from amongst my fore-fathers,[15] went in search of offering, then, O sons of Sudhanvan, because of the grandeur of their conduct, you have come to the abode of the sacrificer, making libations.

(3) *Tr.* Savitṛ has given you immortality, when you had come to warn this god, who is never hidden (on the subject of the prepared libations). This cup of the Asura (Tvaṣṭṛ), this unique cup, destined for the sacred beverage, you have made it fourfold.[16]

(4) Tr. Having accomplished their works with promptness,[17] the officiating priests[18]—though they were mortals—the Ṛbhus, the sons of Sudhanvan, have obainted immortality, endowed with the shining lustre of the sun; during the entire course of the year they have been presented with the offerings.

(5) *Tr.* Just as one measures a field, the Ṛbhus have measured with a sharp instrument onc single cup, which they had to offer; they who (are) well-praised, (who are) desiring only an[19] equal part, (who are) aspiring for a living amongst immortals.

(6) *Tr.* Let us offer homage to these men of the luminous space, with knowledge,[20] as one offers clarified butter

with the ladle; the Ṛbhus who have obtained the rapid springs from this divine protector,[21] have obtained a share in the light of the heaven.[22]

(7) *Tr.* Ṛbhu is our supreme master, younger by his force.[23] May Ṛbhu be a refuge for us, a rich dispenser in abodes and foods. O Devas with your succours, on a favourable day, may we be able to vanquish the troops of those, who do not make libations.

(8) *Tr.* O Ṛbhus, with the help of a hide you have formed a new[24] cow. A second time you have united the mother with her calf, O Men.[25] Sons of Sudhanvan, with your benevolent act, you have rejuvenated your parents, exhausted by life.

(9) *Tr.* Indra, helped by the Ṛbhus, come to our help with the horses, in the battle.[26] Make us possess varied riches. May Mitra and Varuṇa, Aditi, Sindhu and the Heaven and the Earth, give us this well-being in abundance.

I—111

(1) Tr. Working with knowledge, the Ṛbhus have fabricated a chariot rolling well; they have formed the tawny horses, full of manly vigour,[27] carrying Indra. They have brought back youth for their parents; they have produced for the calf its mother, staying by its side.

(2) *Tr.* Create for us, for the sacrifice, a shining offering for maintaining strength and vigour,[28] a nourishment assuring a good posterity, so that we live with a race of men all made up of heroes. Give us a propoitious abundance, for our force.

(3) *Tr.* O Ṛbhus, create for us a great opulence. Produce opulence for our chariots,[29] for our horses, O you courageous men. May every day every creature make our opulence grow, giving victory. May we vanquish in combats strong men related or unrelated.

(4) *Tr.* I call to our help, Indra, dominating far and wide, the Ṛbhus, so also Vāja[30] and the Maruts, to the libations of

Soma. I call Mitra and Varuṇa, so also the Aśvins. May they be our guides towards fortune, towards the meritorious act of sacrifice and also towards victory.

(5) Tr. May Ṛbhu make riches abound among us for the combat.[31] May Vāja, vanquisher of the enemies, protect us. May Mitra and Varuṇa, Aditi, Sindhu the Earth and the Heaven accord us this welfare in abundance.

I—161

(1) Tr. Is he the eldest, is he the youngest, who has come to us ?[32] What message has been sent to us from the side of the gods ? What have we to say ?[33] We have not at all done any damage to the cup, which is of illustrious origin.[34] O Agni, who come as a brother, we certainly proclaim the excellence of this wood.[35]

(2) *Tr.* "From one cup you have made four. The Devas have prescribed you thus. O sons of Sudhanvan, that is why I have come to say that to you, if you do this,[36] you will become participants, in the sacrificies in company of the Devas."

(3) *Tr.* These are the works about which they spoke to Agni, their messenger:—[37] "A horse is to be made, so also a chariot, at the same time, a cow is to be made. Two old relations (i.e. parents) are to be rejuvenated." After these tasks, O brother, we have come towards you, other gods[38] by the sacrifice." (Or. f.n. "After having accomplished these works, in your favour, we have come to the help of the sacrifice)."

(4) *Tr.* O Ṛbhus, having accomplished all that you have put the question.[39] "Where has he gone, he, who had come as messenger to us ?"[40] When Tvaṣṭṛ saw the four cups, already produced, at that instant, he disappeared in the middle of the women.[41] (f.n. With the reading 'yasya' the translation will be, "Where has he gone, he whose messenger has come to us)."

(5) Tr. When Tvaṣṭṛ has said, "Let us strike these, who have done damage to the cup, reserved for beverage of gods !" Then the men,[42] all together took[43] other names in the sacrifice. Henceforward their mother has delighted them with other names.

(6) *Tr.* Indra has yoked his bay-horses and the Aśvins their chariot; Bṛhaspati[44] approached the cow with diverse[45] forms. Ṛbhu, Vibhvan, Vāja ! You have gone to the gods. Excellent by your works, you have gained the fortune of sharing the sacrifices.

(7) Tr. By your offerings, with the help of a hide, you have formed a new[46] cow. You have rejuvenated these relatives (parents) decrepit by age. You have made them young. O sons of Sudhanvan, from one horse, you have created another. Yoking your chariot you have gone close to the gods.

(8) *Tr.* The Devas have said to you,[47] "Drink this water, or drink today this juice that has been purified with the Muñja grass.[48] O Sons of Sudhanvan, if you do not desire either of this at the instant, be full of joy at the Third libation."

(9) Tr. One of you said, "The waters,[49] it is these that are the best." The other said, "The fire, it is this that is the best." To those, who had spoken thus the other said, "It is the lightning."[50] (f.n. rather the cloud, that attracts the lightning). Pronouncing true words, the Ṛbhus have fashioned the four bowls.

(10) *Tr.* One makes blood flow like water[51] on the earth, the other disposes the flesh, separated by means of a sharp instrument. One has drawn from the body, cut into pieces, the excretion for throwing it away. In which manner have the parents come to the help of their sons ?

(11) Tr. O Ṛbhus,[52] you have produced grass for us on high places. You have brought waters in the valleys by your benevolent action. O virile beings ! You reposed at the

house of the sun, who can never be hidden, for such a long time (that) you do not appear today.

(12) *Tr.* While you pass around the existing things by covering them with clouds,[54] where have your parents stayed during the extension of waters ?[55] By a curse you annihilated him, whosoever stops you.[56] You have responded to him, who had offended you in speech.[57]

(13) *Tr.* O Ṛbhus, while you were still sleeping, you put the question "O sun, you who cannot be hidden, who instigated us to this action of pouring down rain ?" The sun says[58] to a dog, who awakens, (That is to say in consideration of the wind, Vāyu, filled in the air). "It is, he who excites you. The year being completed, you have today shown the world,[59] O Ṛbhus."

(14). *Tr.* The Maruts come from the high heaven, Agni from the earth, the wind comes from the air, Varuṇa comes from the churned waters, all desirous of you,[60] O sons of the force.[61]

III—60

(1) *Tr.* O men ! your near ones, desirous of sacrifice, by their intelligence,[62] have fully accomplished such works by the knowledge of their fruits.[63] These are the works by which, O sons of Sudhanvan, redressed with a lustre worthy of them,[64] you have attained a felicity honoured by the sacrifices.[65].

(2) *Tr.* Due to the efforts by which you have produced the four cups, due to the wisdom with which you formed a new[66] cow with the help of a hide, due to the intelligence by which you have fabricated the bay horses of Indra (Harī), you have obtained, O Ṛbhus the divinity in enjoyment.

(3) *Tr.* The Ṛbhus have obtained the company of Indra, Sons of man, active[67] workers, they have not seen the life[68] escaping. The children of Sudhanvan you have obtained immortality, authors of good actions, accomplishing the sacrifices, due to the efficacy of the works.

(4) *Tr.* You come in company of Indra in the same chariot, at the time of libation. At the same time you bring with you the prosperity of men.[69] O officiating priests, Ṛbhus, Sons of Sudhanvan, Your good works, so also your forces, these are not at all to be equalled.[70]

(5) *Tr.* Indra, joined to Ṛbhus, masters of nourishment,[71] make flow, by seizing it with your hand the Soma, extracted and[72] filled. O Maghavan,[73] inspired by our prayer, rejoice in the house of the sacrificer with the Men, Sons of Sudhanvan.

(6) *Tr.* Indra, accompanied by Ṛbhu and by Vāja, rejoice in these places of our libation, by associating yourself with the ceremony.[74] O you praised by several, these days have been fixed for you,[75] and at the same time the offerings of the Devas have been established in accordance with the sacrifices of men.

(7) *Tr.* Indra, assisted by the Ṛbhus, giving nourishment,[76] dispenser of food, come here in front of the invocation of one, who sings of you in the sacrifice, during the offering of libation, in favour of men, come with hundred intelligent and rapid[77] horses, you of thousand eyes.[78]

IV – 33

(1) *Tr.* I send to the Ṛbhus the praise as a message. In return for this poured out libation,[72] I ask them for a cow, giving white milk. Led with the speed of wind by the rapid coursers,[80] traversing the airs, these skilled workers have penetrated the entire[81] heaven in an instant.

(2) *Tr.* When the Ṛbhus had rendered homage to their parents[82] by their intervention, by their co-operation and by their good works, they have obtained immediately the company of the Devas. Endowed with intelligence[83] they have brought an abundance of boons to the thinking[84] being.

(3) *Tr.* They, who have rejuvenated their parents, lying decrepit by age like two broken[85] posts – May Vāja,

Vibhavan, Ṛbhu, companions of Indra, endowed with a charming[86] form, protect our sacrifice !

(4) *Tr.* Every year when the Ṛbhus have saved the cow,[87] every year when they have formed its flesh,[88] every year when they have preserved lustre of this cow, by such actions they have obtained immortality.

(5) *Tr.* The eldest said, "Make two cups." The second amongst them in age said, "Let us make it into three." The youngest said, "Make it four." O Ṛbhus, Tvaṣṭṛ has praised this speech uttered by you.[89]

(6) *Tr.* These men have spoken a true thing and indeed they have done it.[90] That is why the Ṛbhus have come to take part in this offering. Tvaṣṭṛ will desire these four cups shinking like the light of the day,[91] if he sees them.

(7) *Tr.* When during twelve days, the Ṛbhus rested themselves, sleeping in the hospitable abode of the sun who can never be hidden, making the fields fertile, they made the rivers flow, then the plants grew in the desert[92] and the waters subsisted in the valley.

(8) *Tr.* May the Ṛbhus, who have made a chariot, rolling well, stopping at the will of man,[93] who have formed a cow, mother of all, endowed with all forms—may they, who are strong, in protection,[94] strong by their works, having skilled hands, produce riches for us.

(9) *Tr.* The gods have approved of their works. They have become resplendent by the action[95] and by intelligence (f.n. or by an active or operative intelligence) Vāja, became the benefactor, the favourite of all gods, Ṛbhukṣan of Indra, Vibhvan of Varuṇa.

(10) Tr. You, who have formed the tawny horses with intelligence, by celebrating them with chants.[96] (f.n. Could one translate his as: rejoicing in chants with intelligence ?) You, who have made for Indra the two horses, yoking themselves well to the chariot, give us boons. Augment our riches, O Ṛbhus, desiring our prosperity, just as a friend desires it.

(11) *Tr.* It is then that the Devas established for you, the libation of the day, so also the joy that it procures. They do not do it, except as a favour to the man, tired by work[97] (three more interpretations (i) They are not in vain for the help of a man, who is fatigued. (ii) In our sacrifice-Ṛtam—the Devas are to the help of a man, who is fatigued (iii) In this ceremony, of ours, for the help of a man, who is fatigued by work.) Give us, thus, the riches, O Ṛbhus, in the Third libation.

IV—34

(1) *Tr.* Ṛbhu, Vibhvan, Indra, come for dispensing riches,[98] towards this sacrifice that we offer you.[99] Now the goddess Dhiṣaṇā has given you this libation of the days and at the same time the intoxicating joys of refreshment have come for you.

(2) Tr. You, who know the human birth,[100] rich in food, O Ṛbhus, rejoice in company of Ṛtus.[101] For you have arrived the intoxicating joys of the libation, so also the intelligent[102] invocation. Make the riches, accompanied by male progeny, come to us.

(3) *Tr.* For you, O Ṛbhus, has been prepared the sacrifice, which you have accepted as do the men,[103] full of a lively lustre. May the libations, desirous of rendering homage[104] to you, be kept in your presence. O Vāja and your brothers, stay in the sun, the culminating points of the luminous[105] heaven.

(4) Tr. O men, may the favour of riches from your side be presently accorded to me, the mortal sacrificer[106] and faithful servant. Drink O Vājas, O Ṛbhus, I offer you this Third and great libation for your joy.[107]

(5) Tr. Come to us, O you Vājas, so also Ṛbhukṣan,[108] O Men, praised in the subject of great riches.[109] These libations have gone towards you at end of the days, like the cows towards their abode.

(6) *Tr.* O Sons of force, come towards this sacrifice, ivited with praise, associated with Indra, endowed with wisdom[110] cherished as equal of him, to whom you belong.[111] Drink of the sweet liquor, O you, who give treasures.

(7) *Tr.* Come, drink the Soma, O Indra, accompanied by Varuṇa ! Come, you, who are invoked by praises,[112] with the Maruts. Come with those, who drink first,[113] and even with them, who drink at the time, marked for the ceremony.[114] Come in company of women and wives of gods,[115] dispensers of riches.

(8) Tr. Satisfy yourselves with the libation O Ṛbhus, associated (in the sacrifice) with Ādityas, associated with Parvatas,[116] associated with Savitṛ powerful among gods,[117] associated with rivers, bearing wealth.[118]

(9) *Tr.* May they drink first,[119] the Ṛbhus, who by their succours have satisfied the Aśvins, who have rejuvenated their parents, who have produced a new cow, who have created the two horses (of Indra), who have fashioned armours[120] for the Devas, who have separated the heaven and the earth,[121] these men, full of power,[122] who have accorded happy generations.

(10) Tr. You, who give abundant opulence in cows, (who are) rich in force,[123] conferring a male posterity, ensuring an abode provided with abundant nourishment,[124] you, O Ṛbhus, who are the first to drink the libation, full of joy, give such opulence to us, as well as to those, who celebrate your liberality.[125]

(11) Tr. Do not go away fram us. May we never leave you thirsty with an ardent thirst. Come O Ṛbhus, always honoured.[126] Satisfy yourselves joyously in this sacrifice, with Indra, with Maruts, with the resplendent beings, with a view to give the treasures. O Devas.

IV—35

(1) *Tr.* Come here, O Sons of strength! Children of Sudhanvan Ṛbhus, do not go away. In this place, in this Third

libation, which is offered to you, may the sacred liquor causing joy, reach you, so also to Indra. the dispenser of treasures.[127]

(2) *Tr.* May the gift of riches come here from the Ṛbhus. The beverage of extracted Soma has been prepared for you,[128] because you have divided a single cup in four by your activity, by your excellent work.

(3) *Tr.* You have divided the cup in four parts. You have said,[129] "O friend, honour this libation." That is why, O Vājas. O Ṛbhus, endowed with skilled hands, come in the path of the immortal[130] heaven. Come to join the assembly of Devas.

(4) Tr. Of what nature was this cup, that you divided in four parts by fortunate wisdom ?[131] Now extract the libation for your joy. Drink O Ṛbhus, this sweet juice of Soma.[132]

(5) *Tr.* By your action, you have rejuvenated parents. By your action you have produced the cup, destined for the beverage of the Devas. By your action you have produced the bay horses agile in their march, carrying Indra, O Ṛbhus, masters of the treasures of food.

(6) O you masters of nourishment,[133] procure riches accompanied by numerous posterity, for him, who, at the close of the day, extracts for you, for your joy, a libation full of savour,[134] O you Rbhus, dispensers of favours, full of joy.

(7) *Tr.* Possessor of bay-horses, drink the morning libation. The libation of the midday belongs to you alone. Come to drink that of the evening, in company of the Ṛbhus, whom, O Indra, you have made your companions,[135] because of their good works.

(8) *Tr.* You, who have become Devas by your good actions and who have stopped[136] while soaring like falcons[137] in the heights of the luminous heavens, give us wealth, O Sons of force, Children of Sudhanvan, you have been made immortal.

(9) *Tr.* Because, by your holy actions you have procured this Third libation, accompanied by riches,[138] you, O Ṛbhus, you who have skilled hands, come, drink this juice, ready for you, with the senses penetrated with joy.[139]

IV—36

(1) *Tr.* The chariot, which you have produced (for the Aśvins) without a horse, without a bridle,[140] provided with three wheels, worthy of praises, traverses the etheral space. This great work is the testimony of your divinity, so also that by which you sustain the heaven and the earth.

(2) *Tr.* You, who are animated by good thoughts, have prepared this chariot rolling well smoothly, unjolting, only by skilful planning. We call you O Ṛbhus, Vāja and others, so that you come quickly to drink this libation.[141].

(3) *Tr.* It has fallen on you, O Vājas, full of power,[142] this grandeur worthy of being celebrated in the midst of the Devas, because you have rejuvenated your parents and made them walk,[143] parents, bent by age[144] and exhausted by a long oldage.[145]

(4) *Tr.* You have divided one cup into four parts. With the help of a hide you have formed a new cow by the merit of your sacrifices ! Also you have obtained immortality amongst the Devas. Such an action, worthy of you, O Vājas, O Ṛbhus, should be celebrated promptly by praises.[146]

(5) *Tr.* May riches, followed by a supreme glory, come to us from the Rbhus, the riches which these men, praised because of food,[147] have produced. The chariot made by Vibhvan and others should be praised in the sacrifices.[148] The one whom you protect, O Devas, can see[149] far into the distance.

(6) *Tr.* He, who is full of force is rapid in his march.[150] The sage is praised by words of praise. The fearless man

repels the enemies and is invincible in the combats. He receives an abundance of riches. He obtains a male posterity, he, whom Vāja, Vibhvan and Ṛbhu have protected.

(7) *Tr.* Your excellent form, remarkable to the eye, has manifested itself to us. May you accept[151] this praise that we offer you, O Vājas, O Ṛbhus. You are prudent, wise,[152] intelligent.[153] We glorify you by this prayer.

(8) *Tr.* You, who, by your songs of praise know all[154] the things useful to men,[155] procure for us O Ṛbhus, a fortune full of lustre and power, sustenance of force, an excellent luck, so also abundant nourishment.

(9) *Tr.* Produce for us in this sacrifice a posterity, in this ceremony, a fortune, a glory rich in heroes, O you dispensers of well-beings.[156] Give us O Ṛbhus, this varied nourishment, due to which we can be known above others our contemporaries.[157]

IV—37

(1) *Tr.* O Vājas, O Ṛbhukṣan, you who are Devas, come to our sacrifice by the routes, which the chariots of the Devas[158] traverse. Come, so that you establish the sacrifice in the propitious moments of the days among these generations of men, issued from Manu,[159] O you, who rejoice in the libation.

(2) *Tr.* May these liquors of sacrifice be an object of joy[160] for your heart, (f.n. Alternatively-May these libations of Soma be for your intelligent heart). May, they, well accepted, shining with diverse[161] good things, arrive on this day. May the extracted libations, quite full, be borne towards you. May they please you for force and vigour, which they procure.[162]

(3) *Tr.* This offering, repeated thrice, aggreeable to Devas, I present it to you, with the purpose that it may be an invocation of praise to you, O Vājas, O Ṛbhus, like Manu in olden times, I offer you the juice of Soma,

associated with human generations, enjoying the sacrifice in company of men, endowed with long days.[163]

(4) *Tr.* O Rbhus, whose horses are big and stout, whose chariots are shining, be present bearing the jaws of iron.[164] Masters of good riches, proteges of Indra, Sons of force, this excellent libation, has been recognised as yours for your joy.

(5) *Tr.* O Rbhus, for an abundant[165] nourishment, we invoke your troop, full of force in the combat, well-united, endowed with power, always liberal, provided with horses.

(6) *Tr.* Certainly the one from amongst the mortal beings, whom you protect, O Rbhus, you and Indra, may he have the well-being in return by means of his sactifices.[166] May he take part, in the ceremony with the speedy horses.

(7) *Tr.* O Vājas, O Rbhus, inform us of the paths which lead to the sacrifice. Wise ones, well-invoked, make us traverse all the regions of the space.[168]

(8) *Tr.* O Vājas, O Rbhus, O Indra, O the Truthful ones (Aśvins), procure for us the men who praise you, the riches of horses in abundance for our well-being.[169]

VII—48

(1) *Tr.* O Rbhus, O Vājas, O men, endowed with riches, drink this libation presented by us. While you advance, may your active,[70] strong, powerful horses make your chariot roll, the chariot, worthy of men.[171]

(2) *Tr.* O Rbhus, strong with you, powerful with you, who are powerful, may we conquer with your force, the forces[172] of our enemies. May Vāja help us in the combat. With Indra, associated with you, may we vanquish Vṛtra, the common enemy.

(3) *Tr.* These Devas vanquish by their power the nemerous troops of the enemies, whosoever they may be, destroying all the enemies in the combat. May Indra, Vibhvan, Rbhu,

Vāja, our master[173] annihilate by violencc, the power of our enemy.

(4) *Tr.* O Devas, procure for us abundance promptly. Be fully ready to come to our help, all loved equally by us. May these beings, worthy of praise,[174] give us nourishment. Protect us, ceaselessly, O Ṛbhus, with your propitious succours.

Footnotes

1. We will distinguish by the use of italics the passages of the translation which are meant for the comprehension of the text in paraphrase and which base themselves most often on the authority of the Indian Commentator. The notes will help us to expose the reasons for which we sometimes deviated from the interpretation defended by Sāyaṇa.

2. The word Śamī which denotes here the works which earn happiness, the offerings, and the libations is ranked in the Nighaṇṭu (II. 1) amongst the 26 nouns signifying action (Karma) in general, and especially in the religious language of the Veda—the sacrifice and the acts which accompany it. Stevenson has translated this line in another manner in his dissertation (p. 25 and p. 168). "These are they also who pervade our sacrificc by purificatory rites."

3. According to the ancient meaning of these descriptive dissertations, a chariot is described here which rapidly describes the curves of its route and which offers a convenient seat to its driver. It is with this restriction that the scholiast interprets the epithet *sukha*, fortunate.

4. The word '*sabar*' taken here as a synonym of *kṣira*, milk, seems to be a word of a very ancient formation, which soon fell into disuse, perhaps, it was drawn from the root

Samb (*Śamb, Sāmb*) reassemble', 'join.' by means of the neuter suffix as, in a way so that the final of the word sabas could have been changed into '*ar*' by an euphonic irregularity becoming a resonant and perhaps *sabar* had been employed in the compounds such as *sabardughā*. (See RV I, 121,5). *Sabardughāyāḥ paya utsriyāyāḥ*. On the other hand, would it be just to research the etymology of the word in a radical analgous to the root su whose meaning is multiple in Sanskrit? Would it be impossible to discover some analogy between the form sabar and the Latain soboles by directing the philological research in this sense?

5. At this place, the gloss attributes the efficient knowledge of the authentic formulate of the prayer to the Ṛbhus. It suposes the accomplishment of duties prescribed by the part of the Veda called Caraṇa (lit. march) and by the others. There is a dissertations devoted to the distinction of branches *śākhās* schools according to which the texts of the Vedas are divided; this dissertation has *Caraṇa vyūha* as title, a term which should be translated by the words—'Collection of regulations or observations' (Cf. Coler. Misc. Essays I p. 14; Roth Zur Lit etc. pp. 15-17, p. 55-57).

6. Rosen (Adnot p. XL VI) has already explained the word *Visṭī by* an instrumental singular by rejecting the explanation of the scholiast, who makes it nominative plural of a verbal adjective : It appears plausible to compare *visṭī* with *visṭvi* which figures amongst the names of action (*karma*) (Nighaṇṭu II, 11). The same termination of the instrumental is justified by other examples in the Veda. (Kṛtv, *Kṛtyā*, *Karmaṇā*) in the hymn of Dīrghatamas (Book II, Adhyāya 3, Varga 4. stz. 3).

7. The Ṛbhus are named here along with the divinities who have share like them, in the 3rd libation to each day. Sāyaṇa bases his interpretation with a curious passage of *Sūtras* or axioms of Aśvalāyana, a sage placed in the confines of vedic antiquity and the historic origins of Brahmanism.

8. We propose to examine specially this fact of the dividing of the cup, by examining the entire history of the myth.

9. According to Sāyaṇa, the part thus denoted 3 orders of riches serving the sacrifice, the riches called superior, average and inferior. They relate to a number of 7 sacrifices in each order. The 1st class of sacrifices concerns the consecration of the perpetual fire (*Agnyādheya*). The 2nd the victims consumed on the altar (*Upāsanahoma*); the 3rd (Agniṣṭoma) and the other ceremonies which are accomplished by the libations of Soma—The ancient word *Suśasti* is used here in the sense of praise and of hymn which are most often proper to the word *praśasti* in the Veda. See the note of Weber. Vājas. spec. p. 19.

10. The epithet of *vahnayaḥ* (*vahni*) could also signify guides, directors of sacrifices and perhaps making the sacrifices advance, and succeed as Stevenson had wished while translating as 'prosperers of sacrifice.' (p. 25).

11. The root dhṛ which takes in the causative form (*dhārayāmi*) the general meaning of taking, possessing, retaining, is used in an absolute manner to signify 'possess life,' 'retain vital breath.' *Prāṇān cf.* westergaard. Radices ling samscrite S.V.

12. The noun for deed *apaḥ* (Lat. Opus) has here a very large meaning, the collective meaning of the religious act responding to diverse types of sacrifice such as *Agniṣṭoma and* ceremonies such as the consecration of fire (Nigh. II, 1) This first expression of the stanza above all refers, it appears, to the observation of the Vedic ritual.

13. *dhīti* which has the meaning of prayer or invocation, in relation with the verb *śasyate*, as *dhītayaḥ* (preces) in the hymn 25, stz. 16 book I of the RV—*ucatha* is a word particular to the Vedic language of a usage less frequent than the work *uktha*, which has the same meaning as prayer, hymn, praise. This is a neuter noun formed from the same root vac with the help of the suffix *atha* (*vac paribhāṣaṇe uṇādiko athak-pratyayaḥ-sch*).

14. The commentator explains the compound *viśvadevyaḥ* in his grammatical notes in the following manner—*viśvadevyaḥ* : *div ārho mārgo devyaḥ chandasi veti ya pratyayaḥ. Viśve sarve devyā yasmin some ityādi.*

15. The word *āpi,* plural āpayaḥ denotes the fathers, the ancestors, who have ensured the perpetuity of the family and the present generation. It is drawn from the root āp to obtain to attain, with the help of suffix *uṅādi* (*āpayaḥ*) (īpnoteraunādika i pratyayaḥ-sch.); Cf the form of dative case āpaye in st. 20 of the excerpt of the Vāj. Saṁhitā puplished by Dr. Weber (Part I, p. 45) the word āpiḥ is commented upon here by bandhuḥ, relative and compared to neuter āpyam, society. The editor has taken care to indicate the passages of Nirukta which throw light on these terms.

16. The noun *bhakṣaṇa*, nourishment, food, affects here, by opposition, the value of a verbal adjective serving as epithet. The cup is thus said to be suitable to contain the libtation of soma nourishment and beverage of celestial beings.

17. *viṣṭvī* which one encounters among the nouns of Nighaṇṭu signifying action, II) seems to be used here with the grammantical value of a gerundive under this ancient form of instrumental (tvī analogous to *tvā*), the noun could belong to the root vis (3 cl) having the meaning of to accomplish (perficere) as M. Westergaard (Radices S.R. Perficiendo opera) has understood. *taraṇitvena* is an adverbial form, similar to the two words *turṇiḥ* and *taraṇis* signifying rapidly, promptly (Nigh. II 15 *kṣipranāmāni*).

18. *vāghataḥ* which will be explained with difficulty here as signular and which perhaps may be only a substitution of the regular form of plural, vāghantaḥ is ranked amongst the synonyms of *ṛtvij* in the Nigh. III 18. The word appears to have been drawn from the same root *vah*. 'to bear' as that in the word *vahni* (*vahnayaḥ*) cited earlier (I 20, 8) bearer of offerings. See the explanation given in this sense by Devarājayajvan, commentator of Nighaṇṭu

(Rosen Adnot p. xii). RV I 3, 2; I 31, 14; I 36, 13; 40, 4; 48, 7.

19. This concerns the moment of mythical history, in which, the Ṛbhus are represented as taking part with the libations of the ancient Devas.

They desire only a just part of the juice of Soma, so also the divine nourishment, of which the offerings of the mortals, and above all clarified butter, formed part

20. 'vidman' could designate in the Veda a reflexive knowledge, the conscience of knowing. It is explained in the Bhāṣya by the word *jñāna*, knowledge (RV I 31, 1 *vidma ā* "cum is scientis"—Adnot Rosen or by the word *vedana* (see the sanskrit Gloss on the passage).

21. In this place the poet calls the sun (*sūrya*), protector, guardian of the whole universe, the word pitṛ retakes thus the etymological value that the modern philology has attributed to it by drawing it from the root pā to save, to guard, to nourish (cf. Bopp. Glossar Sansc. alt p. 217). The Ṛbhus, by becoming the rays of the sun have acquired the faculty of spreading themselves and penetrating every where with rapidity.

22. According to the scholiast the wellbeing attached to the enjoyment of celestial lustre, is the enjoyment of the divine nourishment of Soma.

23. The second interpretation which Sāyaṇa brings in makes Indra intervene in this stanza and gives him the epithet 'shining from afar.' This is the forced meaning that the Vedic exegesis has given of the word Ṛbhu as we will show in the course of these researches. The repetition of the word Ṛbhu—it appears to us-removes the possibility of this second interpretation.

24. We will return later to the examination of this point of the myth, repeated in almost all the hymns to the Ṛbhus but explained more particularly in the gloss of Sāyaṇa on this hermistich. The resurrection of the cow is one of

the marvellous acts attributed to the children of Sudhanvan.

25. The word naraḥ which serves to invoke the Ṛbhus in this hymn and in several others has been able to denote the sense of men (males), which it has conserved in classical Sanskrit. It is possible to draw it from an ancient root *nṛ* to conduct, to direct and to assign to it in consequence a meaning fully antique. It is by reason of the etymology that Sāyaṇa has explained it most often by the word *netāraḥ*; guides. He has even, in this place and in others determined the hieratic sense, which he has attachd to it, by adding '*yajñasya netāraḥ*' guides or directors of sacrifice.' We have seen the same epithet of the Rbhus commented only once by Sāyaṇa in this most general sense of 'man' *manuṣyāḥ* (*III 4, 7, 1*). We do not know if it is necessary to have recourse to, besides the derivation indicated at the moment, a hypothesis of an ancient form *anṛ*, following the analogy of the Greek stem whose form would be reputed as more organic. M. Benfey, who is the author of this hypothesis had desired to draw the two words from *an* identical root 'an' to 'respirate' 'athmen,' and it would thus be one of the premier nouns of a man, a qualification expressing the faculty of respiration (Grish-wursellexion—A Dictionary of Greek roots Vol. I, p. xiv, p. 122).

26. We have preferred the second interpretation of Sāyaṇa, because of the known sense of *vājasāti*, noun for combat in the poetic language. (Nigh II ,—Vājasātau). Moreover we see it preferred by Rosen. The first interpretation would come to this 'satisfy us by food in the dispension of the nourishment.' This difference is due to the numerous senses that the authors of the Veda have attached to the word *vāja* and its derivatives as we will have occasion to show later in the philological examination of other passages. We admit with Westergaard that '*aviḍḍhi*' is a second person-singular of the Imperative aorist of the root '*av*' to save to protect (Radice Linga, Sansc. p. 255).

27. The epithet *vṛaṣaṇvasū* refers to the male energy, with which the horses of Indra are endowed and of which they have in themselves the inexhaustible source, according to the image used by the poet. The verbal adjective *vṛṣan* is used in the same meaning in several places of the RV (I 10, 10; I 16, 1; 54, 2; I 55, 4).

28. '*kratu*' has a multiple use in the vedic texts, sometimes it plays the role of an adjective meaning dispenser, liberal (RV I 17, 5 lit.—perfector), sometimes it has the value of a substantive, may be with the sense of action, and by analogy of sacrifice (Nigh II 1; RV I 55, 8), may be with the sense of force, power, which belongs here to the antique form of the dative kratve (cf. RV I 19, 2; I 69, 1).

29. The word '*ratha*' in plural seems to be taken here in a collective sense, which does not revolt against the practice of the poetic thought with the ancient people; it designates the collection of chariots or, if one so desires, the chariots of the tribe and at the same time those who mounted them or drove them; as in the language of the epics ratha would have signified at one and the same time the chariot and the hero. Even here the sole term *ratha* has comprised—it appears to us—the active part of the Aryan tribe, charged with the direction of the chariot, which were necessary for the transport of the most feeble part of the families of shepherds during their frequent migrations or in the moments of war or battle. The chariots have been used at the same time by the Hindus to conserve, during the long marches in traversing barren or dry places, the food-stuffs which formed the principal riches of the voyaging tribes suddenly quitting cultivated or naturally fertile places.

30. The name of Ṛbhu or of Vāja placed in plural represents the three Ṛbhus, always associated in their history. Sāyaṇa observes in the gloss on this passage and similar other passgages that Vibhvan, the second of the sons of Sudhanvan is supposed to be included in the names of

these two brothers, elevated in the invocations of Veda to value of a patronymic and sacred name. See chapter VII Sec. I.

31. By the sole word '*sāti*' the vedic poet means the reunion of all material well-beings, which assure force against the exterior enemies and triumph in the combats. The word '*sāti*' can be derived, on the authority of Pāṇini, from the roots *śan* and *san*, which are often confounded in the Veda, with the general sense of giving. It has taken, turn by turn, the analogous meanings of the gift, acquisition, possession, enjoyment, fortune, as the texts, which precede, furnish examples. (Cf. RV I 4, 9; I 6, 10; I 36, 17).

32. For understanding the begining of this hymn well, it is necessary to know that it consists of a dialogue between Agni and the Rbhus. We only indicate at present the subject of this dialogue, whose allusions are explained by the gloss of Sāyaṇa, because we will take up again later the facts contained in it by collecting around, from the same point of view, the diverse elements of the myth of the Ṛbhus. It is sufficient for us to remark here that the poet has given the speech to the Ṛbhus, who perhaps on seeing Agni dressed in a form similar to theirs, cannot further distinguish each one from amongst themselves, and ask themselves if he is the eldest or the youngest of the three brothers. They call him by the word 'brother' and justify themselves, in advance, from the reproach of having destroyed the famous cup of divine libations.

33. kad (*kat*) figures in this locution as the ancient form of the interrogative pronoun in neuter gender and the same form has equally fulfilled the role of a conjunction (Cf. I 121, i—*kadittha*). While *kim* drawn from another stem *ki* has prevailed in Sanskrit, other languages have preserved more of testiomony in favour of a primitive use of neuter singular of the stem ka. While the classical language of India has preserved it only in the interrogative pronoun *kaccit*, the Zend offers it to us in the interrogative participle *kat* and Latin in the relative pronoun

quad—See Bopp. Var. Gr. des Sanskrit, Zend, Greisch, Ltain etc.(3rd edition, Berlin 1837, pronomina pp. 558-559).

34. The cup is thus designated as "issue of a great race," *mahākula* it was the work of Tvaṣṭṛ, the celestial artisan, whose name figures more than once in the hymns to the Ṛbhus, as that one of the important personages mixed with their history.

35. We believe that druṇa (*druṇaḥ*) can be interpreted in this passage as genitive singular of the substantive '*dru*' which would have been used primitively, rather in neuter than in masculine. One knows that the masculine from *druḥ* belongs to the classical language in the sense of wood or tree and figures among the synonyms of *druma* with which it has a common root '*dru*' to run, to flow (cf. Amarakoṣa II 4, 1, 5, Ed. Loiseleur Vol. I p. 80). If we are inclined to take druṇa as a substantive it is in consideration of its relation with *bhūtim* which determines it and at the same time because of the full construction of the second line divided in two hemistiches. We do not know if it would be so natural to relate *druṇa* as adjective of a member of the phrase, which preceds and that in the capacity of a second adjective, while it is separated from the first, *mahākulaḥ* by the vocative '*Agne bhrātar.*'

36. Agni replies to them by recalling the message, with which the gods have put him in charge, concerning the works, procure to the virtuous and just mortals the enjoyment of to immortality and of divine gifts. The marvellous works, which have been enumerated by the authors of every hymn are taken back from a sort of inspiration of gods transmitted, not long before by the god of Fire and repeated to the Rbhus by the same god when already they have been admitted-or if one prefers-when they desire to be admitted to the participation of sacrifices.

37. Here the Ṛbhus recall the principal objects of the message of the devas and the works, which they have faithfully accomplished. They have gone by the way of sacrifice,

according to the masters of the heaven. They acknowledge to the new brother, whom they see in Agni that they owe this glorification to their labour. We remark in passing as one of the peculiarities of the antique language of the Veda the use of the second person of verb in place of the third, which is called the premier in Sanskrit grammar. The present example is furnished to us by the word *abravītana*, which replaces the third person of imperative plural, *abruvan* and whose termination '*tana*' is substituted to the regular flexional ending '*ta*' (see Pāṇini VII, 11 45).

38. It appears difficult to us to join vas (*vaḥ*)' to *tāni* by a very strong elipsis, which the commentator Sāyaṇa supposes and according to which it could be translated as : "O brother, after having accomplished the works, prescribed by you (gods), we have come to the help of the sacrifice." The syntax of the Vedic idiom, does it not authorise us to make the form vaḥ the regime of the verb '*emasi*' by substitution of *yuṣmān*, accusative 'plural' of the same pronominal form ? A third interpretation would consider to take the from 'vaḥ' in a sense, which many of the examples, have justified: yuṣmadartham. "After having done these works in your favour, we have come."

39. With these words Dīrghatamas inserts the style of the direct invocation. 'The Ṛbhus,' says the singer, "interrogate one another about the fate of the messenger, when, all of a sudden Agni disappears from the sight."

40. We have read in the place "*yaḥsya*' relying on the pada-text of the hymn, which offers the following orthography. '*kva iti abhūt yaḥ syaḥ*'. The demonstrative pronoun '*sya*' appears to be of a frequent use in the Veda and is preferred in this kind of construction in which it follows the relative pronoun. If one reads '*yasya*' as in the Manuscript 42 (coll-Chambers,) the translation may be modified in this manner, "Where has he gone, he, whose messenger has come to us ?" But perhaps this interpretation loses clarity.

Here has reappeared the fable of Tvaṣṭṛ, the first author of the unique cup. Penetrated with resentment and shame on seeing his work destroyed he is reputed by tradition to have been envious and all of a sudden, he disappears becoming a woman. The root *añj* to manifest, takes, with prefix ni, the neuter sense of disappearing vanishing.

42. It is necessary to understand, following Sāyaṇa that the Ṛbhus are implicitely named in the scornful exclamation of Tvaṣṭṛ and that after the division of the sacred cup the mortal authors, who sacrifice, have imposed with the sacerdatal functions new names of *'hotṛ,' 'advaryu,' 'udgātṛ'*. A text of this nature will show us in the Ṛbhus, the authors of some important innovation in the practices of more ancient cult of the Hindus.

43. The manuscript from Berlin, No. 42, has here 'sacān' to the hemistich and mans. No. 43 sacaṁ, the adverb *'sacā,'* which is used as a synonym for *'saha'* in the vedic texts (RV I 5, 2,; I 7, 2; I 9, 3; I 10, 4; I 40, 1; I 51, 11) meaning together, at the same time. Or can it be derived from the adverbial stem *'sa' 'sam,'* joined to the suffix *ca*, which is found in the adjective *ucca* (elevated) *nīca* (low), but with the condition of the lengthening of the final vowel ?

44. His name signifies, according to Sāyaṇa the protector of the extensive prayer. This, which is applicable without difficulty to the myth of a divine being who has filled the role of a priest of the world of gods, the purohita of the heaven in the most ancient mythology of India, is directly connected with the Veda (see Roth memoir cited on "Brahma and the Brāhmaṇas" Zeitsch I 1 p. 69 onwards; p. 76 onwards).

45. This first part of the stanza should be thus understood on the authority of the commentator. Indra and the other Devas have, by their high destiny, at their disposal the chariot and the diverse objects furnished by you, O Ṛbhus that is to say—these things created by the Ṛbhus, were

destined for the gods and that is why they have evalued their authors a divine recompense.

46. See earlier hymn 110 of Book I (Stz. 8) and later hymn 4, (Stz. 4) of the Adhyāya 7, Book III. This is the place to observe that the three poets have related the same traditional data in the analogous terms.

47. abravītana replaces here as earlier the third person '*abruv an*' Sāyaṇa gives as the subject of this verb the name of Devas, whom he supposes to internene for presenting to the Ṛbhus the choice of several of the oblations, which are placed in the liturgic day. It is the libation of the evening, as all the texts establish, which has been conceded to the Ṛbhus, associated with Indra and Savitṛ.

48. The poet has desired to distinguish in this place the Soma prepared according to the ordinary rities and special libation in which the Soma is purified or clarified with the help of the plant called Muñja, le Saşcarum Muñja of Roxburg (Wilson Dict)—The scholiast informs us that the mountain Mujāvat was, above all, celebrated for use in submitting the juice of asclepiacle acide to a more refined preparation. One knows also that the fibres of the same plant served to form the three cords of which the girdle of a Brāmaṅa should be composed, following the rules.

In a text of the Kāṭhakopanışad (Chap. VI Stz. 17, Ed. Poley. 111), there is a question in a comparison, of the plant Muñja, of which are extracted fibrous twings icckhiās after taking out its envelope by removing its sheath. We should add that Sāyaṇa quotes a second curious but less plausible interpretations according to which the Ṛbhus address this speech to their thirsty horses.

49. The excellence of waters is consecrated by a great number of antique texts belonging to the religious literature of the Vedas. We have already related and appreciated formerly some of these passages (See Chap I S 1) We restrict ourselves to mention a famous śloka to which the scholiast

makes allusion according to the code of brahmanic legislation. The being existing by itself, having resolved to itself to emanate diverse creatures from its substance, produced, first the waters, in which it has deposited a germ.

50. The word *vadharyantīm*, used here, derives from an ancient noun *vadhar*, analogous by its meaning to the word sabar which we have met with earlier (see the note on I 20, 3). *vadhar* is one of the Vedic nouns for thunderbolt *vajra* (Nigh II 20) and serves to form a verbal adjective, to which the scholiast attributes the value of desiderative. Sāyaṇa applies the epithet to a cloud making the thunder-bolt march, to the row of clouds (*megha-paṅktiḥ*), whose sides the thunderbolt pierces in order to make the waters of the rain gush forth; the cloud attiring the thunderbolt, the cloud, the vehicle of the thunderbolt.

51. Redressed with the quality of *ṛtvij* the Ṛbhus are here represented accomplishing the immolation of a cow. The blood of the animal is named by the poet *śoṇa*: The words which Sāyaṇa explains by the synonymous words *śoṇam* and *śoṇā* (subst. nt and fem) signify red colour of the blood. The faulty form *śroṇām* is that which the manuscripts, to which we have access, bear—The second interpretation according to which Sāyaṇa makes *śroṇam*, the epithet of *gām*. a cow, modifies the sense singularly—The one leads towards water, the lame, deformed cow. The adjective takes thus, the ordinary meaning, which it has in the classical language.

52. This stanza consecrates one of the essential points in the myth of the Ṛbhus, the mixture of a naturalistic element, which one could rather call human : In this hymn, Dīrghatamas passess more than once the order of facts to the other, as he abruptly passess from the recitative to direct invocation. The Ṛbhus are assimilated in similar passages to the rays of the sun. They do not at all appear during the night. They are reputed as sleeping, while the sun is enveloped by darkness. They pour down on the earth

humidity with floods of rain which the Indian imagines as flowing down from the sphere of the luminous rays: From the word of the Śāstra of Manu. "*Adityājjyayate vṛṣṭih.*" *From the sun* is born the rain. The singer supposes that the the Ṛbhus are sleeping while the sun, always the master of the sovereign lustre, hides his rays to the earth.

53. The second line of the stanza 11 is referred to by Yāska in the passage of Nirukta XI 16, concerning the Ṛbhus, according to the explanation of Stz. 4, I 110. We will take back later collectively the points, relatedly necessary for the understanding of the myth. We observe only that the name of the sun is translated in two manners by the commentator, '*agrāhya*' one, who cannot be seized, or rather that which is without doubt better, '*agopanīya*,' one who cannot be concealed or repelled. One can only be struck by the antique character of this expression, so interpreted. The *ṛṣi* Dīrghatamas saluates the sun as the hearth of light and of life, which cannot be hidden even for a moment. The primitive poetry has not at all possessed a more grand and brighter image to paint the indefectible power of the sun in the battle of elements and the triumphant march, that it persues in non-interrupted succession of days and years.

54. The Ṛbhus are spoken, as fully in sleep, in the bosom of the sun in the course of night, covering the beings placed below them, by the clouds, the precursers of the rain. The poet thus desires to praise them as the authors of fertility of the earth, as the agents, whose beneficial concourse never ceases day or night.

55. If one believes Sāyaṇa the singer takes here the word *pitarā* in the hieratic sense of protectors (*jagataḥ pālakāḥ*) as we have observed earlier (See note on I 110, 6) and he means by this term the sun and the moon who divide the empire of day and of night.

56. The praise is addressed to the Ṛbhus, because they have destroyed by cursing all the malificient beings such as the Rākṣasas who hold the rain-water captive in the heaps of the clouds.

57. These last words also take one interpretation by antithesis. 'You have exalted one who has praised you'.

58. *bastaḥ* here used as a noun for the sun carries the meaning of the author, the ordinator for the earth as Sāyaṇa attributes to it. In all cases the word seems to be drawn from the root 'bas'—(vas-Class III) to be fixed, closed rather established, *vāsaraḥ*, which figures in the nouns for the day in the Nighaṅṭu—(II 9 Diva) would easily be drawn from the same root, though one has more often related vastu and *vastra* to the root '*vas*' to cover, to dress (Cf. Bosen Adno p. vi).

59. Sāyaṇa has thus understood and interpreted the response of the sun to the Ṛbhus. You have poured rain with the help of Vāyu and likewise you have poured it not long before, so that the sun and the moon could not be seen. Now in the season of rain, you render visible the entire world, your reveal it for all. Across these images we can evolve in the spirit of the Hindus a thought of admiration which follows the rays of the sun in their aerial fight against the clouds which spread a veil of darkness on the terrestrial world.

60. The four last stanzas have been composed under the influence of the ideas of materialistic cosmogony. The Devas, who fill the diverse points of space make an alliance by the desire of uniting their action in view of the world. They come towards the Ṛbhus to have part in their function of producing the rain.

61. We will reserve to examine especially the value of this qualification which will come again more than once in hymns to the Ṛbhus. We only remark that it accords well in this place the attributes of vivifying heat and of generative force which the singer of naturalism lends to these new divinities.

62. *Uśijaḥ* is translated by Sāyṇa as 'desiring a part of sacrifice', as he had derived it from the root '*vas*' to desire, to wish. The word *uśijaḥ* is found among the

nouns for a sage in the glossary often cited (Nigh-*medhāvīnāma* III 16) perhaps one could translate it rather saying : endowed with wisdom, because of their desire to a part in the sacrifices.

63. The word '*veda*' receives from the glosses, according to the context the precise meaning of knowledge, *jñāna*. Now it does not figure in the Nighaṇṭu among the nouns for intelligence, prajñā; but figures among those for riches (II 10 dhana). The traditional sense of the word vedas is that of riches in the compound sa-vedas (RV I 93, 9) savedasā and *jātavedas*, 'dives' as Rosen has translated in several cases this epithet of Agni. (IV 1, 1; V 2, 3). To us it appeared plausible to establish in some examples of this kind, the idea of science or knowledge of the kind that jātavedas designates 'one in whom, knowledge is in born' and *viśvavedas*, 'one in whom is all knowledge'.

64. *Varpas* used here in compound is one of the Vedic nouns meaning form (Nigh-rūpa III 16). It has the sense of beauty, of lustre, which is applied to the state of the Ṛbhus, glorified in a manner equal of their marvellous acts.

65. We have adopted in the translation of this passage as that of Stz. 8 of I 20, the second meaning of the word *bhāga* happy lot, felicity. If one takes the first meaning that of portion, share it could be translated thus : you have obtained a part of the gifts of sacrifice.

66. We have given to the word *dhiyā* the sense, which Sāyaṇa conserves to it in accord with the author of Nighaṇṭu (III 9) that of *prajñā*, prudence, wisdom. However, it is not less plausible to take to the substantive 'dhī' the concrete sense of act of meritorious work, which it denotes in a great number of passages (Cf R VI 1, 7; I 2, 2 and 3; I 46, 2) and which the gloss explains sometimes by the work karma on the traditional authority of Yāska (Nigh. II 1). One could then translate-due to the sacrifice, due to the prayer or the offering, in virtue of which...etc.

67. The form *apasaḥ*, which is found equally in the following hymn to the Rbhus) III, 7, 1, 1) is none other than then neuter noun '*apas*' action used as a substantive in the sense of worker or artisan (operator). It is joined by apposition to the name of the Rbhus. The same word is also used as adjective meaning related to the work, concerning the workers (Cf. Rosen Adnot—RV I 12, 3; p. xi).

68. *Dadhanvire* the form of reduplicative perfect (33rd perspl.) drawn from the root '*dhanv*' to run away, to avoid, or rather to go, to advance. (Nigh. gati-karma I 14). If one has regard for the value of this root, or if one is forced to give to this passage a very large interpretation. 'They have gone there beyond. They have escaped from this life.' Sāyaṇa does not seem to have taken into account the etymology of the word, in translating it, as formed from the root dhṛ, to possess, to live : *prāṇān dhārayanti* (See earlier *adhārayanta* I 20, 8).

69. If it may be permitted to paraphrase this second hemistich, one finds in it the expression of the ideas, which follow :—At the instant you have joined to the propitious offering of men desirous of their fruits, that is to say, desiring in return of their praises and their offerings the terrestrial boons and the possesion of the heaven.

70. We have tried to render by this expression the energy of the Sanskrit locution 'pratimai' at once worthy of observation in its antique terseness-pratimai is, rather, as Sāyaṇa desires (*caturthyekavacanam*) the dative singular of a form of infinitive immediately drawn from the root mā to produce, to measure with the prefix *prati* jointed to the prefix *anu*, the same root affects the sense of equalling, being equal (RV I 57, 5), which is convenient for the form *pratimai*. The word tends itself in this place to an elliptical construction in which is understood the idea of possibility. "It is not at all possible to measure your works. That is to say, these are without measure or comparison." Dr. Roth has furnished us another example of the same

construction drawn from the Ṛgveda (VIII, 4)—*Na te dāmāna ādabhe*—'Your worshippers are not to offend'.

71. On the authority of Sāyaṇa himself, the possessive adjective Vājavat can be understood from Vāja, associated with his two brothers Ṛbhu and Vibhvan. In all cases the same word has often served the quality of epithet in the language of the hymn (I 120, 9) and the kind of ambiguity which it can present here has nothing that repels with the spirit of the style of the Vedic poems (See later St. 7 *vājibhiḥ*).

72. The poet calls Indra in order that he drinks with big gulps the liquor of Soma, by emptying the cups which the liquor fills.

73. *Maghavan* is an appalation of Indra, which has passed from the chants of the Veda in the mythological language of the epics. It means possessor of riches in all invocations of the Indian Jupiter, reputed as liberal on the earth as powerful in the heaven.

74. *Śacī* (sub. form) designates in general an action (Nigh II 1 karma), but above all the pious and meritorious act such as that of preparing the libation, of presenting the offerings, of accomplishing every point of ritual in the sacrifice. The same word *śac*, by a striking analogy with the use of the word *dhī*, (See the note on Stz 3 of this hymn) joins to this concrete meaning, the general meaning of intelligence or of knowledge. (Nigh II 9 *prajñā*) derived from the root *śac* to speak, it has marked the gift of speech, revealing intelligence. (Eacunditas—Westergaard, Radices, S.V.). Though some passages of the Veda make mention of the deity Indrāṇi, wife of Indra, we do not believe that she is invoked here, under the name of Śacī. The structure of the phrase, moreover, seems to oppose this mythological interpretation.

75. *Svasarāṇi* is one of the synonyms of the word day 'ahar' (Nigh I 7). This neuter noun means the days, those which come by themselves'.

76. The poet uses in this place the resources of alliteration to express the attribute that he lends to Indra and to Rbhus, the power to dispense the nourishment which maintains the force. It follows the epithet Vājibhiḥ, which we will translate more voluntarily by the words-possessors of force-from the participle *vājayat*, belonging to a denominative verb derived from *vāja*, force, nourishment. Indra is thus invoked as he who provides nourishment for men and who desires their vigour and their well-being (cf. RVI 4, 9·*vājayāmaḥ annavantam kurmaḥ*)—Rosen·nutrimus). The same denominative verb has moreover the meaning of desiring food, condition of force, as in the stanzas 2 and 5 of the Gāyatrī (*vājayantam, vājayantaḥ*) and in the RV I 30, 1.

77. By the adjective '*ketāḥ*' 'endowed with intelligence' would the poet denote the Maruts, gods of wind, companions of Indra, as Sāyaṇa desires? Does it not appear more natural and more plausible to apply the first epithet to the noun of horses, '*aśvaḥ*' as the second epithet '*iṣirebhiḥ*' (prompt, active) forces to understand ?

78. *sahasraṇītha*, epithet of Indra is one of the compounds, which admit tne action of the linguals of the first word on the following; that is why the nasal 'n' of the word *nitha* 'eye' has been changed to the lingual ṇ by the influence of the letter *r* which precedes. The reason of this fact may be found mainly in the value of the proper nouns, which the usage has given to similar epithet-compounds. (See Bopp-critical Grammar of Sanskrit language S 94 annotation—Bohtlingk in his work on the change of the dental nasal to cerebral nasal has minutely analysed the axioms of Pāṇini, concerning this euphonic law. (VIII, 1, 1-39). He has shown its application in the compounds acquiring the meaning of proper nouns (Zeit-schrift fur die kunde des morgenlandes) IV B. p. 358 onwards. Bonn 1842).

79. '*upastire*' is a locative used in the sense of dative, by one of these mutations of cases, very frequent in the style of

the Veda. Upastara, that the scholiast explains by the synonym upastaraṇa, equally drawn from the root *stṛ* to spread 'sternere', denotes the liturgic presentation of Soma, which is displayed in large cups or rather poured on the carpet of grass.

80. '*eva*' adjective formed the root '*i*' to go is an epithet used commonly by the Vedic poets to designate some object, whose name is understood. Thus it is applied to the march in the hymns (RV I 117, 4); (RV I 62, 8), to the winds (I 69, 2).

81. Vāmadeva singing of the deified Ṛbhus as the rays of the sun depicts the rapidity of their course, which permits them to penetrate in an instant the etheral space. He enters, in this manner, in the ordinary spirit of descriptions, inspired by Sabaiam.

82. dhīrāsaḥ adjective derived, from the substantive dhī (fen).

83. *aram*, ancient word analogous to the word *alam*, which has remained in classical language in the state of a participle, may mean praise, homage, honour : *Aram viśvasmai* 'Honour is to every one' (RVI 66, 3). '*Yo asmān arams Sūktaiḥ* adjective derived from the substantive *dhī* (fem) 'intelligence' conserves still in the Vedic idiom its premier meaning of wise, intelligent, (Nigh. III 15 *medhāvī-nāmāni*) while the same word has the meaning of firm, dauntless in the classical Sanskrit. (See later Hymn 4, stz. 7).

84. *manāyai* which can only be the dative singular of a feminine substantive 'mana' which is directly derived from the root 'man' to think, may mean intelligent creature, a being endowed with thought. It is not one of the luminous expressions of the language of antique poetry ? We will relate it to the word, '*manāyu*' which can be interpreted with greater justice only by the words 'to be thinking.' RV I 92, 9—*manāyoḥ*. However Dr. Roth has informed us of a passage from the Ṛgveda, where the same term *manāyuḥ* has received as its synonym (*Stuti-*

kāmaḥ), desirous of praise in the gloss of Sāyaṇa (RV III, Adhyāya VI, SṢkta 13).

85. We will remark here that the image of a pillar has been introduced from early times in Indian poetry but that here it has been also applied in good as well as in bad part. One of the singers of the Veda, says to Agni in an invocation to the fire, "You support men, as an errected pillar does to an abode (RV I 59, 9)."

86. The compound *madhupsarasaḥ* is interpreted in the simplest and the most natural manner by the equivalent word '*manohararūpaḥ*.' Among the very numerous nouns for form or beauty '*rūpa*' in the Vedic texts figures the neuter noun '*psaras*' analogous to the better known words cited by Nighaṇṭu (III 7) such as *apasaḥ*, *psaḥ*, *peśaḥ*. *One reads* for example '*Mahi psaro varuṇasya*.' The great form, the immense body of Varuṇa' (RV I 41, 7.) It appears to us that this word could be explained as one of the affiliated forms of 'psu' 'body' which has its equivalents in Zend *fṣu* curious word to which Mr. Eug. Burnouf has consecrated an ingenious monograph (studies on the Zend texts, third art. Asiatic Journal series III, 1840, Vol. X p. 327 onwards, p. 333). The word, more known, taken for example '*psu*' could draw its meaning from a root, which has the sense of nourishing, in such as the animated beings receive their body from the nourishment that they take, or canserve it by virtue of food. One is related by this kind of researches to a double stem '*psu*' and '*psā*' that one could derive from two roots of classical sanskrit '*sphi*' and '*svi*' with a condition of a series of transformations of metathesis of the same kind by which the word psaraḥ could be traced to a root such as 'spṛ' to protect or rather svṛ, svar to go ?

87. The word '*saṁvatsara*' (a year, the first year of the cycle Cf. Colebr. Misc. Es. Ip. 58). However the repetition of the same formula relates only to the principal moments of the same act, the resurrection of a dead cow. There is nothing in the myth which gives place to believe that the same feat

may be reproduced several times; but the poet uses this course as if he could begin the enumeration of a more considerable series of feats, in order to give more of weight to the fact, which serves the denoument, obtaining of immortality.

88. This text furnishes to us in the word '*mā*' (*mās*, *māḥ*) one of these monosyllables which have soon mostly disappeared in the crowd of the words, richer in formation and in harmony, but which attest the austere simplicity of primitive Sanskrit. The classical Sanskrit has not at all retained this accusative plural of a monosyllabic feminine noun, which the sole neuter, noun *māṁsa*, *māṁsāni* has replaced.

89. This stanza has been translated in Latin by Rosen in his notes on I 20 (Adnot p. XL VII).

90. The poet says that the Ṛbhus have not at all spoken in vain that they would make four cups; they have in reality executed their plan, which has deserved them, being men, a part in the divine prerogatives, the enjoyment of third libation every day.

91. '*venat*' is the imperfect singular of the verbal stem *ven* or vain-in classical, 'to praise,' 'to desire.' (Nigh II 6—*kāntināma*) the sense of other similar passages concerning Tvaṣṭṛ would permit to translate –'to be envious, to bear envy,' since the celestial worker sees with envy a work, which surpassed his, in lustre.

92. The substantive '*dhanvan*' (mas, nt) could have had, in the beginning the meaning of vast extent. It has sometimes meant the world, great space. (RV I 35, 8). Sometimes it has served to designate the atmosphere, the space of the air (Nigh I 3—*antarikṣa*), sometimes it has expressed the idea of a desert land, of the places dry and barren (RV I 38, 7). The same word has persisted in classical Sanskrit in the sense of desert, a land without water (Wils. Dict) "*Samānau marudhanvanau*" - (Amara-koṣa II, 1, 5). *Dhanvan* (mas, nt), on the other hand is one of the synonyms for the noun for bow, the neuter *dhanuḥ*.

93. We believe that in this Tatpuruṣa-compound, the word *nara* does not have only the etymological meaning of leader (*netṛ*) but that it denotes a man as in many of the passages of these hymns. The root *sthā* has preserved its long vowel in the second member of the compound according to the analogy that the use of the roots ending in long vowels presents in the Vedic language (See the examples in Rosen Adnot p. VII).

94. It appears to us conform more to the spirit of this stanza, which describes the works of the Ṛbhus, to attribute to *avas* the sense of help or protection, which it frequently has in the Vedic language. (RV I 17, 1-2-6; I 22, 6; I 42, 5; I 46, 12; I 117, 19), while the scholiast interpretes the word *avas* in the sense of nourishment (Nigh. II 7 anna).

95. We have preserved in the word *kratvā* the general sense of action that the Vedic language furnishes (See earlier the note on stz. RV I 111, 2) Meanwhile we will propose in the manner of a conjecture to consider *kratvā* as a verbal adjective, qualifying *manasā* and to translate consequently 'by an active operative, intelligence (capable of executing).'

96. We have followed on this point the construction indicated by the scholiast, who explains the *ukthā* as a from of the instrumental. If this form is not different from the Vedic form of nt. plural (*ukthāni*) can it be applied to other cases of nominative and accusative ? One would need other examples to prove this. Could not one find a meaning more conforming with the antique poetry on the nature of the chant and of poetry by combining the three words.—'*medhayā ukthā madantah*' and by translating 'rejoicing in the songs by intelligence ?' In these poetic texts the word *ukthā* characterises the hymns, of which the Ṛgveda is compoted. (*Bahvarcānām śastrāṇi*—RV I 5, 8 the Commentary). This sense is justified by a great number of passages I 2, 2; I 8, 10; I 10, 5; I 27, 12; I 47, 10; I 54, 7) *uktha* is formed by means of the suffix *tha* which remanis only in a few words, e.g. in the nt. subst. *riktha* fortune.

97. Here still we have desire to reproduce, in the beginning, the interpretation, which resorts to the gloss of Sāyaṇa in which na is reputed as adverbial negative particle and *ṛte* plays the role of preposition as in classical Sanskrit (without, beyond, with the exception of). It seems to us that one could defend another interpretation of the passage by giving to *ṛte* the value of an adverb and the sense of 'vainly' 'uselessly' deduced by the analogy of the meaning of the preposition. 'They are not in vain for the succours of a fatigued man.' But there is a third explanation of this text, which could have more verity. One could read : *na(ḥ) ṛte* by restituting to the neuter substantive *ṛta* the sense of sacrifice, of ceremony of pious act, which it bears most often in the Vedic poetry (see for example RV I, 1, 8 Adnot Rosen I 13, 6; I 14, 7; I 23, 5; I 34, 10; I 36, 19; I 44, 14; I 46, 14; I 47, 1, 3 and 5). One could persue in this way the following interpretatoin : 'In our sacrifices, the Devas are to the help of fatigued man' or rather one could connect together the two members of the phrase. 'Then the gods have established for you the libation of the day and the enjoyment that it procures, in our ceremony, for the succours of the man, fatigued by work.'

98. *ratnadheya* is considered by Sāyaṇa as a dative, as if this form was equivalent to *ratnadheyāya*, which belonged to the neuter substantive ratnadheya, used later (Stz. 4) and formed in a manner analogous with the word '*somapeya*,' the action of drinking Soma. (RV I 45, 9).

99. *accha* which is an ordinary adverb making a tendency towards a thing, has here the use of a preposition which precedes the accusative *yajñam* with the value of the preposition '*ad*' to. Though this indeclinable word, placed isolatedly, best represents the Latin 'ecce' whose euphonic elements it contains, it determines the idea of movement, when it is constructed with a verb, that expresses itself. One can see on this second meaning of the word, the rule of Pāṇini I 4, 69. (*acchagatyarthe vedeṣu*) and the observations of the scholar-editor of 'Hindu grammarian,' M.O.

Bohtlingk on the hymns of the Ṛgveda (Sect 1, Stz. 2), in one of the recent publications of Sanskrit chrestomathie—St. Petersburg 1845 p. 369). The prosodic accent makes the final 'a' long in the measured stanzas of the Veda, where we find several examples of it. (RV I 38, 13; I 44, 4).

1 00. We have searched to combine in this formula the two meanings, which Sāyaṇa draws from the words : ('*vidānāso janmanaḥ*). It is useless, it appears to us, to understand here the idea of possession of divinity or of enjoyment of Soma. The verbal root *vid* 'to know,' 'to acquaint' often admits in the Vedic texts the noun of the thing in genitive rather than in accusative (See Westgaard. Rad. Ling, Sansc p. 175). It is not, therefore, doubtful that one could relate to the participle as its regime the genitive *jāyamāṇāh*, which could express the idea of mortal birth, of life among men. If the word *janman* could be used in the capacity of an adjective marking possession, as a synonym of the term *janmavantaḥ* as Sāyaṇa uses in the second place, the analogy of the grammatical flexions would demand the form *janmanaḥ* responding to the masc. nom. plural.

101. The Ṛtus are the divinities in number of three or of four, which mark the great divisions of time by relation with the religious ceremonies with which we occupied ourselves in Chap. I S 1.

102. The word *purandhiḥ*, of which the etymological explanation has been attempted by Rosen P XVII) could have the concrete sense of a hymn, of praise or invocation, sign of a complete intelligence as in the hymn I 97, 19 '*Athā yuvāmid-ahvayat-purandhiḥ*' and in the chant called Gāyatrī (III 4, 11, 5).

103. Manuṣvat is an adverbial locution which lends itself to several interpretations; but we have adopted the most natural one, which has the only defect of remaining a little vague (Cf RV 31, 17 *manuṣvat*).

104. We have, in this place followed the scholiast, who calls the libations of soma personified by the poet '*jujuṣāṇāḥ*,' that is to say, '*sevamānāḥ*,' rendering a cult of veneration; but while the root *juṣ* is used many a time in the Veda with the active sense of agreeing, of receiving favourably (RV I 91, 10; I 118, 7) it could be susceptible to take a passive and reflexive meaning, above all when it concerns inanimate objects, to which poetry lends sentiments. That is why we will translate voluntarily the participle *jujuṣānāḥ* by this paraphrase : 'desirious of being received, of being agreed.'

105. To us the ajective *agriya* seems to be taken in the meaning of 'the first' 'the excellent' (*śreṣṭha* RV I 13, 10), though the classical ajective is drawn equally from '*agra*' head 'summit.' Rosen has translated by 'agregius' the word agriya understood as the sun in an ancient text (Adnot P LIII). No doubt that epithet is related to the Ṛbhus, envisaged as the rays of the sun.

106. The verbal root *dhā* takes the sense of venerating, adoring, rendering a cult when it is found joined in conjugation to the prefix *vi*. Westgaard has furnished, in support of this sense several examples drawn from the Vedic books (Radices—p 11). We are content by mentioning here that the form *vidhema* is given by the author of Nighaṇṭu (III 5) among the words which express the act of adoration (*paricaraṇa-karma*).

107. We dare sustain only that the words *martyāya*, *madāya*, which end the two lines of this stanza offer an example to rhyme, whose very ancient use in poetry of the Oriental nations one has searched to prove; but they give us at least a very remarkable application of these assonances, which have not at all been strangers to the composition of the sacred chants of India. There is in the measured portions of the Veda, which are most numerous, a certain symmetry which is not exempt from calculation—it may not be the work on the part of the poet—but which has lent such a great harmony to the chant or to the recitation, as a great help to memory (Cf. Etudes pp. 43-45).

108. Choosing among the denominations of the Ṛbhus Vāmadeva names this time the name of Vājaḥ to the two brothers, Vāja and Vibhvan, and he names the eldest Ṛbhukṣan as has already been seen in the preceding hymn (stz. 9).

109. *gṛṇānāḥ*, the present participle by means of *gṛ* (9th class) to resonnate, to sing, has frequently the sense of praising, celebrating in the Vedic stanzas (See the explanation in the Radices of Westgaard). We observe that the same participle has very often affected a passive meaning as in this stanza (RV I 35, 10; I 62, 5, I 117, 11; *sūnormānena gṛnānena gṛnānāḥ*). We prefer this mode of expression, in spite of the difficulties, which the juxtaposition of the gentitive '*maho draviṇaso*' offers; because it accords best with the nature of an invocation, which supposes the divinities to be praised because of the boons that they have dispensed. Sāyaṇa maintains the active sense by translating —*mahad draviṇaṃ stuvantaḥ*, 'praising, glorifying a big treasure.'

110. *sūrayaḥ* is frequently used in the hymns as an epithet denoting the sages, the poets (RV I 48, 4; I 51, 15; I 54, 11; I 61, 3). It could have been taken rather rarely in the meaning of soldier or warrior (RV I 119, 3). The word has remained in Sanskrit in the restricted sense of pandit or scholar. One finds the form *sūrayaḥ* among the ancient nouns for a singer *stotṛ* (Nigh III 16. See later hymn 5, line 7).

111. The Ṛbhus are well-merited by Indra by their eagerness to execute the works, that this god had demanded from their ability. When the moment of their deification has arrived they are lifted in the celestial world of the master, whom they had obeyed in their mortal life. They have taken place in the court of the Indra and have come following his course, on the earth to drink of Soma in the third libation of every day.

112. This epithet of Indra *gīrvaṇaḥ* recurs often in the hymns of Ṛgveda (I 5, 7; Adnot—Rosen 1, 10, 12; I 45, I 57, 4).

In accord with the etymology proposed by Sāyaṇa it means-charmed by praise, honoured by prayer. The same substantive '*gir*' 'speech' enters in the formation of other compounds of an analogous value. We cite, for example, '*girvāhase*, which is elevated, exalted by prayer (RV I 61, 4—*girvāse*). The entire stanza is not wanting in a certain art of construction. The lyrical style in it is full of firmness and vigour.

113. The divinities called '*agrepāh*' are those, who drink in the first rank, who have right to take a place in the first part in the libations, who arrive at the head of others. In this number are Indra, Varuṇa, so also the Maruts. We believe that a distinction of this kind has been established by the poet, when he has placed at the commencement of the second line the word *agrepābhiḥ*, that we have translated literally with a view to preserve better the simplicity of the original text.

114. Under this name of *ṛtupāḥ* are denoted the divinities named earlier (Stz. 2) to whow one offers the sacrifices at the decided moments of a year. The compoundword expresses a speciality of the Vedic cult on which the commentators have not missed to insist. In ovder to grasp it better, here we will give place to a gloss of Sāyaṇa on the word '*anṛtupāḥ*, epithet of Indra. "*Anṛtupāḥ na kevalam ṛtuṣveva pibati. Anṛtuṣvapi babuśaḥ somam pibannityarthaḥ* (RV III 3, the passage communicted by Dr. Roth).

115. We have not believed to be able to reproduce the interpretation of the scholiast according to which these terms taken to the letter formed a kind of compound called dependant and named 'Tatpuruṣa.' Sāyaṇa has consequently translated '*gnāspatnayaḥ*' with these words : *Strīṇām pālayitryaḥ*, 'Protectors of women.' If one makes it a copulative 'Dvandva' compound one perceives a mythological data, which forms well an alliance with the conceptions of the Veda on the constitution of divine races. It concerned the personifications of female principle, soon associated by the people to the history of gods of

nature and distinguished as women or wives. If one understands the words, *gnāspatnayaḥ* as possessive Bahuvrīhi compound one could find the meaning, very close to this given mythology. The 'Devas who have women for wives', and justified by the passages of the hymns, where are named "the women, the wives of gods. (RV 61, 8; *gnāḥ devapatnīḥ*)." The Nighaṇtu (V 5) gives, '*devapatnayaḥ*' as one of the denominations used in the liturgic style of the Veda. It is in all cases incontestable that *gnā* a women, the mother who gives birth (root *jan*), is a noun expressing suddenly a kind, while *patnī* characterises a specis a decided class, the wives recognised as legitimate wives. The second of these two words, has retained this meaning in some legal sort in classical Sanskrit. It is true that the word *gnā* has disappeared from the language after the Vedic epoch; but its primitive use is confirmed by the similar words, which other ancient languages have retained. Zend *gena*; Persian—*zen*; Armenian-*gin* (*gnaj*-stem of plural gann-nom. *gankh*), Greek and Dorian. It remains for us to take into account the form *gnāḥ* juxtaposed to the second member of the compound *patnī*, or it is not rare in the Veda that the consonant '*p*' and '*k*' admit before them one of the dental or lingual sibilants as one sees it in the proper nouns Bṛhaspati, Brahmaṇaspati etc. and in the orthography of the words *tamasa-spāram*, *tavasaskṛtāni* etc. Now in the example, with which we are occupied, there has been an attraction stronger than this kind of *Sandhi*, attraction which has euphonically placed the sibilant 's' to its following labial 'p'.

116. The Devas named here Parvatas seen to be not different from the divinities which preside over lunar days, denoted in the classical language as *parvan*, *parvāṇi*. Meanwhile we cannot pass in silence over one of the special meanings of the word *parvata* in the Vedic stanzas, that of a cloud which, in fact is one of the synonyms of *megha* (Nigh. I 10, RV I 19, 7; I 54, 10). One knows that the same word has preserved the meaning of a mountain in the monuments of literary centuries.

117. It appeared natural to us to see in the word daivya rather a sort of superlative than a simple adjective derived from Deva. It moreover denotes that which belonged to or that which is related to Devas (RV 45, 9 and 10)—*daivyaṃ janam*. It expresses here the nature of that which is divine by excellence or in the Indian sense that which is eminently resplendent. The sun is, in this sense, as the poet says, essentially divine

118. See the thoughts which we have presented in Chap. I S I on the cult of waters and in particular of the rivers.

119. This invocation that Sāyaṇa desires to add for completing the construction of the stanza '*te agrepāḥ*' is in the spirit of the stanzas that precede, and leads well to an enumeration, poetic but almost complete of the works attributed to the three sons of Sudhanvan.

120. The neuter noun *aṁsatra* which Sāyaṇa comments by kavaca may not mean only the armour but the whole suit of armour, adopting all parts of the body. The word is derived, without doubt from the substantive *aṁsa* 'shoulder' and in general 'part' (root *aṁs* to divide). If one takes it in a more restricted sense aṁsatra would denote the armour of metal which is supported by the shoulders of the warrior. The stem *aṁsa*, derived from homogenous *añc*, has a double meaning. It is related to these words of the Gothic ams, *amas*, (Pott. 'Etymological researches' Vol. II p. 290) Latin *axilla*, *aissella* (Bopp. Gless. Sansc. S.V.) to which respond the forms *ansala* or *anśala* of ancient German and *achsel* of modern German, analogous to Sanskrit *aṁśala*. 'strong', 'robust'. The suffix *tra*, in the word *aṁsatra* could contain, under an abridged form the idea of protection or safety, belonging to the '*trā*'. If one lends such a value to the suffix the vedic word could mean 'protecting the shoulders or the limbs' as the word *tanutra*, or even *tanutrāṇa* means the armour, protecting the body.

121. The word *ṛdhak*, joined in the second line to *rodasī* is an ancient adverbial form, which has the same value as the

adveb *pṛthak*—meaning separately (‘*-rdhak-prthak*’-Nairukta-śabdasaṅgraha—Ms). The idea of isolation, of separation has been drawn from the formation of two words from the verbal roots, which possess the meaning of growing and augmenting. One can be related to the root ṛdh as the other to the roots *Pṛth* and *prath* (to spread). The adverb *pṛthak* presents a veritable antithesis of meaning with the adjective *pṛthu* ‘large’, which has the same root. Its termination expressing a dminutive has in some sort taken back the root upto a contrary idea. On the comparison of these two terms see the first memoir of Dr. Höfer (Baitrage zur Etym. IB p. 75).

122. We understand the word *vibhvaḥ* not as the name of one of the Ṛbhus but as the Vedic form of nom. pl. of the masc. noun *vibhu* ‘master) (pl. *vibhvaḥ*). The same form is found still later in the hymn IV of Vāmadeva (stz. 3). It has remained probable that the poet has preferred this word, presenting with the name of one of his gods, a great resemblance of formation and of euphony.

123. *Vājavat* should be understood here as the physical force that the nourishment serves to contain, but not as the same gift of nourishment, which one of the following epithets specifies. We establish moreover that the substantive *vāja* has had the meaning of force before that of food.

124. The compound *purukṣu* is formed from an ancient masculine noun *kṣu* nourishment, food Nigh II 7 *annanāmāni*). We find the same word in another compound *kṣumat* ‘Pervaded by food’ RV I 31, 13).

125. The substantive *rāti* (derived from the root rai to give, of which the verbal form *rāti* is found in the Nighaṇṭu III 20-*dāna-karmāṇi*) means very often gift, wealth (for example RV I 11, 3-6, 8; I 34); but it has appeared to us susceptible to take in this place the value of an abstruct noun. Meanwhile we have observed the use, sufficiently frequent of the same word as a noun of action, giver, dispenser, liberal (RV I 23, 8; I 29, 4; I 52, 3; I 60, 1) if one adopted this other meaning of the word one could translate. “To

those who celebrate the author (or the authors) of all these gifts."

126. The laudatory epithet *aniḥśastāḥ* not scorned, not mistaken is remarkable by the union of two negative expressions serving to indicate the highest degree of affirmation, the enjoyment assured of honours and of praises. The kind of diverted expression is in all cases in the taste of the antique poetry and the Indian poems could offer quite curious examples of it. We will quote only only the compounds quite known (*anavadyāṅga* mening 'he who is accomplished under the relation of physical beauty, he whose body is irreproachable, he whose form cannot be subject to any blame'. *anavadyāṅgī* is one of the epithets with which the epic poet has composed the portrait of Damayantī in the episode of Nala.

127. It is on the authority of the scholiast that we have translated '*ratnadheyam*' as an epithet of Indra in which could reappear the active sense of the verbal root *dhā*. It seems possible to maintain the value of a substantive-compound given otherwise (RV I 11, 1 and 4) to the same term by constructing the second line in the following manner :—"In this libation, which is offered to you (resides) the dispensing of riches. May the libations causing joy come to you, as towards Indra." One would be borue to deduce this by analogy from the full composition of the following stanza.

128. The scholiast recalls here that the enjoyment of the sacred beverage was accorded to the Ṛbhus by Prajāpati inspite of the opposition of the Devas, as the legend, which we will relate in full, later (Chapter VI) establishes.

129. These words of the Ṛbhus seem to be addressed to Indra for inviting, to take with favour the libation, which will be hereafter presented in the new cups.

130. We are content in this place to the bearing, which the explanation of Sāyaṇa assigns to the word '*amṛta*' the heaven, the abode fixed for the peaceful enjoyment of immortality. In other passages '*amṛta*' just as *amṛtatva*

has meant 'gift of an immortal life'. Later on we will search out if *amṛta* of the Vedic stanzas has ever been understood, as in the mythological poem, as a beverage reserved for the gods, as a celestial ambrosia communicating immortality.

131. *kāvya* (sub. nt) expresses a work accomplished by the wise ones (*kavi*). Sometimes the word is applied to a poetic production, to the composition of a sacred chant; sometimes it characterises the superior capacity, which is the exclusive part of enlightened men. It is the kind of wisdom, which Sāyaṇa defines in his gloss by the noun '*kauśala*'.

132. Somyasya is the reading furnished by the consulted manuscripts. If this word is an adjective derived from the noun *soma*, should not one read : *saumya*, *saumyaya* ?

133. '*vājāsaḥ*' could be translated thus :—Masters, possessors of force. Meanwhile the word could be taken without difficulty as collective name of the Ṛbhus often used in the invocations; *Vājāsaḥ* does not differ from *vājāḥ*, as by the Vedic termination plural in the masculine nouns of the 1st class.

134. *tīvra* meaning 'sharp' in general can it not be understood as a libation which excities thirst and stimulates hunger, somewhat by its odour or by the sight of the limpid and savoury waters ?

135. Let us observe in this stanza a fact of the Vedic orthography, the change of the final 'i's of the masculine accusative plural in 'r' before a sonant. *Sakin-r-yān* in place of *sakhin-yān*. (cf. RV 33, 3, I 46, 1). The insertion of the latter 'r' has a place by a law, analogous to that which makes an euthonic 's' follow the dental letter 'n' before surd-consonants (Bopp. Krit, Gr. S. 65). One can believe in a predominence of the sound r in the primitive laws of Sanskrit euphony, though several other languages had retained without alternation the sound of the sibilant *s*. The exception which the rotasism of the laconic dialect

among the languages of Greece forms has already been pointed out more than once. (cf. Bopp Verg. gramm. Comparative Grammar. p. 22).

136. The form of the reduplicative perfect '*niṣeda*,' belonged to the verbal root '*sad*,' which, joined to the prefix *ni* takes the sense of staying, stopping. See in Westgaard the example drawn from the RV (Radices pp. 178-179).

137. The comparison of the flight of the hawk is used with a sort of preference by the singers of the Veda when they desire to depict the agileness of the course, the rapidity or even the impetuosity of the march. We venture to indicate the numerous passages, which the first book of RV furnishes in support of this observation (RV I 33, 2 *Na śyeno vasatim patāmi.* I 32, 14; I 93, 6; I 98, 1 and 4). We will add that the word *śyena*, which contains the root *syai* to move has become metaphoric noun for a horse, for a rapid courser; one reads *śyenāsaḥ* among the nouns for a horse; Nighaṇṭu (I 14 aśva). It is not less true that the ordinary sense of the word is that of a falcon (a hawk, a failon, Wilson). The author of the Amara-koṣa (II 5) ranks the falcon in two classes of birds, neighbours of each other those of columbine and those of sparrow-hawks (Ed. Loiseleur I p 119, p. 121).

138. The scholiast relates the epithet to the nature of the libation, which he speaks as agreeable, abundant in Soma, due to the gifts of the authors of the sacrifice; but to us it appears to conform more to the ordinary sense of *ratnadheyam*, so also to the spirit of the Vedic cult, to see in the epithet the expression of hope of future well-being that the sacrificer expects from the recognition of his gods. This is why we have translated '*ratnadheyam*' as a sort of apposition, which has this value, 'giving riches, making gift of opulence, conferring enjoyment of boons.'

139. Though we believe as incontestable the meaning of 'sense,' 'sense-organs' given in this passage to the word *indriya*,

we will observe that the same word has, in some texts of the Veda, the meaning 'superior' 'sovereign' which belonged to its root and to the primitive noun *'indra,'* master (Cf RV I 57, 3—indriyaṁ jyotiḥ) and that in other passages it has the meaning of strength, fortune, opulence, *'indriyaṁ'* (sub. nt) is comprised among the synonyms of *dhana* in the glossary of Yāska (Nigh I 10). It is used in the sense of power (RV I 55, 4) and of opulence (ibid, 11, 2) so also in that of male-force (Vāj. Saṁh. Specimen-Stz. 22—Scholiast—*vīryam*).

140. The epithet *anabhiśuḥ* depicts the marvellous chariot, which advances without the help of horses and reins. The substantive *abhiśuḥ* has meant in the masculine a ray or rather a rein (Cf Amara-koṣa III 4, 29) pragrahe (*raśmau*); in the feminine it has taken the sense of a finger, instrument, which acts or directs and this sense will be justified by the Veda. (Cf. RV I 38, 12, Nigh II 5—*Aṅgulināma*) in the small dictionary Nairukta-Śabda-Saṅgraha the word *abhiśuḥ* has *bāhu* arm as the synonym.

141. Out of the two particles which follow in the second half of stanza—the first one 'u' (ū by position) is rather an expletive—the other 'nu' which is most often interrogative particle (*num*) or explanatory (*nam*)—fulfil, in the style of the Veda the function of an adverb with the meaning of quickly, rapidly. Nigh. II, 15—*kṣipra-nāma*, RV I 53, 1, I 120, 2. 'to be speedy.' It is plausible to join this adverb to the principal preposition, and not to the subordinate as the scholiast desires.

142. We are borne to take the word *vibhvā* for the Vedic form of Masc. pl. *vibhavaḥ*, masters, powerful ones, in stead of seeing there a variant of the proper name of one of the Ṛbhus as Sāyaṇa understands.—*vibhu* literally means penetrating everwhere, present in all places. This value comes to that of the word Viṣṇu, which is not strange to the Veda, if one judges by the 1st book of the hymns.

143. The substantive *caratha* expresses a march, the action of marching. It belongs to the class of the Vedic words,

formed by means of the suffix *atha* analogous to the *Uṇādi* suffix *tha*. Cf. ucatha, synonym of *uktha*. (RV I 110, 1).

144. The word '*jīvri*' which is already presented earlier (RV I 110, 8) cannot be derived by a regular derivation from the root '*jīv*' to live; it seems rather a reduplicative form drawn from the root *hvṛ* to be curved, to suffer; from which the aspiration would have disappeared before the group of two consonants. The substantive *jīvrin* (dual *jivrī*) would have been equivalent of an ancient form Jihvrin.

145. The word *jurā* is used here, in compound with the adverb *sanā*, derived from the root jīṛ 'to get old;' similar to the other adjectives and participles expressing in a varied manner the idea of oldage or of decrepitude, and frequently used in the Veda : *jīra*, old (RV I 44, 11), *jarā*, destroyer, (RV I 46, 4) *jujurvaḥ*—accessible to oldage. (RV I 37, 8, *jaraṇa*) RV III, 7, 1, 3), *jarat*, *jarantā* (RV I 3, 4, 7).

146. The word *śṛṣṭī* explained as an adverb, synonym of the adverb *kṣipram*, rapidly in a list of the Vedic words, already cited Nairukta-śabda-saṅgraha. Nevertheless *śṛṣṭī* figures in some texts with the value of a substantive, meaning gift. recompense, wealth, for example *śṛṣṭīvāno* (RV I 45, 2) *śṛṣṭīmat* (RV I 93, 112; cf. I 69, 4). Following this particular use of the word could not one establish another construction and recognise another sense in the second line the recompense, it is this praise, that is addressed to you ? In this case the form *ukthyam* would take back the value of neuter substantive, which other passages justify (CF. RV I 52, 9).

147. We have preserved to the substantive *śravas* in the compound of the first line the sense of glory or lustre which Sāyaṇa assigns to it according to the etymology and on the authority of numerous examples. We restrict ourselves to recall the epithet of the fire in I 1. *citra-śravastamaḥ* (Stz. 5). In all cases we will believe it more natural to take in this place the word *śravas* in the sense

of nourishment, food, to which would correspond the compound *vāja-śṛtāso* which moreover the use of the Vedic vocabulary (Nigh II 7—*anna*—RV 1, 11, 7; I 31, 7; I 34, 5; I 43, 7 : I 64, 2; I 51, 10, I 113, 6) does not at all protest. In consequence we will translate 'a treasure, accompanied by excellent food.' Cf later *śravas* stz. 9 of the same hymn. We should no more share here a doubt that we have in the subject of interpretation of the word vāja translated by Sāyaṇa '*anna*'—*vājaiḥ*. This doubt has been solved in our spirit, above all by the presence of the three divine names in the same stanza. Would it not be just to believe the name of Vāja inserted in the compound of the first line and called to the third quarter by the symetrical structure of the whole passage ? But on the other hand would not there be something affected and too distorted in the following paraphrase : May it come to us from the Ṛbhus, this wealth, eminently glorious, which the men, made celebrated by Vāja have produced. The chariot manufactured by vibhavan may be praised in the sacrifices :—?

148. The word *vidatha* used in the Veda in singular and in plural is one of the antique nouas for sacrifice in Sanskrit (Nigh III 17. *yaja*; RV I 40, 6 *vidatheṣu* 'in sacrifices', I 56, 2; 117, 25). It seems difficult to go back, with surety to the primitive sense of this word, which may have been derived from the root *vid* to know (suff. *atha*) as moreover, the unique sense of a scholar or a sage, that it has preserved in literary languages. We venture to interpret *vidatha* in a double sense active and passive, which the Vedic usage of the root *vid* justifies. On one hand, the sacrifice is the action which acquaints to the man the gods by their benefits (Cf. RV I 11, 6 *viduṣte*); on the other *vidatha* is an act to which the gods are attentive in order to take their part of the offerings and to recompense the sacrifice (Cf. RV I 42, 7 to 9, *kratuṃ viduḥ* I 43, 9).

149. *vicarṣaṇiḥ* seems to us fulfil here,—whatever may be the etymological sense of the word—the role of verbal adjective, meaning, he who sees from a distance, who

discovers from all corners. We meet in the Nighaṇṭu (III 11) among the forms, which express the action of seeing (*paśyati-karma*) the words *vicarṣaṇiḥ*. So also the form *vicaṣte*. The word *carṣaṇiḥ* already by itself denotes seer, (Schcl—*draṣṭā* RV I 46, 4). It is moreover used in the Veda as one of the qualities, which express the general idea of man. (Nigh II 3 *manuṣya*).

150. The substantive *arvan* which seems to be derived from *ṛ* to go is used here in the meaning of an adjective marking movement. It is taken more often in the Veda as a sunstantive, denoting a horse (Nigh I 14 aśva RV I 8, 2; I 27, 9, I 43, 6; I 93, 92; I 116, 17).

151. *jujuṣṭana* is an antique form of imperative aorist, drawn from the root *juṣ* to favour, to accept. See the examples collected by Westgaard (Rad. ling sanscr p. 285). On the termination tana Cf. Pāṇini VII 1, 45.

152. We have already insisted earlier (Chap I S 11) on the antique meaning of wise, intelligent, peculiar to the word *kavi* and consigned in the Vedic vocabulary (Nigh III 15 *medhāvī*). We add to the authority of the stanzas quoted, that of a passage from the Ṛgveda, (I 31, 1) where the Maruts are called *kavayaḥ*, wise ones, prudent (sagaces—Rosen).

153. The explanation given to the word *vipaścit* by the commentator of Nighaṇṭu (Cf. III 15) Devarājayajvan had been related by Rosen in his note in the hymn I 4, 4, (p. XV) : the idea of antique wisdom is perfectly expressed by this term 'assembling, reading the discourse,' 'vip' and the analogous from *vipa* seem to have been in the number of primitive nouns for the speech in Sanskrit. The redactor of the Amara-koṣa has retained the two words *kaviḥ* and *vipaścit* among the nouns for a wise man (Book II, Chap. 7, Stzs 4 and 5). We point out, in addition qualificative *manaścit* which the cited glossary gives (III 15).

154. On the use of the preposition pari with the ablative see pāṇini II 3, 10. *pañcamyapāṅga-paribhiḥ Cf. Bopp.* Krit. Grammar S 620.

155. The Vedic adjective *narya* means peculiar to a man, useful or favourable to men. The word is applied to demostic animals, which compose the wealth of the peoples of shepherds and agriculturists : *catuṣpade naryāya* RV I 121, 3. It is equally susceptible to a native meaning and becoming thus an epithet of the gods, a synonym of the Vedic compound *nṛmanas*. Cf. RV I 63, 3, to Indra, *naryaḥ*. Compare the compound *nṛcakṣas* 'giving light for men' (RV I 22, 7).

156. The participle *rarāṇa* from the verbal root rā to give has the general sense of giving with liberalty. (RV I 117, 24). The present from *rāti* is cited conjointly with the form *rāsati* in the Nighaṇṭu (III 20 *dānakarma*).

157. The expression *aticitayema* may be related to the idea of a life, prolonged by food, beyond the ordinary term, a sort that the men, cherished by gods survive to their contemporaries and leave a memory ever celebrated in the numerous posterity that they have obtained. In the translation we have intentionally retained the simplicity, a little vague, of the Sanskrit terms.

158. In interpreting epithet *deva-yānaiḥ* in a manner more precise than what Sāyaṇa does, we have desired to take into account the meaning of a chariot that the word *yāna* ordinarily possesses in the texts.

159. *viśaḥ* means in general men in the Veda RV I 66, 2 *vikṣu.* It is used more rarely in the collective sense of human creatures of human generations as one can understand it in the present passage, so also in the third stanza of the same chant Sāyaṇa has translated this time with precision, *vikṣu* by prajāsu. Rosen had quite well remarked that *viśaḥ* is a feminine noun (Adnot. RV 125, 1. Cf. 178, 3 *mānuṣīviṭ-hymn* I 72, 8 ; ibid 121, 1. *viśām Aṅgirasām III Adhy* 8, 3 5 26.—*mānuṣirviśaḥ-viś* would have previously meant a house, if one takes into account the etymology of the word, the use of zend *viş* in the sense of a house, an bode, where one enters'. *viś* from where is derived *vaiśya* has been applied to a man, living in the house (Cf. Burnouf—Yasna

Vol. I p. 46. note 62. (Observations on the comparative grammar of Bopp. p. 48). Nevertheless it is conforming to the spirit of every nation of antiquity to consecrate to its profit, a privilege almost in general terms of language. The word viś has denoted in the Veda only civilised people to the exclusion of all other. This, which is confirmed to us by a fully peculiar concordance of meaning that a word of ancient Persian, fully different from the Zend viṣ presents. In the cuneiform inscriptions of Persépolis the word (acc.) means the people faithful to Darius, the nation of the Parsis, the dominating race, placed at the centre of the great monarchy and protected above all others, by Ormuzd. See Lassen—'Old Persian Inscriptions' 1845, pp. 27-30, p. 112 (Zeitscrift de Kunde de Morgenl, Journal of the Oriental knowledge—Vol. VI).

160. In stead of interpreting *manase* as a second dative furnishing the attribute of the first preposition (*tatprītaye*)—(scholiast), would it not be just to join to the substantive *hṛde*, the word *manase*, taken as adjective and serving as epithet ? "May these libations of Soma be for your intelligent (capable of experiencing the joy that they procure) heart."

161. Though we have translated the compound *ghṛtanirṇijāḥ* in accordance with the exegesis of Sāyaṇa we should observe here that this term denotes a literal sense, which, perhaps, offers greater justice. "Taking the form of rain, that is to say, flowing as the waters of the rain." *nirṇik* has the sense of form or appearance in the Vedic idiom (Nigh III 7 rūpa—RV I 113, 14 species).

162. On the sense of force which we give here to the word *kratu* in spite of opinion of the scholiast see earlier RV I 111, 2 and the note which concerns the same expression *kratve dakṣāya*.

163. We believe that the term *bṛhad-diva* depicts the enjoyment of long flashes of the days, the enjoyment which is so lively in the meridional climate, and which the gods, in the thought of the Hindus, give by preference to those

who sacrifice. It appears to us hat the poet has rather decided this kind of well-being in stead of interpreting it as Sāyaṇa desires as the vague expression : endowed with a superior lustre : The preceding epithet *uparāsu* could very well be related to this general idea of wellbeing, above all, if one could understand it as a compound formed, from the prefix *upa* and the substantive *rai* nominative masc. '*rāḥ*' riches. "Enjoying well-being, possessing opulence." This second explanation of the compound *uparāḥ*' appears to us to conform more to the etymological laws than explanation of the scholiast, who traces it to the verbal root *ram*, to rejoice. We do not see here from which application, could there be the sense of 'regions of space.' (Nigh I 6 *diṅnāmāni*) to the word *uparāḥ*.

164. *ayaḥ-śiyrāḥ* literally means those who have nostrils or jaws of iron. One finds the same epithet given to Indra in several vedic chants (suśipra RV I, 9, 3 and I 101, 10) and one can compare it to *sunāsau* epithet of Aśvinau in the hymn, which is contained in the first book of the Mahābhārata (Stz. 723). The word *ayas* 'iron' is equally used in other compound, for expressing a superior and invincible force, such as that of Indra : *ayodaṁsṭra*, with teeth of iron (RV I 88, 5) *āyasa*, covered with iron I 56, 3).

165. We deviate from the gloss of Sāyaṇa in separating the words *ṛbhum rayim*, and in giving thus to the verb invoke (*havāmahe*) a double direct regime (see the examples of this construction in 'Radices' of Westgaard). Meanwhile we will propose to the verb 'to give' the word *rayim* as unique regime by relating it fully to the series of epithets, which the Veda often applies to the idea of riches and which are taken moreover by Sāyaṇa in their most material sense. It is convenient that the elipsis of the words *'bhavatāṃ gaṇam'* proposed by the scholiast, has moreover something of force to separate the same, from the syntax, so concise, of the Vedic stanzas.

166. The root *san*, from where is derived the substantive *sanitṛ* (*sanitā*) has double meaning of giving and receiving, as proved by the examples collected by Westgaard (Radices).

167. The dative *yaṣtave* belongs to ancient form of the substantive *yaṣtu* (the action of the sacrificer, the accomplishment of the sacrifice), whose complete declension has disappeared from the language after the Vedic times. The curious traces, of this class of faminine noun in '*tu*' in the published places of the Veda have been pointed out more than once.

168. The plural substantive *āsāḥ* is among the number of nouns for the space in the cited glossary (Nigh I 6 *diṅnāma*). One can compare to this locution, which ends this stanza, the following passage of the RV atariṣma tamasaspāram (I 112.6).

169. The faminine substantive *maghatti* can thus denote the dispensing of boons, liberality. Thus Sāyaṇa has translated by making use of the words *dhana—dānāya*. Is not the word composed from *magha*. ancient noun for riches (Nigh. dhana) and by contraction of *ātti*, itself contracted form for *ādatti*, which one could suppose as formed in a manner analogous to the participle *ādatta* ?

170. The word *arvācam* expresses the action of marching towards a future aim as in these passages of the RV : *arvācā vāṃ saptayaḥ* (I 47, 8). arvācam daivyam janam (I 45, 10).

171. We take here the word *kratu* in plural as a verbal adjective, meaning active, capable of acting, accomplishing the action. Already we have pointed out earlier in I 111, 2-note, analogous example, which a text of the RV (I 17, 5) has furnished and which Rosen has related to Greek.

171. We have attempted to reproduce by one such repetion of words, the effect, which the poet has desired to attain in this line by continued alliteration.

173. Without doubt, it is useless to demonstrate that in the first line of this stanza *aryaḥ* can only be an ancient form of

the accusative plural of the masculines substantive *ari*. But in the second, the word *aryaḥ* is nothing but the nominative singular of the masculine substantive *arya*, master, lord, which the Vedic idiom uses in a manner, quite distinct from the nouns of analogous form—Nigh II 22 *īśvara* RV I 81 6; I 33, 3. Let us add that the substantive *arya* has remained in the classical Sanskrit with the meaning of master and with that of artisan (Amara-koṣa III 4, 24 *svāmi-vaiśyayoḥ*-Nevertheless *aryaḥ* in the second passage cited from the first book of the Ṛgveda, has been taken as genitive singular of the substantive *ari*, substituted for the form *areḥ*. (Cf. Kuhn Rec. in Jahrb. für Wiss. Krit 1844, p. 127). Itwould be necessary for joining it here to the word *śatroḥ* to suppose a plenoastic construction very rare in the veda.

174. *vasu*, *vasavaḥ* has the literal sense of grand, great, excellent, eminent; but we have desired to preserve and reproduce in the French text the precise and possitive sense, which the gloss of the scholiast indicates.

III

S.A. Langlois

I 20

To The Ṛbhus

Note : The Ṛbhus form a class of divinities. Following the opinion of Mr. Néve these would be ancient mortals elevated to the rank of goods. Sons of Sudhanvan, of the race of the Aṅgirasas, they are three in number : Ṛbhu, Vibhvan, Vāja. It is to be believed that they established a sort of cult in honour of the rays of the sun, with whom they are personified in their capacity of gods ? The legend attributes to them that they have restored to life a cow (i.e. the sacrifice), that they have made their two old parents young again (i.e. they have led the sacrifice of the morning, which gives back life to the heaven and the earth), that they have prepared the horses for Indra, a chariot for the Aśvins (i.e., they have celebrated the sacrifice in their honour), and finally that they have divided into four the cup of Tvaṣṭṛ. (ie. they have established four libations in place of one). I would believe that Ṛbhus are not the ancient divinised *Ṛṣis* but they are the rites themselves, the ceremonies defied. I confess that the hypotheses are a very simple thing, above all with the philological instrument. I would give an example, which the name Ṛbhus itself furnishes to me. Grgmmar informs us first how the vowel '*ṛ*' is metamorphosed in '*ar*'. Then the consonant '*bh*', for the value of its sound corresponds to '*ph*' or '*f*'. From these two facts it results that the 'Ṛbhus' quite naturally could have converted into '*Arphous.*' And this word immediately calls to mind the name *Orphe*, priest and poet, who has presided over the ancient Greek civilization.

(1) *Tr.* In honour of a divine race the mouth of the priests sings this hymn, which should bring the generous recognition (of these gods).

(2) *Tr.* It is they whose thought has created the radiant horses of Indra, for whom the speech is sufficient to yoke to his chariot. They have pervaded the sacrifice with (holy) ceremonies.

(3) *Tr.* They have constructed for the truthful Aśvins a happy chariot that makes tour (of the world). They have produced a cow that gives milk.

(4) *Tr.* The Ṛbhus, powerful by their prayers and their justice, have made their father and mother young.

(5) *Tr.* The libations are addressing themselves to you and to Indra, whom the Maruts as also the brilliant Ādityas accompany.

(6) *Tr.* These are the Ṛbhus who have divided in four parts the cup[2], still new, of the divine Tvaṣṭṛ. *Note* No. 2 The wooden cup of sacrifice called '*camasa*'.

(7) *Tr.* With our praise, taking these into account, receive for the religious (father of the family) three kinds of offerings in seven different[3] sacrifices.

Note—or else 'the three times seven different offerings.' On the occasion of this stz. the commentator explains that in the receptacle of the sacrifice there are three kinds of offering, which he qualifies as the superior, the mediocre and the inferior offerings. He also distinguishes three classes (vargas) of sacrifice, the *Haviryajñas*, the *pākayajñas* and the *Soma-saṁsthānas*. He cites that the sacrifices belong to each of the classes, these sacrifices in which the Ṛbhus had been probably invoked. Moreover he says that there are seven offerings called the Hotras, and are accompanied by the exclamation 'vaṣaṭ'.

(8) *Tr.* Charged with (our sacrifice) the Ṛbhus have lived by persevering in the wellbeing and have obtained a part of the sacrifice, offered to the gods.

I 110

(1) *Tr.* I have fully prepared for the the (holy) work. A new hymn is chanted in honour (of the divine beings). The sea (of Soma) has been poured for all gods. O Ṛbhus[1], rejoice yourselves in our homages. *Note* See I 20, note 1.

(2) *Tr.* O Sons of Sudhanvan, you who like me descend from Aṅgiras, did not have your part in the offerings. In order to procure it you proceeded to the house of the generous Savitṛ. You (rightly) counted on your merits.

Note : The Ṛbhus have been elevated to the rank of the gods and have had their part in the offerings and in the invocations. They have been identified with the rays of the sun. It is with this idea that this strophe is to be understood. We have seen that the poets of the Ṛgveda have divinised under the denomination *'deva'* the diverse parts of sacrifice and the formulea of prayers. Would not the Ṛbhus be the rites used for transferring the light of Agni in the Sun ? Would they not be the rays of sacrifice leaving in order to illumine the disc of the sun ? One can conceive how the authors of this part of the ritual might have left their name to these ceremonies and by such confusion the idea has been spoken out that the human beings have received the title of the gods.

(3) *Tr.* Savitṛ gave you immortality when you had come to place yourselves in service of (the god) who can never be concealed. It is then that you have divided in four parts,[3] the cup of Asura[4], which contained the offerings and which was unique. *Notes* 3 See 120, note 1. *4—asura* used here for a name of the sun.

(4) *Tr.* The Ṛbhus, the priests accomplishing the holy ceremonies, though mortal have obtained immortality with their deligence. These Sons of Sudhanvan (established) in

the solar disc and brilliant like the star of the day are invoked by our prayers.

(5) *Tr.* As one divides the earth with a sharp instrument, the Ṛbhus have divided the cup of the sacrifice. The praised ones, equal (to other gods) in might, they obtain, among the mortals, the offerings, which they have desired.

(6) *Tr.* Thus in honour of these Princes of the air, we offer the prayer by means of knowledge, just as one offers butter of sacrifice by means of the (sacred) ladle. The Ṛbhus, uniting themselves with the lively lustres of the father (of nature), raise themselves to the sky in order to nourish the sun.

(7) *Tr.* To us Ṛbhu is a master, whose force is always new. Ṛbhu gives us nourishment and treasures. He is our refuge, our benefactor. O gods, with your help, may we be able to attack the armies of the impious on a favourable day.

(8) *Tr.* O Ṛbhus you have covered a (new) cow with the hide (of a dead cow), and thus created a mother for a youg calf.[5] O noble Sons of Sudhanvan, in a pious intention you have given youth to your parents, decrepit under the weight of age.[6] *Notes 5*—The legend narrates that the cow of a *ṛśi* happened to die and that seeing the calf separated from its mother the pious person addresses the Ṛbhus. It is they who prepare another cow, whom they cover with the hide of that one which was dead. 6 See I 20, note 1.

(9) *Tr.* O Indra, come with the Ṛbhus. Give us our part in the nourishments, which you dispense (to the human beings). Accord us abundance of all diverse boons. May Mitra, Varuṇa, Aditi, the Ocean, the Earth and the Heaven protect us equally.

I 111

(1) *Tr.* The Ṛbhus, clever workers, have constructed (for the Aśvins) a chariot, whose routes are marvellous. They have given for the chariot of Indra, the coursers which pour

a treasure of abundance. They have created youth for their parents. They have created a new mother for a young calf. *Note*—

See I 20, note 1 and 110

(2) *Tr.* In favour of our sacrifice give us abundant nourishment. In favour of our homages ond offerings give us an opulence, that numourous children sustain. (Arrange) that we may be surrounded by heoric people. For our welfare surround us with force and might.

(3) *Tr.* Noble Ṛbhus, give us riches, give us chariots, horses, give us victory. May our power be lauded every day. May we be strong in the battles, alone or aided by our friends.

(4) *Tr.* I call Indra to our help. (I call) Ṛbhukṣans, the Ṛbhus, the Vājas[2], the Maruts, Mitra and Varuṇa, the Aśvins. May they come to drink our Soma and may they give us riches, piety, victory. *Note*—Vāja means sacrifical offering. This seems to confirm our view (that they are personified rituals.)

(5) *Tr.* May Ṛbhu, by his force guard us against the danger. May the victorious Vāja save us. May Mitra, Varuṇa, Aditi, the Ocean, the Earth and the Heaven protect us equally.

I 161

To the Ṛbhus[1]

Note—The Ṛbhus are the gods, who, it is said, represent the rays of the sun and whose cult is less ancient than that of other divinities. It would appear that before being recongnised as gods, they were human beings on the earth. Their legends, as one can see in the hymns themselves, would appear to indicate that they invented several ceremonies and founded a sort of a new cult. See page 254, note 1. The details of this legend could be related to a sort of religious revolution; but they are quite obscure, so that it would de difficult to express a definite opinion on this subject.

(1) *Tr.* (The Ṛbhus speak) "O You, the best and the youngest of us, in order to announce what have you come to us ? What have we spoken ? We do not blame the vessel of libation, which we find quite distinguished, O Agni,[2] our brother, we have disputed over the superior nature of the vessel."

Note—Agni, in charge of carrying the offerings, addressed to the gods is naturally their messenger according to the Ṛbhus, who have the claim to arrive to this elevated rank. They desire to have also the honours of the vessel of libations, reserved for Agni alone. They are three and the gods consent to this that they should prepare four vessels out of that one, which their artist Tvaṣṭṛ had prepared.

(2) *Tr.* (Agni speaks) 'Make into four this bowl, which is unique.' This is what the gods have said to you. It is with this intention that I have come to you. O Sons of Sudhanvan, if you act like that, you will be worthy of sharing the honours of sacrifice with the gods.

(3) *Tr.* (O Ṛbhus, you have responded favourably to the message of Agni (and he has added). 'It is necessary for you to construct the rapid[3] chariot (of sacrifice). And at the same time brothers, fashion a cow.[4] Restore youth to these two old[5] ones. Well, let us go'.

Note—3. This expression 'rapid chariot' is known. It refers to the preparations of sacrifice. 4. The sacrifice of the Ṛbhus is inter-rupted. In other words their cow is dead; because the cow is the sacrifice. It is the question of making her revive. 5. Who are the two old ones, the father and the mother of the Ṛbhus, if not the heaven and the earth, whom the rays of the sun must renovate ?

(4) *Tr.* O Ṛbhus, when you had executed this order, you have asked, "Where is the messenger today, who had come to find us ?" Meanwhile, Tvaṣṭṛ on seeing the four bowls

that had been prepared, has shown himself in the midst of the women (in charge of the preparations of the sacrifice).

(5) *Tr*. 'Kill,' cried Tvaṣṭṛ 'kill them, who have blamed the bowl, which serves towards the libations of the Devas.' They invent new invocations. It is necessary for these invocations that the mother of the family furnishes them with new libations.

(6) *Tr*. Now Indra has received from you the two horses, the Aśvins the chariot, Bṛhaspati, the cows of all forms.[6] O Ṛbhu, Vibhvan and Vāja, whose works are excellent and who have claimed a part in the sacrifice, you have come, you have joined the Devas. *Note*—By the sacrifice the gods receive a chariot i.e., the honours and the presents which accompany it. Bṛhaspati is a form of Agni and his cows are the sacrifices of diverse sort.

(7) *Tr*. From the hide (of a dead cow) you have made a living one. By your operations you have restored these two old ones to youth. Sons of Sudhanvan, from one horse you have drawn another horse. Yoking these to your chariot, you have come to the Devas.

(8) *Tr*. O Devas, you have spoken to them, "Drink these libations. Drink from this draught purified by Muñja.[7] Sons of Sudhanvan, if you so desire you can still exhilarate yourselves in the liquors offered in the third sacrifice."[8]

Notes—7, Muñja is a plant whose twigs could serve to purify the beverage or to wash away the impurities, which might have mixed with it. Another explanation would recognise the mountain Mujāvat, which produces the plant of Soma. 8. Otherwise the Third Savana, of the evening.

(9) *Tr*. "The libations are abundant," says one (of the assistants) "Fire is ardent," says another. Several others occupy themselves with the cow (of sacrifice) or fill the cups with the formulae of use.

(10) *Tr.* This one here brings rice, water, (the drinks prepared from milk of the cow), that one there arranges the meats, that come out from the kitchen. Another takes away the filth. At last assisted by their children, the father and the mother of the family take their place.

(11) *Tr.* O generous Ṛbhus, it is due to your good offices that we owe the greenary in high places, water in low places. As long as you sleep in the bosom of this (god), who can never remain hidden,[9] you remain unknown to the world.

Note—This god is Agni or Sūrya.

(12) *Tr.* When mixed (with the sun) you pervade the airs, then the venerable father and mother of the family[10] honour you all over. Misfortune to him, who holds your arm.[11] Glory to him who sings of you. *Note*—10. The translation uncertain; because these two persons could also be the heaven and the earth, parents of the world helping the Ṛbhus, all over. 11—the arms of this kind of gods—It is their rays—Holding the arm is perhaps also inconveniencing the sacrifice.

(13) *Tr.* Fortunate Ṛbhus, you have put this question, "(O god), who can never remain hidden, who is he that has awakened this world and (has given) us (a signal) ?" (The god) spoke to you that it was the dog[12] who breaks the silence of night. And in the star that traverses the space you have illumined the world. *Note*—According to Sāyaṇa the dog that breaks the silence of night is the wind; but it can be recalled that there is a bitch named Saramā, which is none other than the prayer, whose voice, in the morning awakens all the beings for the sacrifice.

(14) *Tr.* The Maruts go in the sky, Agni on the earth, the wind in the air, Varuṇa in the waters and the seas, desiring you all over, O children of force.[13] *Note*—Agni is fourth Ṛbhu and reciprocally the Ṛbhus become the forms of Agni, who is—as is known—'child of Force.'

III 60

To the Ṛbhus and Indra

Note—The text calls them by the word *Auśjiaḥ*

(1) *Tr.* Noble Sons of Sudhanvan, you, who have the power to confound your enemies, here are our priests,[2] who are your parents by the (holy) thought. With sacrifice they renew these marvellous works which have made you obtain a part in the offerings. *Note*—See Volume I P 254, Note 1.

(2) *Tr.* O Ṛbhus, by that skill with which you have divided the cup (of sacrifice), by these pious skills with which you have covered an (old) cow with a (new) hide, by that (sacred) thought with which you have fashioned the blue horses (of Indra), you have merited the title of the Devas.

(3) *Tr.* The Ṛbhus have acquired the friendship of Indra. Grandsons[3] of Manu, pious sons of Sudhanvan, they have come as workers (of sacrifice). They have obtained the name of 'immortals' by their attention to (sacred) ceremonies and to religious works. *Note*—That is to say 'born of human race' Sudhanvan, their father was the son of Aṅgiras, who, following mythology owed his birth to Brahmā. There is a probable relation between the name *Sudhanvan* and the verb *dhanvati.*

(4) *Tr.* You come to our libations on the same chariot as Indra. You partake with him the offerings of your servants. O Ṛbhus, learned Sons of Sudhanvan, there is nothing comparable to your force and to your good actions.

(5) *Tr.* O Indra with the Ṛbhus for whom we fill in the offerings, receive in your hands this Soma which is filled in your honour. Indra, invoked with the prayer in the house of a faithful servant, rejoice yourself, as also these noble Sons Sudhanvan.

(6) *Tr.* Indra, accompanied by the Ṛbhus and ever flowing with our offerings, (come) to our sacrifice. You, whom the world celebrates, may be happy with 'Śacī'[4] (whom we have adorned for your sake). The ceremonies full of a (pious) eagerness,[5] associating themselves with efforts of the Devas and of Manu,[6] are hurrying up for you. *Notes*—4. I am far away from the sense that the commentator gives to '*svasarāṇī*.' He translates this word by '*days*' '*ahānī*.' 6. That is to say of the mortals, of whom Manu is the father.

(7) *Tr.* O Indra, you who give force, come with the Ṛbhus, endowed with force, (like you). Be attracted to our sacrifice by the praises of the poet. Come towards the sons of Āyu, with hundred rapid and luminous (horses).[7] You who have thousand means of making us happy, (receive) our sacrifices and our offerings. *Note*—7. These horses are the rays of the morning, 'keta' or of the sacrifices. See earlier Lecture III 55—Note 48.

IV 33

(1) *Tr.* I send to the Ṛbhus my hymn as a messenger. I invite the cow (of sacrifice) to give milk of libation (in their honour). May the Ṛbhus, speady as the wind, the (clever) workers, shoot foreward without delay in the celestial course. *Note*—See Vol 1 p. 254, note 1.

(2) *Tr.* May the Ṛbhus, pervading the world in their brilliant works, achieve to adorn the two (great) parents. May they quickly find the friendship of the Devas. May they, in their wisdom, bring honour and prosperity to the pious person.

(3) *Tr.* It is they who have renovated youth to their two ancestors, feeble and decrepit like two pillars. May Vāja, Vibhvan and Ṛbhu, friends of Indra and strengthened by the honey (of Soma), be the guardians of our sacrifice.

(4) *Tr.* The Ṛbhus guard the (sacred)[2] cow for the whole year. They give a new stoutness to her flesh the whole year. The whole year they have borne her splendour. And it is by such works that they have obtained the title of 'the

Immortals.' *Note*—I suppose that this cow is the flame of sacrifice, which should also be the flame of the sun.

(5) *Tr*. The eldest said, 'Make two cups' The second, in his turn, said, 'Let us make three of it.' The youngest cried, 'Make four of it.' O Ṛbhus, Tvaṣṭṛ has approved of your speech.

(6) *Tr*. 'Well' said the Ṛbhus. And they have done as they proposed. In this manner they have accomplished the '*Svadhā*.' On seeing these four cups shining like the light of the day, Tvaṣṭṛ has approached it with pleasure.

(7) *Tr*. While the Ṛbhus have received the hospitality for twelve days in the residence of the god, who can never remain hidden,[3] (one could believe them to be) asleep. Then they have fertilised the earth. They have led the Sindhus. It is because of them, that plants grew in the desert-places and waters have filled the valleys. *Note*—The Ṛbhus, in their capacity as the rays of the sun rest conncealed there for twelve days. This is the time of the rains. Then they seem to be working towards the fertility of the earth. See Volume I p. 375.

(8) *Tr*. The Ṛbhus have formed the chariot (of sacrifier), which rolls happily, being directed by the sage, and this cow[4] which assumes all forms and which sets every thing in motion. May these useful auxiliaries, these excellent workers, endowed with a fortunate hand, be designed to prepare treasures for us. *Note* 4—By this word the poet designates the sacrifice with its various forms and its efficacy.

(9) *Tr*. Adorned by their works and by (the fruits) of their thought, the gods have applauded their works. The industrious Vāja is devoted to all gods, Ṛbhukṣan[5] to Indra, Vibhvan to Varuṇa. *Note*—It is probable that the person Ṛbhukṣan is the same as Ṛbhu. The word Ṛbhukṣan is also an epithet of Indra.

(10) *Tr*. The Ṛbhus, exhilarated (with Soma), have created two blue horses for Indra, docile to be yoked and sung by

poetry. O Ṛbhus, give us lustre and all the boons of opulence. Work for our welfare (as a friend works for the welfare) of his friend.

(11) *Tr.* On this day the Devas have offered the libations and and the exhilarating beverages to your friendship, on condition that it would not show itself fatigued. O Ṛbhus, give us your blessings in this third sacrifice.

IV 34

(1) *Tr.* O Ṛbhu, Vibhvan, Vāja and Indra come to our sacrifice and (take your part) in our offerings. At this moment the divine prayer has presented you the libations of the (sacred) days. All these exhilarating beverages are united for you.

(2) *Tr.* (Be born) to the life of which you have experience. The choice meads have been presented to you. O Ṛbhus, rejoice yourselves in the company of the Ṛtus. All these exhilarating beverages are united for you, along with the (sacred) hymn. Send us opulence accompanied by happy descendants.

(3) *Tr.* O Ṛbhus, this sacrifice has been prepared for you and you have received it in all your splendour as Manu (did formerly). All that you can love is presenting itself before you. Come you all, whom (we call) Vājas from the name of your youngest.

(4) *Tr.* Now generous Ṛbhus, shower your boons on the mortal who serves and honours you. Drink O Vājas. It is for you, it for your pleasure that the third sacrifice is celebrated with pomp.

(5) *Tr.* Noble Vājas and you Ṛbhukṣan, come to us. We sing of you for your munificence. May the libations towards the end of the day go to you, as the cows go to their stable.

(6) *Tr.* Sons of force, called by our homages come to this sacrifice. Accompanied by Indra, you dispensers of

riches, partake of his pleasures and drink of our sweet (Soma).

(7) *Tr.* O Indra, we praise you. Come with Varuṇa come with the Maruts in order to rejoice (yourselves) and in order to drink our Soma. Come here to rejoice yourselves along with the wives (of gods) admitted in the first place on convenient moments to the share of the libation, (with these wives) who possess rich treasures.

(8) *Tr.* O Ṛbhus, come and share the joy of (our sacrifices) with the Ādityas, with the Parvatas,[1] with the divine Savitṛ, with the Sindhus, who (also) possess rich treasures.

Note. We have seen elsewhere (vol. I p. 545, note 5) that *parvata* was the cloud personified. Sāyaṇa identifies this word with '*parvan*' and says that the author here designates the periods of the month, to which this name is given.

(9) *Tr.* The Ṛbhus have given their succours to the Aśvins and to the (grand) parents, and to the cow (that was dead). They have created the two horses (of Indra) and fashiened the armours (for the gods). They have developed the Heaven and the Earth. Intelligent masters, they themselves have a beautiful posterity.

(10) *Tr.* O Ṛbhus, you possess a strong opulence of herds, of foodstuff, of family, of treasures. You be the first ones to the joyous cup of our libations. Give us your boons, to us and to those who sing of you.

(11) *Tr.* Do not go away. We want to satisfy your thirst in this sacrifice, O generous Ṛbhus. If you desire our offerings, we invite you to rejoice yourselves with Indra, with the Maruts, with our brilliant protectors.

IV 35

(1) *Tr.* O Ṛbhus, Sons of Sudhanvan, Offsprings of Force, come near here. Do not go away. In this sacrifice we

present you our offerings. May the beverages, which make Indra happy, come to be for your welfare also.

(2) *Tr.* May the offerings in honour of the Ṛbhus be brought. May Soma be poured in the cups. It is you, who in your pious works, in your happy doings, have divided the unique cup (of sacrifice) in four.

(3) *Tr.* You have divided the cup in four parts. You said (to Agni), "Friend, make this distinction." Thus O Vājas, O Ṛbhus, with industrious hand, you have entered on the way of immortality. (You have obtained) the rank of Devas.

(4) *Tr.* What was the nature of the cup, which your wisdom has divided in four parts? Take these libations which inspire joy. Drink, O Ṛbhus, of this sweet Soma.

(5) *Tr.* By your skill you have fashioned youth for the two (grand) parents. By your skill you have prepared a cup, which had to serve the gods for libation. By your skill you have formed the two rapid horses, which carry Indra, O Ṛbhus, you, who are honoured by choice-meads.

(6) *Tr.* O Generous Ṛbhus form a strong and vigourous opulence for him, who towards the end of the days, offers for your pleasure numerous libations in raptures of your joy.

(7) *Tr.* O Indra, borne by blue horses, drink the libation of the Morning. The sacrifice of the Midday is entirely yours. Drink (the libation of the Evening) with the Ṛbhus, possessors of rich treasures, who have become your friends, by their good works.

(8) *Tr.* You have made yourselves Devas by your good works and like hawks you have seated yourselves in the sky. Sons of Sudhanvan, Offspring of Force, shower on us your treasures, you, who have oblained the title of the Immortals.

(9) *Tr.* O Ṛbhus, having industrious hand, if by your happy works you have prepared this third sacrifice, which we

accompany with rich offerings, may these libations be for you. Drink of it so that all your senses may find satisfaction.

IV 36

(1) *Tr.* This magnificient chariot, which rolls on three wheels amidst the airs, having need neither of the reins nor of the horses, has just come to birth. O Ṛbhus, you traverse the heaven and the earth thus. And this is the great testimonial of your divine knowledge.

Note—Allusion to the three positions of the sun.

(2) *Tr.* It is you who, in your wise meditations, have created chariot on beautiful wheels incapable of deviating from the trodden track. O Ṛbhus, also called Vājas, we invite you to libations of this sacrifice.

(3) *Tr.* O Ṛbhus, O powerful Vājas, a noble and glorious testimonial for you among the Devas was that you have rendered young and vigorous the two (grand) parents, that were old and infirm.

(4) *Tr.* You have divided one cup into four parts. By your works you have covered a cow with a (new) hide. These are your claims for glory. O Ṛbhus, O Vājas, it is thus that you have obtained a name of 'the Immortals' among Devas.

(5) *Tr.* The most glorious, the most abundant opulence is that which the Ṛbhus give, which the illustrious Vājas produce. The (fortune) which Vibhvan produces and which you protect becomes an object of envy. It deserves to be celebrated in the sacrifices.

Note—I have not believed that one can understand here the word '*camasa*' (cup) or '*ratha*' (chaiot) as the commentator does.

(6) *Tr.* He whom Vāja and Vibhvan protect, he whom the Ṛbhus defend, is strong and dauntless. He is wise and

prudent. He is valiant, a clever archer invincible in combats. He possesses the ornament of riches and has the advantages of male-family.

(7) *Tr.* Your beauty develops itself before your eyes and with it our hymn. O Vājas, O Ṛbhus, accept our homages. You are full of prudence, wisdom, knowledge. It is you whom we invoke in this sacrifice.

(8) *Tr.* Listen to our prayers. You know which are the good things convenient to human beings. O Ṛbhus, give us a rich and brilliant opulence, an abundance, strong and virile.

(9) *Tr.* Give us family and riches. Bring for us here the glory of heroes. O Ṛbhus, give us fruitful and varied resources, which can assure us superiority over all others.

IV 37

(1) *Tr.* O divine Vājas, and you O Ṛbhukṣan, come to our sacrifice by the ways which the gods traverse. Receive the sacrifice offered by these offsprings of Manu. And in your recognition give us the cheerful days.

(2) *Tr.* Take these sacrifices to heart. May they today please your soul. May the forms (of libations) of pure butter present themselves to you. By pleasing you may they augment your force and skill.

(3) *Tr.* O Vājas, O Ṛbhukṣans[1], (the offerings) reserved for the gods at the moment of the Third sacrifice are presented to you, and so also the hymn that praises you. Like Manu, I, surrounded by the people and their glorious chiefs, pour Soma for you.

Note—The word *Ṛbhukṣan* is in plural here.

(4) *Tr.* (Adopted) sons of Indra, Offsprings of Force, be robust and beneficient. Mounted on a brilliant chariot you push forth your sturdy horses and your face is strong like iron. This last sacrifice has been founded for your welfare.

(5) *Tr.* O Ṛbhukṣans, we ask of you an opulence worthy of you, which gives us force in the combat and supports us (in the peril), which should be full of glory, generosity, happiness and good horses.

(6) *Tr.* O Ṛbhukṣans, may the mortal, whom you and Indra protect be distinguished in his works, liberal in the sacrifices, famous for his horses.

(7) *Tr.* O Vājas, O Ṛbhukṣans, point out to us the ways of sacrifice. Honoured sages, (give) us the force of being vanquishers everywhere, from whichever corner of the heaven (the evil comes).[2]

Note—I do not think the poet intends here supernatural power to traverse the celestial regions. It will be a literal translation, but it does not seem to be justified at all.

(8) *Tr.* O Ṛbhus, O Ṛbhukṣans, and you O Indra and you truthful[3] (gods), give us mortal powers of treasures, of horses and all that which goes to make magnificient man.

Note—That is to say the Aśvins, called Nāsatyas.

VII 48

(1) *Tr.* O opulent priests, O Ṛbhukṣans,[1] exhilarate yourselves in our libations. May the strong and powerful horses lead towards us your chariot, which moves only for the welfare of the human beings.

Note—These are two names of the Ṛbhus. At VII 37, 2 the poet uses these as denoting two classes of the divinities. *Ṛbhukṣans* is also an epithet of Indra and here it is joined with the adjectival word *suśipra*, which refers to the god of sky. *Ṛbhukṣan* makes the plural *Ṛbhukṣanaḥ*.

(2) *Tr.* O Ṛbhus, with you (each of us is) a Ṛbhu. Powerful with (you, who are) powerful ones, may we, by your force, triumph over the forces (of our enemies). May Vāja save us amidst the combats. With Indra as our ally may we vanquish Vṛtra.

(3) *Tr.* These (gods) overturn numerous armies, as they want. May they destroy all our enemies in the combat. May Indra, Vibhvan, Ṛbhukṣan and Vāja make, from the spoils of our adversary, riches of the father of the family.

(4) *Tr.* O gods, fashion our fortune. All of you participate in the joys (of the sacrifice), and be of help to us. May Vasus give us abundance. Support us ever with your benedictions.

IV

H.H. Wilson

I 20

(1) Tr.—This hymn, the bestower of riches has been addressed by the sages, with their own mouths to the (class of the divinities), being born.

Notes—'*devāya janmane*,' literally, to the divine or brilliant birth : but the scholiast explains the latter as *jāyamānāya*, being born or having birth, and the former as *devasaṅghāya*, a class of divinities, i.e. the Ṛbhus, about whom it is said that they were pious men, who, through penance, obtained deification *manuśyāḥ santastapasā devatvaṁ prāptāḥ*. Thanks to the learning and industry of Mr. Néve, of the university of Louvain, we are fully acquainted with the history and character of the Ṛbhus, as they appear in the different portions of the Ṛgveda. 'Essai sur le mythe des Ribhavas.' Their origin, and actions are also narrated in the Nītimañjarī, as well as in the notes on this and similar passages. The Ṛbhus were the three sons of Sudhanvan, a descendant (the Nītimañjarī says a son) of Aṅgiras, severally named Ṛbhu, Vibhu and Vāja and styled collectively, Ṛbhus from the name of the eldest. Through their assiduous performance of good works *svapas* (su-apas)—they obtained divinity, exercised superhuman powers, and became entitled to receive praise and adoration. They are supposed to dwell in the solar sphere; and there is an indistinct identification of them with the rays of the sun; but whether typical or not, they prove the admission, at an early date of the doctrine that men might became divinities.

(2) Tr.—They, who created, mentally, for Indra, the horses that are harnessed at his words, have partaken of the sacrifices performed with holy acts.

Notes—śamībhiryajñamāśata—Mr. Néve renders it as : 'Ils ont obtenu le sacrifice par leur ouvres meritoires' : Mr. Langlois' Ils ont entoure le sacrifice de ceremonies (saintes)' Mr. Stevenson. 'They pervade our sacrifice by purificatory rites'; Rosen, literally, 'ceremonies sacrificium acceperunt.' That three simple words should admit of this variety of rendering shows the vagueness of some of the Vaidika expressions, The sense seems to be, they have pervaded, appropriated or accepted, the sacrifice offered (which last word is understood), with usual implements and observances (*śamībhih*, ceremonies); as Sāyaṇa explains : "*Grahacamasādiniṣpādanarūpaiḥ karmabhiryajñamasmadīyamāśata* (*vyāptavantaḥ*)." They have pervaded (or accepted) our sacrifice, performed with those acts which are executed by the means of tongs, ladles and other (utensils employed in making oblations). The expression may, perhaps, obscurely intimate the invention of the implements so used, by the Ṛbhus; their modification of one of which, at least, is subsequently referred to (stz. 6), while other expressions imply mechanical skill.

(3) Tr.—They constructed for the Nāsatyas, a universally moving and easy car and a cow, yielding milk.

Notes—takṣan for *atakṣan*; literally, they chipped, or fabricated, so, in the preceding verse, they carved (*tatakṣuḥ*) Indra's horses. There, it is said, they did so mentally (manasā); but, in this verse, there is no such qualification; and the meaning of the verb implies mechanical information. The Ṛbhus may, have been the first to attempt the bodily representation of these appendages of Indra and Aśvins.

(4) Tr.—The Ṛbhus uttering unfailing prayers, endowed with rectitude and succeeding (in all pious acts) made their (aged) parents young.

Notes—satyamantrāḥ, having or repeating, true prayers, i.e. which were certain of obtaining the objects prayed for. There is some variety in the renderings, here also; but it was scarcely necessary, as the meaning of what the verse implies is clear enough. *viṣṭī* for *viṣṭayaḥ*: according to the scholiast *vyāpti-yuktāḥ*, in which vyāpti means, encountering no opposition in all acts, through the efficacy of their true or infallible mantras. *akrata*, from *kṛ*, to make, generally; not as before, *atakṣan*, to make mechanically.

(5) Tr.—Ṛbhus, the exhilarating juices are offered to you along with Indra, attended by the Maruts and along with the brilliant Ādityas.

Notes—According to Āśvalāyana, as quoted by Sāyaṇa, the libations offered at the third daily (or evening) sacrifice are presented to Indra, along with the Ādityas, together with Ṛbhu, Vibhu and Vāja, with Bṛhaspati and the Viśvedevas.

(6) Tr.—The Ṛbhus have divided into fous, the new ladle, the work of the divine Tvaṣṭṛ.

Notes—Tvaṣṣṛ in the pauranic mythology is the carpenter or artisan of gods. So Sāyaṇa says of him : He is a divinity, whose duty with relation to the gods is carpentry—'*devasam-bandḥ takṣaṇavyāpāraḥ*. The same may be said of his calling the Rbhus the disciples of Tvaṣṭṛ—The act ascribed to them of making one ladle into four, has, probably, reference to some innovation in the object of libation rather than the mere multiplication of the wooden spoon used to pour out the Soma juice. The Nītimajarī says that Agni coming to sacrifice which the Rbhus celebrated, became one of them, and therefore they made the ladle fourfold, that each might have his share.

(7) Tr.—May they, moved by our praises, give to the offerer of the libation, many precious things, and perfect the thrice seven sacrifices.

Notes—trirā saptāni—The scholiast considers that *triḥ* may be supplied to precious things, as meaning best, middling, worst : or *tri saptāni*, seven sacrifices, as classed under three heads. Thus one class consists of the *Agnyādheya* (seven ceremonies in which clarified butter is offered on fire); one class consists of *pākayajñas* in which dressed viands are offered to the

Viśvedevas and others) and one comprehends the *Agniṣṭoma* class (in which libations of Soma juice are the characteristic offerings).

(8) Tr. Offerers (of sacrifices), they held (a mortal existence); by their pious acts they obtained a share of sacrifices with gods.

Notes—adhārayanta, they held or enjoyed, is all that the text gives. What they held is not specified. The Scholiast supplies *prāṇān*, vital airs, life; his addition is in harmony with other texts; *martāsaḥ santo amṛtatvamānaśuḥ*—Being mortals, they obtained immortality. Their partaking of sacrifices is also repeatedly stated : *Saudhanvanā yañiyam bhāgamānaśa.* By the sons of Sudhanvan was a sacrificial portion acquired (see vol. III p. 106, note 2) *Ṛbhavo vai tapasā somapīthamabhyajayan.* The Ṛbhus won, by devotion, the drinking of soma among the gods.

I 110

(1) Tr. O Ṛbhus, the rite formerly celebrated by me is repeated again; and the melodious hymn is recited in your praise. In this ceremony the Soma-juice is sufficient for all the gods. Drink of it, to your utmost content, when offered on the fire.

(2) Tr. O Ṛbhus, when you, who were amongst my ancestors, yet immature (in wisdom), but desirous of enjoying (the Soma libation), retired to the forest, to perform (penance) then, Sons of Sudhanvan, through the plentitude of your completed (devotions), you came to the (sacrificial) hall of the worshipper Savitṛ.

Notes—Sudhanvan, the father of the Ṛbhus, was a descendant of Aṅgiras : so is Kutsa; therefore, they are related, as Kutsa is the son of Aṅgiras, it seems not very consistent to call them his kinsmen of a former period. (*prācāḥ or pūrvakālīṇāḥ*) Rosen calls them 'sapientes'; but this is an evident inadvertence; as the epithet is apākāḥ, unripe, *aparipakvajñānāḥ*, 'immature in wisdom.' In the preceding verse Savitṛ (su to offer oblation) might mean merely the presenter of oblations; but here we have, evidently, the sun alluded to.

(3) Tr. Then Savitṛ bestowed upon you immortality, when you came to him, who cannot be hidden and represented (your desire) to partake of the libations; and that ladle for the sacrificial viands, which the *asura* had formed single, you made fourfold.

Notes—asura—Tvaṣṭṛ, as in a former passage. See p. 48 Note b.

(4) Tr. Associated with the priests and quickly performing the holy rites, they, being yet mortals, acquired immortality, and the sons of Sudhanvan, the Ṛbhus, brilliant as the sun, became connected with the ceremonies (approprieted to the different seasons) of the year.

(5) Tr. Lauded by the bystanders, the Rbhus, with a sharp weapon meted out the single sacrificial ladle-like a field (measured by a rod)—soliciting the best (libations) and desiring (to participate) of the sacrificial food amongst the gods.

(6) Tr. To the leaders (of the sacrifice), dwelling in the firmament, we present, as with a ladle, the appointed clarified butter and praise with knowledge, those Ṛbhus, who, having equalled the velocity of the protector (of the universe, i.e. the sun) ascended to the region of the heaven, through (the offerings) of the (sacrificial) food.

Notes—nṛbhyaḥ i.e. *yajñasya netṛbhyaḥ*; as in the text—*Rbhavo hi yajñasya netāraḥ*. "The Ṛbhus are the leaders of the sacrifice." On which account they obtained immortality. Or the term may be connected with '*antarikṣasya*,' which precedes in the text and may means as Rosen has it 'to the chiefs of the firmament (aeris regibus).' *Piturasya*—A text of the veda identifies the Ṛbhus with the solar rays (*Ādityaraśmayopi Ṛbhava ucyante*). The Ṛbhus are indeed said to be the rays of the sun.

(7) *Tr.* The most excellent Ṛbhu is in strength our defender, Ṛbhu through gift of food and wealth is our asylum. May he bestow them on us. Gods through your protection, may we, upon a favourable occasion over-throw the hosts of those, who offer no libations.

(8) *Tr.* Ṛbhu, you covered the cow with a hide and reunited the mother with the calf. Sons of Sudhanvan, leaders (of sacrifice), through your good works you rendered your aged parents young.

Notes—A story is related that a *ṛṣi*, whose cow had died, leaving a calf, prayed to the Ṛbhus for assistance, on which they formed a living cow and covered it with the skin of the dead one, from which the calf imagined it to be its own mother, *yuvānā pitarā* see I. 20.

(9) *Tr*, Indra, associated with the Ṛbhus, supply us, in distribution of viands, with food and consent to bestow upon us wonderous riches. May Mitra, Varuṇa, Aditi, the Ocean, the Earth and the Heaven preserve them for us.

Note—*Vājebhirno vājasātāvāvīddhi* may also be rendered 'protect us in battle with your horses.'

I 111

(1) *Tr.* The Ṛbhus, possessed of skill in their work, constructed (for the Aśvins) a well-built car; they formed the vigorous horses bearing Indra. They gave youthful existence to their parents; they gave to the calf its accompanying mother.

(2) *Tr.* Prepare fully for our sacrifice resplendent sacrificial food, and for rite and for strength such nourishment as may be the cause of excellent progency, so that we may live (surrounded) by vigourous descendants. Such wealth do you confer upon us for our benefit.

Notes—*ṛbhumat* explained as 'having much light;' for according to the Nirukta etymology ṛbhu means 'much light' from uru 'much' and bhū to shine.

(3) *Tr.* Ṛbhus, Conductors (of sacrifice), bestow ample sustenance upon us, upon our chariots, upon our horses. Let every one daily acknowledge our victorious wealth and may we triumph in battles over our foes, whether strangers or kinsmen.

(4) *Tr.* I invoke the mighty Indra for protection, and the Ṛbhus, the Vājas and Maruts to drink Soma-juice; also both Mitra and Varuṇa and the Aśvins; and may they direct us to opulence, to holy rites and to victory.

Notes—'*Ṛbhukṣaṇam Indram*' might mean 'Indra, who is Rbhukṣan;' of which *Ṛbhukṣaṇam* is the accusative. In the following expressions Ṛbhūn and Vājān, plural accusatives, we are to understand, according to the commentator, the three sons of Sudhanvan-Ṛbhu, Vibhu and Vāja.

(5) *Tr.* May Ṛbhu supply us with wealth for war. May Vāja, victorious in battle, protect us and may Mitra, Varuṇa, Aditi, the Ocean, the Earth and the Heaven be propitious to this (our prayer).

I 161

(1) *Tr.* Is this our senior or our junior who has come (to us). Has he come upon a message (from the gods) ? What is it we should say ? Agni, brother, we revile not the ladle, which is of exalted race. Verily we assert the dignity of the wooden (implement).

Notes—According to the legend cited by the commentator, the three Ṛbhus being engaged in a sacrifice and about to drink Soma-juice, the gods send Agni to see what they were doing; observing that they exactly resembled each other, Agni assumed the like form, and it is to this that the stanza refers in calling him 'brother' and questioning his comparative age. One purpose of Agni's visit is stated in the next verse to be the order to convert the one spoon or ladle (*camasa*), used for drinking the Soma-juice, or for libation, into four. See I. 20.

(2) *Tr.* Make fourfold the single ladle; so the gods command you; and for that purpose am I come. Sons of Sudhanvan, if you accomplish this, you will be entitled to sacrifice, along with the gods.

(3) *Tr.* Then said they in answer to Agni, the messenger (of the gods) Whatever is to be done whether a horse, a car or a cow or the two (old parents) are to be made young-having

done all these acts, brother Agni, we are then ready to do what you desire.

Notes—These marvels have been related in the preceding hymns of the Ṛbhus see I. 20, 110, 111.

(4) *Tr.* So doing, Ṛbhus, you inquired, where, indeed, is he, who came to us as a messenger ? When Tvaṣṭṛ observed the one ladle become four, he was immediately lost among the women.

Notes—Gnāsvantarnyānaje—Sāyaṇa explains the verb merely as '*nyakto abhūt*,' the combination of ni and añj is not common, and has not been given by westergaardī but it is possibly the converse of *vyañj* 'To bc manifest', 'to be concealed, indistinct or invisible' *Gnā* is a synonym of *strī* but in what sense it is here used is not very evident. Sāyaṇa explains as '*striyamātmānamamnyata*.' He, Tvaṣṭṛ fancied himself to be a woman i.e. he felt humbled, as feeble as a female.

(5) *Tr.* Then Tvaṣṭṛ said, "Let us slay those, who have profaned the ladle (designed) for the drinking of the gods; then they made use of other names for one another, as the libation was poured out, and the maiden (mother) propitiated them by different appalations.

Notes—According to the scholiast this legend accounts for the origin of the names of the chief officiating priests; in order to evade the indignation of Tvaṣṭṛ, the Ṛbhus assumed the titles *Hotṛ*, *Adhvaryu* and *Udgātṛ*, by which an individual enegaged in pıiestly functions at a scrifice is to be always addressed, and never by his own name. d—The force of the term kanyā 'a maiden,' is not explained. Sāyaṇa expounds it as 'a mother, self-engendering' *svotpādayitrī mātā*.

(6) *Tr.* Indra has caparisoned his horses, the Aśvins have harnessed their car. Bṛhaspati has accepted the omniform (cow). Therefore Ṛbhu, Vibhvan and Vāja go to the gods. Doers of good deeds enjoy your sacrificial portion.

(7) *Tr.* Sons of Sudhanvan, from a hideless (cow), you have formed a living one. By your marvellous acts you have

made your old parents young. From one horse you have fabricated another. Harness now your chariot and repair unto the gods.

(8) *Tr.* They (the gods) have said, 'Sons of Sudhanvan, drink of this water (the Soma-juices) or drink that which has been filtered through the Muñja grass. Or if you be pleased with neither of these, be exhilarated (by that which is drunk) at the third libation'.

Note—The first two libations intimate that the Ṛbhus may be participants of the libations offered at the dawn, at the noon. The third libation applies to the evening sacrifice. the right of Ṛbhus to share in this being acknowledged elsewhere. see I 20.

(9) *Tr.* "Waters are the most excellent" said one of them. "Agni is the most excellent", said another. The third declared to many the Earth (to be the most excellent) and thus speaking true things, the Ṛbhus divided the ladle.

Notes—vadharyantī is said by the scholiast to mean either 'a line of clouds' or 'the earth.'

(10) *Tr.* One pours the red water (the blood) upon the ground; one cuts the flesh, divided into fragments by the chopper; and the third separates the excrement from other parts. In what manner may parents (of the sacrifice) render assistance to their sons ?

(11) *Tr.* Ṛbhus, leaders (of the rains), you have caused the grass to grow upon the high places. You have caused the waters to flow over to low places; for (the promotion of) good works as you have reposed for a while in the dwelling of the unapprehensible (Sun). So desist not today from (the discharge of) this (your function).

Notes—Throughout the remaining stanzas the Ṛbhus are identified with the rays of the sun, as the instrument of the rain and the cause of fertility. Sāyaṇa quotes Yāska as his authority—'*Ādityaraśmayopi Ṛbhava ucyante*'—Nir. XI. 16. *Agohyasya gṛhe—Agohya* is also, upon the authority of the Nirukta, name of the sun, who is not hidden '*agūhanīya*' or according to Sāyaṇa '*agrahaṇīya*'—not to be apprehended literally or metaphorically. idam nānugacchatha—Sāyaṇa explains the compound verb-anusṛtya na gucchatha-'having come forth go not away without doing this, 'idam,' your office of sending down rain for as long a period as you repose in the solar orb. 'Yāska's explaination following Aṅgiras, seems to be a truism. "As long as you are there, you are not here" "*Yāvat tattrn bhavatha na tāvadiha bhavatha*".

(12) *Tr*. As you glide along enveloping the regions (in clouds) where, then, are the parents (of the world) ? Curse him who arrests your arm. Reply sternly to him, who speaks disrespectfully (to you).

Notes—The parents of the world-the sun and moon, the protectors of the world, which during rains, are hidden by the clouds. *pra* prefixed to *brū* may mean, either to speak harshly or kindly, to censure or to praise.

(13) *Tr*. O Ṛbhus, reposing in the solar orb, you inquire : who awakens us; unapprehensible (the sun) to this office of sending rain ? The sun replies—The awakener is the wind and the year (being ended) you again light up this world.

Notes—'*Śvānam bodhayitāram*' might be rendered : the awakener is the dog; but the commantator explans '*śvānam*' *by* "*antarikṣe svapantam vāyum*" *cd*—You have made this world today luminous, after the year has expired i.e. The rainy season being passed, the rays of the sun and the moon are again visible.

(14) *Tr*. Sons of Strength, the Maruts, desirous of you, coming, advance from the sky, Agni comes to meet you from the earth; the wind traversers the firmament. Varuṇa comes in the seas gathered water, in which they search for you.

III 60

(1) *Tr*. Your connection with (the consequences of acts), O Rbhus, is here (acknowledged) by the minds of all; desiring their share (of sacrifice). O Men, they have come with a knowledge (of their claims) to those (rites). The Sons of Sudhanvan, with the devices with which they are

victorious over the foes, they have accepted the share of sacrifice.

Notes—'*Vo bandhutā*' might mean 'your affinity or friendship'; but the scholiast explains. 'They, who connect acts with their fruits—'*Badhnanti phalena karmāṇi.*' *Yajñiyam bhāgamānaśā*—Sāyaṇa here explains the verb as if it were in the second person plural of the reduplicative preterite—'*yūyam vyāptāḥ stha.*' You have pervaded—the veda conjugating as in the *Parasmai-pada* in stead of *Ātmanepada*, as is usual. So in the third stanza we have *samānaśuḥ* in stead of *samānaśire*, the passage has been cited in the note of I. 20.8 and is translated somewhat incorrectly there. In I. 161.6 we have '*yajṇiyam bhāgamaitana*' explained also as *prāpnuta* '*obtain.*' see I. 20, I. 111—Grammar 2nd Edition p. 241.

(2) *Tr.* The faculties, by which you have divided the ladle, with that intelligence, wherewith you have covered the (dead) cow with a skin, with that will by which you have fabricated the two horses (of Indra); with those means, O Ṛbhus, you have attained divinity.

(3) *Tr.* The Ṛbhus, the performers of (good) works, the grand sons of a man, have obtained the friendship of Indra. They have perpetuated (existence). The sons of Sudhanvan have attained immortality. Performers of pious acts influencing (the results) through their devotion (they attainted divinity) by their works.

Notes—dadhanvire-as in the former case, *adhārrayanta* (I. 20.8) has no accusative. The scholiast, as before, supplies *prāṇān*, 'vitality' meaning 'immortal life' as follows. *cd*-see I. 110.3.

(4) *Tr.* Go with Indra in his chariot when the libation is poured out and be welcomed) with honour (by the worshippers) desiring (your favour). Ṛbhus, Sons of Sudhanvan, bestowers (of the rewards of pious acts) your virtuous deeds, your faculties are not to be measured.

(5) *Tr.* Indra, along with the food-bestowing Ṛbhus, accept with both hands (the cup of) the effused Soma-libation. Maghavan, excited by worship rejoice with the human

sons of Sudhanvan in the dwelling of the donor of the offering.

(6) *Tr.* Indra praised by many, associated with the Ṛbhus and with Vāja exalt with śacī, at this sacrifice. These self-revolving days are devoted to thee as well as the ceremonies (addressed) to the gods and the virtuous acts of men.

Note—śacī may mean *karman* 'act or rite.'

(7) *Tr.* Indra, with foodbestowing Ṛbhus, rewarding worshippers with food, come hither to (receive) the reverential praise of the adorer, with a hundred quick going steeds, the indications (of the Maruts). Come to the burnt offering of the sacrifice, yielding a thousand blessings to the sacrificer.

Notes—'Ṛbhubhir Vājibhir vājayan' implies a quibble upon the word Vāja, which is the name of one of the Ṛbhus, put for all, but which, in its more usual sense means 'food'.

IV 33

(1) *Tr.* I send my prayer as a messenger to the Ṛbhus. I solicit (of them) the milch-cow, the yielder of the white milk, for the dilution (of the Soma-libation); for they, as swift as the wind, the doers of good works, were borne quickly across the firmament by rapid steeds.

Note—As applicable to the deified mortals, this alludes to their being transported to the sphere of the gods. If the rays of the sun are to be understood, it implies merely their dispersion through the sky.

(2) *Tr.* When the Ṛbhus, by honouring their parents with renovated (youth) and by other works, had achieved enough, they there-upon proceeded to the society of the gods; and considerate they bring nourishment to the devout (worshipper).

(3) *Tr.* May they, who rendered their decrepit and drowsy parents, who, lay like two dry posts, again perpetually

young, Vāja, Vibhvan and Ṛbhu, associated with Indra, drinkers of the Soma-juice, protect our sacrifice.

(4) *Tr.* In as much as for one year the Ṛbhus preserved the (dead) cow, in as much as for one year they invested it with flesh, in as much as for a year they continued its beauty, they obtained by their act immortality.

(5) *Tr.* The eldest said, "Let us make two ladles." The younger said, "Let us make three." The youngest said, "Let us make four." Tvaṣṭṛ, O Ṛbhus, has applauded your proposal.

(6) *Tr.* The men (the Ṛbhus) spoke truth, for such (ladles) they made and thereupon the Ṛbhus partook of that libation. Tvaṣṭṛ, beholding the four ladles, brilliant as day, was content.

(7) *Tr.* When the Ṛbhus, reposing for twelve days remained in the hospitality of the unconcealable (sun), they rendered the fields fertile. They led forth the rivers, plants sprang upon the waste and waters spread over low places.

Note—See I. 161. 11.

(8) *Tr.* May those Ṛbhus, who constructed the firm-abiding, wheel-conducting car, who formed the all-impelling multiform cow, they, who are the bestowers of food, the doers of great deeds, and dexterous of hand, fabricate for us riches.

(9) *Tr.* The gods were pleased by their works, illustrious in act and in thought. Vāja was the artificer of the gods, Ṛbhukṣan of Indra, Vibhvan of Varuṇa.

(10) *Tr.* May the Ṛbhus who glorified the horses (of Indra) by pious praise, who fabricated for Indra his two docile steeds, bestow upon us satiety of riches and wealth (of cattles), like those who desire prosperity for a friend.

(11) *Tr.* The gods verily have given you the beverage at (the third sacrifice of) the day and its exhilaration; not through regard, but (as the gift of one) wearied out (by penance). O Ṛbhus, you, who are so (eminent), grant us verily, wealth of this third (diurnal) sacrifice.

Note—'narte śrāntasya sakhyāya'—is the phrase of the text. Sāyaṇa says "*Na sakhitvāya bhavanti devāḥ.*" "The gods are not through friendship." '*śrāntāt tapoyuktāt ṛte*' "except one wearied by penance," which would seem to apply to the worshipper; but again he says, "*Ete śrāntāḥ. Ato daduḥ*" They wearied out, therefore gave."

IV 34

(1) *Tr.* Ṛbhu, Vibhvan, Vāja and Indra, do you come to this our sacrifice to distribute precious things; for the divine ward has indeed now desired the drinking (cf. the Soma) on the (appointed hours of the) days; therefore the exhilarating draughts are collected for you.

Notes—dhiṣaṇā devī—In the Aitareya Brāhmaṇa it is said, Prajāpati said to Savitṛ, "These are thy fellow-students. Do thou drink with them."

(2) *Tr.* Resplendent with (sacrificial) food, prescient of your (celestial) birth, be exhilarated O Ṛbhus, along with the Ṛtus. The inebrating draughts are collected for you as well as pious praise. Do you confer upon us riches with excellent posterity.

Notes—'vidānāso janmanaḥ, is explained as "*Jananasya devatvalakṣaṇasya, devatvaprāptiṁ jānantaḥ,*" 'knowing the attainment of deification.'

(3) *Tr.* This sacrifice, Ṛbhus, has been instituted for you; which you, who are eminently resplendent, have accepted after the manner of men; before you, have the propitiatory (libations) been placed; for Vājas you are entitled to precedence.

(4) *Tr.* Now, leaders (of rites) the treasure that ought to be presented is to be given to the mortal performing (the sacred rite), the offerer (of libation). Drink Vāja, drink Ṛbhu, I present it to you at the third solemn (diurnal) ceremony for your exhilaration.

(5) *Tr.* Vājus, Ṛbhukṣans, leaders (of rites) come to us eulogising exceeding wealth; these draughts (of Soma) proceed

to you at the decline of the day, like newly-delivered cows to the stalls.

(6) *Tr.* Sons of Strength, come to this sacrifice, invoked with veneration; givers of precious things, associated with Indra, with whom you are intelligent, participate in being gratified (by the libation) drink of the sweet Soma-juice.

(7) *Tr.* Sympathising in satisfaction with Varuṇa, drink Indra, the Soma-Juice; drink it thou, who art entitled to praise, sympathising with Maruts. Drink sympathising with the first drinkers, with the drinkers, (at the sacrifices) of the Ṛtus, sympathising with the protectresses of wives (of the gods), the givers of wealth.

Notes—sajoṣasaḥ—It is not easy to find an equivalent for '*sajoṣasaḥ*' although the sense is obvious enough. '*Sajoṣā Indra Varuṇena somam pāhi*' is literally 'Indra, who art copleased with Varuṇa, drink the libation' implying that they both derive the like satisfaction from the beverage which they imbibe together. *ṛtupābhiḥ* is explained as—'*Ṛtuyājadevaiḥ*'—the deities to whom the Ṛtu sacrifice is dedicated. *gnāspatnībhiḥ-gnāḥ* is usually rendered as the wives of the gods. The compound is here explained as '*strīṇām pālayitryaḥ*. "The female protectors of women." It may imply the goddesses; but there is no authority for such an interpretation.

(8) *Tr.* O Ṛbhus, be exhilarated, sympathising with the Ādityas, sympathising with the Parvatas, sympathising with the divine Savitṛ, sympathising with the wealth-bestowing (deities of) rivers.

Note—'Parvatebhiḥ' "*parvavadbhiḥ parvaṇyarcamānair-devaiḥ*" "a sort of deities to be worshipped at the *parvas*, certain periods of the month as the New Moon and the Full Moon etc."

(9) *Tr.* Ṛbhus, who, by your assistance (gratified) the Aśvins, who (renovated your) parents, who (restored) the cow, who fabricated the horses, who made armours (for the gods), who separated the earth and the heaven, and who

the all-pervading, leaders (of rites), accomplished acts (productive of good results).

Notes—svapatyāni cakruḥ—According to the scholiast—'*svapatana*' *sādhanāni karmāṇi*—acts, the means of accomplishing their good affspring or consequences. According to Sāyaṇa, the relative '*ye*' refers to the antecedent in the next verse, '*te agrepāḥ*,' they, the first-drinkers the Soma being first offered at the evening sacrifice to the Ṛbhus.

(10) *Tr.* Ṛbhus, who possess wealth, comprising cattle, food, progeny, dwellings and abundant sustenance, do you, who are the first drinkers (of the Soma) bestow upon us, when exhilarated, that wealth and upon those who laud your liberality.

(11) *Tr.* Ṛbhus, do not go away, let us not leave you thirsting : (be present) unreproached at this sacrifice; be exhilarated, deities, along with Indra, along with the Maruts, and along with other brilliant (divinities) for the distribution of wealth.

IV 35

(1) *Tr.* Come hither, Sons of Strength, Sons of Sudhanvan, Ṛbhus, keep not away. May the exhilarating juices proceed to you at this scrifice, after the munificent Indra.

Notes—Indramanu-Indramanusṛtya or *Indramanugamantu.* 'having followed Indra' or 'May they come after Indra' Or it would be more consistent to render it as 'May they come after you to Indra'. See Note on IV. 34.9.

(2) *Tr.* May the munificence of the Ṛbhus come to us on this occasion (since) there has been the drink of the effused Soma, in consequence of one ladle having been made fourfold, by their dexterous and excellent work.

(3) *Tr.* You have made the ladle fourfold and have said (to Agni) "Assent (to the division)". Therefore you have gone, O Vājas, to the path of the immortals, dexterous-handed Ṛbhus, (you have joined) the company of gods.

(4) *Tr.* What sort of ldale was that which, by your skill you made into four? Now pour forth the Soma for their exhilaration. Drink Ṛbhus, of the sweet Soma-libation.

(5) *Tr.* By your (marvellous) deeds you have made your parents young; by your deeds you have made the ladle (fit) for the drinking of gods; by your deeds you have made the two horses, the bearers of Indra, swifter than (an arrow frcm) a bow, Ṛbhus, who are rich in sacrificial food.

(6) *Tr.* Distributors of food, Ṛbhus, showerers (of benefits), exhilarted by (Soma draught) fabricate wealth, comprising all posterity, for him, who pours out for your exhilaration the acid-libation at the decline of the day.

(7) *Tr.* Drink, lord of horses, Indra, the libation offered at dawn; the noon-day oblation is alone for thee; but (in the evening) drink with the munificent Ṛbhus, whom, Indra, thou hast made thy friends by good deeds.

(8) *Tr.* Do you, Sons of Strength, who have become gods by (your good deeds), soaring aloft in the sky like falcons, bestow upon us riches. Sons of Sudhanvan, you have become immortals.

(9) *Tr.* Dexterous-handed, since you have instituted, through the desire of good works, the third sacrifice, which is the bestower of weath, therefore, Ṛbhus, drink this effused Soma, with exhilarated senses.

IV 36

(1) *Tr.* The glorious three-wheeled car (of the Aśvins), made by you O Ṛbhus, traverses the firmament without horses, without reins; great was that proclamation of your divine (power) by which O Ṛbhus, you cherish the heaven and the earth.

(2) *Tr.* We invoke you respectfully, Vājas and Ṛbhus, to drink of this libation, for you are the wise sages, who, by mental meditation made the well-established, undeviating car (of the Aśvins).

(3) *Tr.* Therefore Vāja, Ṛbhus, Vibhvan, was your greatness proclaimed amongst the gods, that you made your aged and infirm parents again young (and able) to go (where they would).

(4) *Tr.* You have made the single ladle four-fold; by your (marvellous) acts you have clothed the cow with a (new) hide : therefore you have obtained immortality amongst the gods; such acts, Vājas and Ṛbhus, are to be eagerly glorified.

(5) *Tr.* From the Ṛbhus, may wealth, the best and the most productive of food (come to me) that which the leaders (of the rites), renowned together with the Vājas, have engendered; that which has been fabricated by Vibhvan-is to be celebrated at sacrifices, that which, deities, you protect, that is to be beheld.

(6) *Tr.* He is vigorous, and skilled in war; he is a Ṛṣi worthy of homage, he is a hero, the discomfiter of foes, invincible in battles; he is possessed of ample wealth and (is blessed) with excellent posterity, whom Vāja and Vibhvan, whom the Ṛbhus protect.

(7) *Tr.* An excellent and agreeable form has been assumed by you. (This is our own) praise. Vājas, Ṛbhus, be glorified (by that) for you are wise, experienced and intelllgent. Such we make you known (to be) by this our prayer.

(8) *Tr.* Do you, who are wise, (bestow) upon us in requital of our praises, all enjoyments that are good for man, and fabricate for us Ṛbhus, riches and food, resplendent, invigorating, overpowering (foes), and most excellent.

(9) *Tr.* Gratified (by your worship), fabricate for us, on this occasion progeny and wealth and reputation, with numerous adherents. Grant to us, O Ṛbhus,abundant sustenance wherewith we may greatly excel others.

Notes—'*śravo vīravat*' might be rendered as 'food comprehending offspring,' but as *prajā* has been already specified, the scholiast interprets *vīravat*—'*viros habens*' by "*bhṛtyādibhirupetam*," 'endowed with dependants.'

IV 37

(1) *Tr.* Divine Vājas, Ṛbhus, come to our sacrifice by the paths travelled by the gods, in as much as you, gracious (Ṛbhus), have maintained sacrifiee amongst tne people (the pregeny) of Manu, for (the sake of) securing the prosperous course of days.

Notes—The text has *Ṛbhukṣāḥ,* which is properly the Nom. sing. of *Ṛbhukṣin,* a name of Indra. Here Sāyaṅa identifies it with Ṛbhavaḥ the Nom. pl. of Ṛbhu. In some of the following verses of this hymn the word appears as *Ṛbhukṣaṇaḥ,* in Nom. or Voc. pl. of *Ṛbhukṣin* substituting optionally, the short for the long in the antipenultimate *Ṛbhukṣaṇāḥ* for *Ṛbhukṣāṇaḥ.* See Sanskrit Grammar 2nd edition p. 460.

(2) *Tr.* May these sacrifices be acceptable to you in heart and mind. May today the sufficient (juices) mixed with butter flow to you. The full libations are prepared for you. May they, when drunk animate you for glorious deeds.

(3) *Tr.* As the offering suited to the gods at the third (daily) sacrifice supports you, Vājas, Ṛbhuskṣans; as the praise (then recited supports you), therefore, like Manu, I offer you the Soma-juice, along with the very radiant (deities), among the people assembled at the solemnity.

Notes—cd. The meaning is not very clear. *Upara* is explained as those who are pleased or who sport near the worship of the gods—'*devayajansamīpe ramantaḥ.*' *tāsu vikṣu*'—'among such people.' *bṛhaddiveṣu*-Sāyaṇa considers this as an epithet of '*deveṣu*' understood.

(4) *Tr.* O Vājins, you are borne by stout horses, mounted on a brilliant car, have jaws of iron and are possessed of treasures. Sons of Indra, grandsons of Strength, this last sacrifice is for your exhilaration.

Notes—*Vājinaḥ*—'the possessors either of horses or food' is here used somewhat irregularly for *vājāḥ. ayaḥśiprāḥ*—According to commentator, it means as hard or as strong as iron.—'*ayovat sārabhūtaśiprāḥ suniṣkāh*—having good *niṣkas,* a certain weight of gold, if not a coin. 'Son of Indra' Son or Grandson of Strength'—The text has here nouns in the singular and it inconsistently follows with *vaḥ-vas*, you in plural, *agriyam* '*agre bhavam*' would mean the first, the preceding; but Sāyaṇa explains is as '*tṛtīyam savanam*,' which is most consistent with the worship of the Ṛbhus.

(5) *Tr.* We invoke you Ṛbhukṣans, for splendid wealth, mutually co-operating, most invigorating in war, affecting the senses, ever munificent and comprehending horses.

Notes—Such are the explanations of the epithets given to '*rayim*' '*wealth*' *ṛubhum*, *yujam*, *vājintamam*, *indrasvantam*, *sadāsātamam*, *aśvinam*, explained as the text.

(6) *Tr.* May the man, whom you and Indra favour, be ever liberal by his acts and possessed of horse at the sacrifice.

Notes—Medhasātā so arvatā—Perhaps a horse fit for the *Aśvamedha* is implied.

(7) *Tr.* Vājas, Ṛbhukṣans, direct us in the way to sacrifice; for you who are intelligent, being glorified (by us) are able to traverse all quarters (of space).

(8) *Tr.* O Vājas, O Ṛbhukṣans, O Indra, O Nāsatyas, commend that ample wealth with horse be sent to men for their enrichment.

VII 48

(1) *Tr. Ṛbhu*, (Vibhu) and Vāja, leaders of rites, possessors of opulence, be exhilarated by our effused (libation). May your active and powerful horses bring to our presence, your chariot, beneficial to mankind.

Notes—The text has *Ṛbhukṣṇo*, *Vājāh*, the use of the plural implying, according to the scholiast, that the three brothers are intended.

(2) *Tr.* Mighty with the Ṛbhus, opulent with the Vibhus, may we overcome by strength, the strength (of the foes). May Vāja defend us in battle. With Indra, our ally, may we destroy the enemy.

Notes—Ṛbhur ṛbhubhir vibhvo vibhubhiḥ are rather unintelligible phrases : the commentator explains ṛbhu by uru, great and *vibhu, vibhvaḥ* rich or powerful; but he leaves unexplained why the first should be in the singular and the second in the plural. It is an evident play upon words, as in the following *Vājo vājasātau.*

(3) *Tr.* They verily (Indra and the Ṛbhus) overcome multitude by their prowess. They overcome all enemies in the missile-conflict. May Indra, Vibhvan, Ṛbhuksan, Vāja, the subduers of foes, annihilate by their wrath the strength of the enemies.

Notes—uparatāti-upara is explained as '*upala*' 'stone'-'upalaiḥ *pāṣāṇasadṛśairāyudhaistāyate yuddham*', war that is waged with weapons like stones is *uparatāti.*

(4) *Tr.* Grant us deities, this day, opulence; may you all, pleased alike be (ready) for our protection. May the exalted (Ṛbhus) bestow upon us food : and do you (all) ever cherish us with blessings.

Notes—The text has *vasavaḥ*, which might be *Vasus*; but Sāyaṇa explains it as *praśasyaḥ*, an epithet of Ṛbhavaḥ, understood.

V

Hermann Grassmann

I 20

(1) *Tr.* This hymn, which secures treasure, has been prepared by the singers, from their family, in front of the gods.

(2) *Tr.* The clever ones fashioned for Indra, the pair of bay-horses, yoked by word. They obtained sacrifice through their work.

(3) *Tr.* They fashioned for the truthful Horsemen (Aśvins) the chariot that rotates on its flight. They also (fashioned) the cow that pours nectar.

(4) Tr. Through efficacious dictums the truthful Ṛbhus, with efforts, made their old parents young again.

(5) Tr. You accepted the share in feast along with Indra with the troop of Maruts, with the rulers and also with Ādityas.

(6) Tr. You have made in four vessels that new drinking cup, the work of god Tvaṣṭṛ.

(7) Tr. Then O gods, now bestow on us, thrice seven treasures, for him who presses, one after the other for the prayers.

(8) *Tr.* The travellers, through their skill, obtained and held fast the divine share.

I 110

(1) *Tr*, My web was already spun. Again I am weaving it. The sweetest song is recited to praise you. Here is the sea sufficient for all gods. O Ṛbhus, satisfy yourselves with this drink, consecrated with holy word.

(2) Tr. When seeking enjoyment you wandered towards the West and the East, you, who are partly related to me. O Sons of Sudhanvan, after a long journey you came here to the house of the gracious-minded Savitṛ.

(3) Tr. Savitṛ bestowed immortality upon you, because you appeared calling him, the eternally bright one. You have formed into four the cup, in which the eternal gods drink.

(4) Tr. Since you worked assiduously with efficacious prayer, you, the mortals, attained immortality. O Descendants of Sudhanvan, O Group of the Ṛbhus resembling the sun, in course of a year you were filled with prayers.

(5) Tr. The Ṛbhus, the praised ones, entreating for excellence and desiring glory among the eternal gods measured out one wide cup, like a field, with a bamboo-stick.

(6) Tr. We, with knowledge, would like to consecrate to the men of the mid-region a prayer sprinkling it like clarified butter with ladle. The Ṛbhus, who, with their father's victorious strength have obtained his treasure, have climbed up to the region of the heaven.

Note—'asya'—Since it is without accent it cannot be directly connected with 'pituḥ'.

(7) Tr. Ṛbhu is a new Indra to us through his strength. Through good might Ṛbhu is a good donor to us. O Gods, through your favour, make us conquer over the violence of the Soma-less ones on auspicious days.

(8) Tr. O Ṛbhus, you have fashioned a cow out of a hide. You have united the mother once again with her calf. O Heroes of the family of Sudhanvan, through your skill you have rejuvenated the parents, who were infirm through age.

(9) Tr. With refreshment help us in battle to get refreshment. O Indra, along with the Ṛbhus, give us rich gift. May Mitra, Varuṇa, Aditi, the Ocean, the Heaven and the Earth grant that to us.

I 111

(1) Tr. The wise artists produced the speedy chariot, the bay-horses, mighty as bull, who carry Indra. The Ṛbhus fashioned youth for the two parents, the mother for the calf, that united herself with it once again.

(2) Tr. Fashion vigorous youth for the sake of our sacrifice. Fashion for us nourishment rich in progeny, for might and wisdom. And for our group bestow such Indra-might that we shall ever stay with whole heroic family.

(3) *Tr.* O Ṛbhus, O Heroes, fashion for us benefit, benefit for the chariot and benefit for the courser also. May we always obtain benefit of the victory, through which we conquer in battle the friend and the foe.

(4) Tr. I invoke for help Indra, the lord of the Rbhus. I call the Ṛbhus, the Vājas, the Maruts, for a drink of Soma. (I call) both Mitra and Varuṇa, the horsemen (the Aśvins), that they may hasten us to gain, to courage and to victory.

(5) Tr. May the Ṛbhus hasten for us the gain for battle. May Vāja, who wins in battle, help us. May Mitra and Varuṇa, Aditi, the Ocean, the Heaven and the earth grant that to us.

I 161

Introduction—In stz. 1 the Ṛbhus are introduced as speaking, in stz. 2 Agni. The first 7 stzs stand in coherence. Stzs 6 and 7 narrate the deeds which the Rbhus had promised in stz. 3. On the contrary, the following three stzs stand isolated and are to be considered as fragments from hymns. Stz 8 refers to the fact that the Evening-libation is offered to the Ṛbhus. Peculiar is the narration about the yearlong-continuing sleep of the Ṛbhus in the house of Agohya, during which they, although asleep, accomplish heroic deeds.

(1) *Tr.* "Has the youngest, has the eldest been sent to us? Which message does he bring? What have we said? We have not blamed the cup. It is of a good breed. O brother Agni, we have praised the excellence of the wood."

(2) *Tr.* 'You must prepare four cups out of one,' the gods have said so to you. That is why I have come to you. O Sons of Sudhanvan, if you shall have that done, you will be honoured like the gods.

(3) *Tr.* 'You replied to the messenger Agni upon that', "We have to fashion a chariot, a horse and a cow. We must bestow youth on the old ones. When we have accomplished that, then O Brother, we will go to your work."

(4) *Tr.* O Ṛbhus, when you had accomplished that, you asked, "Where has he gone, he who has brought us the message?" When Tvaṣṭṛ saw the four cups ready, he concealed himself, slipping away to the group of women.

(5) Tr. When Tvaṣṭṛ said, "Let us kill these men, who have audaciously profaned the drinking vessel of the gods," then you assumed different forms at the drink, whom thus concealed, a maiden rescued.

(6) Tr. Indra yoked for himself the bay horses and the Aśvins your chariot, Bṛhaspati the wonderful cow. Ṛbhu, Vibhvan, Vāja went to the gods and the good artists had divine honour to their share.

(7) Tr. With wisdom you brought a cow out of a hide. You have rejuvenated the two parents. O Sons of Sudhanvan, you have brought out a horse from another. Yoking the chariot you went to the gods.

(8) *Tr.* 'Drink that water' thus you spoke to us. "Yourselves drink this pool which you have drawn out of the reed." 'O Sons of Sudhanvan, if this is not agreeable to you, then satisfy yourselves on the Third libation.'

(9) *Tr.* One said, "Water is the most glorious." The other said, "No, fire is the most glorious." The third one praised much more the lightning flash. Thus speaking of good things you fashioned the cups.

(10) *Tr.* One leads the lame cow to water. The other cuts well the flesh on the board. The third one sweeps away all dung in the evening. Did the act of the sons please the parents ?

(11) *Tr.* O Men, when you slept in the house of Agohya, through your skill you created for him plants on high lands and water in valleys. O Ṛbhus, do not carry out that work any more today.

(12) Tr. When with closed eyes you crawled through the living beings, where did your dear parents stay at that time ? You cursed him, who, stopping you, held your hand. He who greeted you, you greeted him in response.

(13) *Tr.* O Ṛbhus, when you awoke you asked, "Agohya, say, who indeed has awakened us ?" Then the ram gave out the dog as the awakener. After one year you opened the eyes.

(14) Tr. The Maruts go in the heaven, Agni goes on the earth. Wind goes through the air. Varuṇa goes through the floods of the sea. O Sons of Strength, they all are searching for you.

Note—The stanza stands isolated. It might have belonged to an old hymn, addressed to the Ṛbhus, (the Sons of Strength).

III 60

To the Ṛbhus, the divine artists

Introduction—The Rbhus, the Sons of Sudhanvan i.e. of the one equipped with a beautiful bow, are mythical creatures, who through their artistic works, have obtained divine honour and immortality. Generally the three are named : Ṛbhu or Ṛbhukṣan, Vāja and Vibhvan. As the three directors they are also designated the divine creatures, called with the same names. They carved four cups out of the one prepared by Tvaṣṭṛ. They fashioned for Indra the two golden-coloured horses. They severed the hide from the cow and out of it prepared the wonderful cow of Bṛhaspati. They rejuvenated their parents and fashioned for the horsemen (Aśvins) three-wheeled chariot, which rolls around the world in one day. Preferably the Evening-libation (the Third libation) is offered to them.

(1) Tr. Here, O Men, is the relationship for you, according to your mind. With wisdom the eager ones have leart all that, through which artifices you, O Sons of Sudhanvan, long ago, always finding the means, have attained divine honour.

(2) Tr. The skills, through which you have fashioned the cups, the craft through which you severed the cow of its hide, the spirit through which you fashioned the pair of the bay-horses, through these, O Ṛbhus, you have obtained divine honour.

(3) Tr. The group of the Ṛbhus has attained friendship of Indra. The Grandsons of Manu made themselves active in quick work. Working with zeal the Sudhanvanas obtained immortality, the artistic ones, with artistic work.

(4) Tr. Come, for the drink along with Indra in the same chariot. The accomplishment of your desires will be to your share. O Pious Ṛbhus, O Saudhanvanas, your high virtues and your exploits are not comparable.

(5) Tr. O Indra, in company of the Ṛbhus and Vājas, rinse the poured out juice, that is pressed through the arms. O mighty one, urged through devotion, intoxicate yourself in the house of the pious one along with the Sons of Sudhanvan.

(6) Tr. O Indra, O praised one, along with Ṛbhu and Vāja intoxicate yourself lustfully, in this drink of ours. These Soma-troughs here are offering themselves to you and the divine customs according to the human laws.

(7) Tr. O Indra, along with the mighty Ṛbhus, come here in haste to the singer's holy song. For the man, come to this sacrificial downpour, with hundred strong achievements and with thousandfold leadership.

IV 33

(The unconcealable in stz. 7 is Savitṛ thought as the Sun)

(1) Tr. I send to the Ṛbhus my speech as a messenger. I wish for white milk in order to be poured over. The wind-winged ones on speedy tours have been active around the heaven in one day.

Note—1 in order to pour over the Soma-drink which must reach the Ṛbhus.

(2) Tr. When the Ṛbhus, working ardently, did service to their parents with wonderful skill, they came to the divine companionship. The wise ones carried wellbeing as its reward.

(3) Tr. They, who rejuvenated their parents, that lay like two broken pillars, may those Vāja, Vibhvan, Ṛbhu together with Indra, the Soma-feasting ones, enjoy our sacrifice.

(4) Tr. Because the —bhus preserved the cow for one year, and artistically formed her flesh through one year, brought fodder to her one year long, through these efforts they became immortal.

Note—bhāsas (nt) (from bhas) fodder (according to GKR).

(5) The eldest said, "Make the cup into two". The younger said, "Let us make three cups". The youngest said, "Make the cup into four". O Ṛbhus, Tvaṣṭṛ was astonished at this speech of your".

(6) Tr. The men spoke truth, since it so happened also. The Ṛbhus carried out these plans of theirs. Of course when

Tvaṣṭṛ saw the four cups shining like the day he became envious.

(7) Tr. When the Ṛbhus revelled resting joyfully for 12 days in the house of the unconcealable one they provided the fields, dischared the streams. The plants occupied the plains, water the valleys.

(8) Tr. The Ṛbhus, who fashioned a chariot, that now rolls and now stands, (who fashioned) the cow with all forms, which stimulates everything, may these Rbhus, with helpful, skilful hands, fashion treasure for us.

(9) Tr. When the gods looked at their work with thinking and understanding, they were pleased with it. Ṛbhukṣan was the artist of Indra, Vibhvan of Varuṇa and Vāja of all gods.

(10) Tr. You, artistically fashioned for Indra the smoothly-yoked bright horses, murmuring sentences, O Ṛbhus, give us good prosperity, treasure. Give us good rest granting it as to a friend.

(11) Tr. They have given you today drink and exhilaration. One cannot be a friend to the gods without effort. Therefore O Ṛbhus give us today treasures in this Third libation.

IV 34

(1) Tr. O Ṛbhu, Vibhvan, Vāja, Indra, come towards this sacrifice of ours, to our offering. For today, at this hour, group of gods has offered this drink to you and all the Somas have hurried towards you.

(2) Tr. O Ṛbhus, you donors of treasures ever since birth, intorxicate yourselves at the time of the sacrifice. The drinks and the fullness of gifts have hurried towards you. Lead towards us wealth equipped with heroes.

(3) Tr. O Ṛbhus, this sacrifice was prepared for you, who received it from human hand. The drinks offered at it are hurrying towards you. O Vāja, all of you be the first here.

(4) Tr. Also O Men, today there was rich gift for you, to your servant, to the mortal worshipper. O Vājas, O Ṛbhus drink (the Soma). The great third libation was given to you in order to intoxicate you.

(5) Tr. O Vājas, O Ṛbhns, O Men, come here to us, delighting yourselves in the great gift. The drinks have come to you at the close of the day as the cows which are oozing milk come to the stable.

(6) Tr. O Sons of Strength, now come here to this sacrifice being invited humbly. O rich ones, O donors of treasures, drink this mead in company of Indra to whom you belong.

(7) *Tr.* O Indra, taking delight in the hymns, drink Soma, in company of Varuṇa, in company of the Maruts, in company of those who drink first and of those who drink later, in company of the wives of gods, who present treasures.

(8) Tr. O Ṛbhus, intoxicate yourselves in company of the Maruts, in company of the high mountains, also in company of Savitṛ, the god, in company of the rivers that present treasures.

(9, 10) Tr. The Ṛbhus, who (fashioned) the horsemen (Aśvins), who (fashioned) the parents, who fashioned the milch-cow for delight, who fashioned the pair of horses, who fashioned the armours and both the worlds separately, the strong men doing good works (i.e.) you O Ṛbhus, who present possession, which is rich in cattle, rich in horses, rich in heroes, rich in material boons and in nourishment, who drink first, you cheerful ones, give that (wealth) to us and to them who offer you gift.

(10) Tr. O flawless Ṛbhus, you were not away. We do not leave you thirsty in this sacrifice. O gods, exhilarate yourselves with Indra, with the Maruts, with the heroes in order to present treasures.

IV 35

(1) Tr. O Descendants of Strength, come here. O Sons of Sudhanvan, O Ṛbhus, do not be away. A rich gift for you is there in this feast. May your drink follows Indra.

(2) Tr. The rich gift of the Ṛbhus has come here. Drinking of the well-pressed Soma has taken place, when through good deed and artlstic works they made four cups out of one vessel.

(3) Tr. You made four cups out of one vessel. "Comrade, be helpful to us" thus you spoke. Then O Vājas, you went on the path of the perpetual ones, to the group of the gods, you Ṛbhus, expert in arts.

(4) Tr. Out of which material was this one cup made, from which you have fashioned four cups through wisdom? Now press Soma for yourselves in order to intoxicate you. O Rbhus, drink of this sweet juice.

(5) Tr. Through artifice you have rejuvenated your parents. Through artifice you have fashioned the cup in which the gods drink. O Ṛbhus, rich in treasures, through artifice you have fashioned the two speedy bay-horses, that carry Indra.

(6) Tr. O Vājas, O Ṛbhus, O lively bulls, rejoicing in drink, fashion wealth associated with all heroes for him, who, at the close of the day, presses sharp Soma for your intoxication.

(7) Tr. O Indra, driving bay-horses, you drank Soma early in the morning. The midday-libation was fully yours only. Now drik along with the Ṛbhus, bestowing treasures, with whom you are allied because of their good actions.

(8) Tr. You. who have become gods through good work and have settled yourselves in the heaven like an eagle, (being like that) give us treasures you born of strength, O Sons of Sudhanvan, you have become immortal.

(9) *Tr.* O artists, the third feast, rich in gift, which you have obtained for yourselves through good works, that O

Ṛbhus, has been poured out here all over, for you. Drink it jointly together with Indra's intoxicating drink.

IV 36

(1) Tr. The majestic chariot, once constructed is three-wheeled, (the chariot) which rolls around the heaven without a horse and without reins. That is the high testimonial of your divine power O Ṛbhus, that you made the heaven and earth flourish.

Note—Through the fact that the Ṛbhus have fashioned the three-wheeled chariot of the horsemen (Aśvins), that rolls around the heaven in one day, they have brought the heaven and the earth to flourish.

(2) Tr. They, full of wisdom, who with the help of deliberation of mind, have fashioned the chariot that rolls froward without slipping, we invite them i.e. you O Vājas, O Ṛbhus, so that you should drink this concoction of the Soma-juice.

(3) Tr. O Vājas, O Ṛbhus, that was your high reputation and your excellence among the gods that you made your parents, who were frail and grown old, young again for vigorous walk.

(4) Tr. With artifice you have made one cup fourfold. You have made a cow newly arise out of a hide. Then there was immortality for you with the gods. O Vājas, O Ṛbhus, this work of your is praiseworthy.

(5) Tr. From the Ṛbhus springs forth the treasure with renown of the first order, the treasure, which the group wellknown through Vāja has created. That, which Vibhvan has fashioned, is praiseworthy in feasts. O gods, he whom you help, he has a lively life.

(6) Tr. He whom Vāja, Vibhvan, the Ṛbhus promote that horse is speedy, that signer is fully of poetic art, that archer is invincible in battle and he receives nourishment of treasures, the strength of a hero.

(7) Tr. The most beautiful, superb ornament, i.e. this hymn was invested to you. O Vājas, O Ṛbhus, accept it graciously. Since you are connoisseurs, wise poets, we invite you with this memorised verse.

(8) Tr. You, who understand it, produce for us from your fully-filled cups all nourishment, agreeable to men and (produce) brilliant treasure, that bestows strength, treasure that is excellent, and (produce) for us wealth, vigourous force of life.

(9) *Note*—(Translation given in the Appendix p. 535. The stz. 8 forms the end of the hymn. The 9th, a superficial repetition is detached even through its extent.)

Tr. Since you bestow on us progeny here and treasure there, create for us renown, rich in heroes, through which we shall surpass all others. O Ṛbhus, present us this manly gift.

IV 37

A

(1) Tr. O Ṛbhuṣons, O Vājas, O Gods, come to this sacrifice of ours by the paths trodden by gods, O cheerful ones, you always accept on favourable days the sacrifice of man in the houses.

(2) Tr. May these sacrifices dipped in ghee be gratifying to your heart, and mind today. May the filled juices delight you and may they inspire you to courage and strength.

(3) *Tr.* O Vājas, O Ṛbhukṣans, as the three-timed god-loved sacrifice and the hymn were ordained to you, like Manu, I offer you Soma in the lower houses, to you, who stay high up in the heaven.

(4) Tr. O Strong ones, since you have stout horses, bright chariot, iron-helmets and beautiful necklaces, O Sons of Indra, Grandsons of Strength, that which is the best offers itself to you in order to intoxicate you.

B

(5) *Tr.* O Ṛbhukṣans, we entreat, Ṛbhu for g ood things, Rbhu, who, as a friend is the strongest in battle, who is like Indra, that presents the most plentiful (thing), who rides a horse.

(6) Tr. O Ṛbhus, the mortal whom you, along with Indra, support must be victorious through prayers, (victorious) through the horse in the battle for treasure.

(7) *Tr.* O Vājas, O Ṛbhukṣans, pave for us the ways so that we go quickly, so that O praised Princes, we cross all directions.

Note – Now I take *Yaṣṭave* as infinitive from *Yakṣ*, in the sense. "Persuing ones aim quickly." The denotation "for the sacrifice" is not suitable in the context.

(8) *Tr.* O Vājas, O Ṛbhukṣans, O Indra, O horsmen (Aśvins), point out to us that treasure and give a horse to the group of men and (give) ample treasure for donation.

VII 48

Introduction—Stz. 4 is addressed to all gods and has been joined later-yet before the winding up of the original collection as it is probable with several closing stanzas of our book, which end with the refrain.

(1) *Tr.* O Vājas, O Ṛbhukṣans, intoxicate yourselves in the Soma-juice of ours, O Mighty heroes. O Rbhus, may the stallions roll the strong chariot on its journey here to us.

(2) Tr. Be Ṛbhu with the Rbhus, Vibhvan with the Vibhus, and strength with the strength, you, who are ours. May Vāja help us in battle to gain booty. May we, in association with Indra, strike the enemy.

Note—Perhaps one has to read Ṛbhu instead of Ṛbhuḥ.

(3) Tr. Since they rule over many through their authority, they conquer all enemies, that approach them. May Indra,

Vibhvan, Ṛbhu, Vāja extirpate the manliness of the wicked enemy.

Note—Viśaḥ is to be added to *pūrvīh* (cf. vii 31, 10) (W.B. to change it to *puru*).

(4) *Tr.* O Gods, (fashion) for us wide space now. May you all united, be to our help. O Gods, good nourishment may be presented to us. Always protect us with your blessings.

VI

Alfred Ludwig

I 20

(1) *Tr.* This most joy-bringing hymn was fashioned with their lips by the Brāhmaṇas for the divine race.

(2) *Tr.* They, who, fashioned for Indra the two bay-horses, harnessed by mere word, by their work they attained the sacrifice.

*Notes—vacoyujau—*Sā.—*Tāḍanādikaṁ vinā vāṅmātreṇa rathe yujyamānau.* with their work-through serving them.

(3) *Tr.* They fashioned for the Nāsatyas an unjolting light chariot. They created the cow Sabardughā.

*Notes—Sukham—*with good hole (in the naval) so that the axle turns lightly in it, what might not have been so easy to achieve at that time. cf. AV IV. 12.7; X. 1.8; III. 508, 521. Yasna XXIX. 6—*azuṭoi manthrem* is the cow herslef.

(4) *Tr.* The Ṛbhus, with their words coming true, the honest dealers, made their parents young again, by means of their alteration.

Notes—The parents – the heaven and the earth, viṣṭī—There can also be a pun on the word, since it can be understood as 'service' also.

(5) *Tr.* Your exhilarating drink came to Indra, accompanied by Maruts, to the kings among the Ādityas.

Notes—Sā. also cities *Āśvalāyana āvahana-nigada* : *Indram Ādityavantam Ṛbhumantam Vibhumantaṁ Vājavantaṁ āhaveti.* cf. I. 164.4 i.e. III. 60.4. *Nivid* to the Ṛbhus—The Ṛbhus, the gods, dexterious in service, the skilful artists should intoxicate themselves with Soma, they, skilled in service, the dexterious artists, with their deft-handed work, they with nimblest quickness, most proficient workers in their work, the most capable in capacity, they, who have fashioned the all-impelling, all-formed cow. They fashioned the cow that was of all forms, they harnessed the two bay-coloured (horses), as they went to the gods. When they were eating, the maiden noticed them. They, capable in work, in one year's time, obtained a share in the sacrifice. The Ṛbhus, the gods should listen to this here. They should exhilarate themselves with Soma. (After this Ludwig has quoted and discussed a passage from Tai. Ar. 13. It has been dropped out here).

Saṁ vo agmata—The expression brings out that Soma is to be thought of as presenting itself in the cups of the Ṛbhus, cf. 1.166.1 i.e. IV. 34.1. The exhilarating drinks came to them with Indra and Maruts. See also IV. 35.7.

(6) *Tr.* They also made newly into four that new cup of Tvaṣṭṛ, the creation of the god.

Notes—camasam—Kat, ŚS X. 3.21.

(7) As such give to us, as the bringers of Soma-sacrifice, delights three times sevenfold to each single one, through good prayers.

Notes—triḥ saptāni—three seven numbers 'seven *pāka, haviḥ* and *Soma yāgas*.' This is without any substance here. It can mean sacrificial drink, if triḥ saptāni does not refer to ratnāni as Grass. took it. Śāṅ B I. 14.5—*Asurāṇām sapta saptāni āvṛjata*. cf. AV VI. 47.3; TS III 1.9.2.

(8) *Tr.* They were efficient as priets. Through their skill they became sharers of the right of sacrifice amongst the gods.

I 110

(1) *Tr.* This holy work of mine, which I had (already) spun (formerly) has been spun again. The sweetest hymn is sung in order to praise (you). Here is the *Viśvadevya-vat.* O Ṛbhus, satisfy yourselves with the *Svāhākṛta* (Soma) i.e. with the Soma brought with the call '*Svāhā*'.

Notes—Tataṁ tāyate—a common expression TB III. 7.6.4 : *Yajñiyā yajñaṁ vicayanti śaṁ ca.* If *vicayanti* is not to be understood as transitive. cf. AB II. 21.2. apaḥ-Sā. '*Agniṣṭomādirūpam*' this can only refer under the circumstances to the action which is restricted in magnitude on the fourth day of the *Abhiplava ṣaḍaha* as *Nivid* for *Vaiśvadeva śastra,* which precedes the *Ārbhavam* and follows a detached *Dhāyyā. Vaiśvadevya vat*—Sā '*Somarasaḥ sarvebhyo devebhyah paryapto yathā bhavati.*' *Svāhākṛtasya*—Sā.— '*Svāhākṛtenāgnau* prakṣiptasya somasya pānena.' ucathāya-in order to praise. Sā.—*stutyāya śasyate i.e. as śastra.*

(2) *Tr.* As you went on searching on a curved band, "In West, in East (are) certainly the relatives of mine," O Saudhanvanas, (thinking thus) after a long wandering about, you came to the house of the liberal Savitṛ.

Notes—Ābhogayam belongs to '*praitana.*' The fact that the poet should seek to share relationship with the Ṛbhus does not at all give any useful element to the stanza. The fact that they came to Savitṛ is motivated through this that they wanted to search for the relatives. But here as also in stz. 4 this can have laid the ground for the erroneous opinion that Ṛbhus might have been human beings. The fact that our opinion viz. that they stand for the seasons is not strange to those times, can be seen from the expression, often recurring in the Brāhmaṇas : Ṛtavaḥ vai pitaraḥ. *Bhūmanā* –SB III. 5.2.11.—*Bhūmā vai rāyaspoṣaḥ*; III. 5.4.4—*Bhūmā vā barhih* (about the abundance of the grass). I. 2.1.7—*Bhūmā vai sajātāh.* cf. II. 1.2.2. and the stz. cited at II. 1.72.6. *Saviturgṛham*—Here Savitṛ seems to be the sun of the year (cf. I. 32.9; SB XIV. 2.2.9.—*Savitre tvā Ṛbhu nat e vibhumate Vājavate*) which is visited by the Ṛbhus at the begining of the year and which moves out of the South for its departure. 'Announcing'—Sā.—'*Apekṣitaṁ Somapānaṁ vijñāpayantaḥ* i.e. Hence forward the sacrificial progress should begin anew.' Savitṛ bestowed immortality upon them, because the symmetrical course of the sun conditions the never-ending symmetrical course of the seasons.

(3) *Tr.* Thereforc Savitṛ gave you immortality, because you came proclaiming him, who cannot be hidden. You have made into four this camasa, the eating bowl of the Asura, that was a single one.

Notes—Asurasya Tvaṣṭuḥ—Savituḥ; *caturvayam-vaya—dvaya*, division in general.

(4) *Tr.* When with alertness they had served at the sacrifice as the priests, they, though mortal, obtained immortality. The Saudhanvans, the Ṛbhus, having the sun as the eye, became introgated in a hymn in the course of a year.

Notes—martāsaḥ—mortal. Here in the sense of temporary. Their excellent achivements guarantee them a return. In the identification of 'temporary' and 'human' there lies an ironical trait, as pointed out by many myths—partly in themselves and party in the manner in which they are handled—point out.

'In one year'—This can be understood thus—Since no individual Ṛbhu among the Ṛbhus was worshipped for himself but all were worshipped together and presented with Soma-drink together, this recognition could come only to their collective performance, which required one year even for its action. Here the third Savana and the Ārbhavam of the Agniṣṭoma are meant.

(5) *Tr.* The Ṛbhus, who were praised and who, desiring the highest glory among the immortals, themselves entreating, measured out like a field, the gaping bowl with a measuring rod.

Note—This is how Ludwig has revised the translation of this stz in vol. IV p. 164.

(6) *Tr.* We desire to offer to the heroes of the firmament the poem by means of our knowledge, just as one offers ghṛta by means of a sṛc i.e. a ladle. (We desire to offer to the Ṛbhus) who, coming with the rapidity of the All-father Savitṛ, have risen to the space of the heaven for strengthening food of Soma.

Notes—It is not admissible to translate as we have done (in vol. I). We do not regret to have followed Sāyaṇa fully, who alone is right.

(7) *Tr.* Ṛbhu is Indra to us, newest by growth; Ṛbhu through strength, the giver of treasures through wealth. O gods, through your favour, may we, on auspicious days overthrow the battles (i.e. the attacks) of those who do not bring sacrificial drink.

Notes—vasurdadiḥ—or the present-making Vasu. sṛc—also masc.; ṛbhu as adjective denotes 'skilful'—*asunvatām*—SB VII. 2.1.9.—*yo vai na sunoti na yajate taṁ nirṛtir ṛcchati. 'Stenasyetyām anvihi.'*

(8) *Tr.* O Ṛbhus, you have formed the cow out of the hide. You have reunited the mother with the calf. O Saudhanvanas, O heroes, through your workmanship you have rejuvenated the old parents.

Notes—By the hide the earth deprived of its vegetation is to be understood. (The other way round, the skin on which Soma is crushed is meant as earth—SB V. 4.11; I. 65.4; VI. 6.2; X. 142.4; TB III. 1.3; AB V. 32.2) '*Iyam vai tvak Ādityatvagasi. Prati tvā pṛthvī vettu*'—Tai. Br. III. 2,63. Often the concept is of a different nature that the plants represent the continuance of the earth. V 41, 11; 1 65, 4; VI 6, 2; X 140, 4; Tai. Br. III 1, 3. The calf is here the spring-time-sun. *Saudhanvanāḥ*—According to Manu X. 23, Kat SS I. 1.10 Sudhanvā—a descendant of *Vrātya vaiśya* from a *Vaiśya* woman.

(9) *Tr.* O Indra, help us with might where strength wins. Efficient like Ṛbhu give us much grant. May Mitra, Varuṇa, Sindhu, Aditi, Pṛthvī and Dyauḥ grant that to us.

I 111

(1) *Tr.* With skill they fashioned the lightly-rolling chariot. They fashioned the excellent bay-stallions, bearers of Indra. They fashioned youthful living for the old (parents). They created for the calf, the mother staying beside.

Notes—Perhaps this hymn directly reported before a battle. *vidmanāpasaḥ* TB III. 1.1. cf. *Hastam* about the *Nakṣatra* with reference to the significance of the appelatives.

(2) *Tr.* Fashion for us, for the sacrifice, efficient vigour (as that for your) spiritual strength. Fashion nourishment that brings good descendants. Create for us this efficiency of our group, so that we live with a family of numerous heroes.

(3) *Tr.* O Ṛbhus, fashion for us gain for the chariot, gain for the horse. O heroes, always present to us victorious wealth, over-powering in battle the related and the unrelated.

(4) *Tr.* I call for help Indra, ruling over the Ṛbhus. I call Ṛbhu and Vāja (and Vibhvan), the Maruts and the two i.e. Mitra and Varuṇa, then the Aśvins. They should send us (help) for gain, for wisdom, for victory.

Notes—dhiye—Perhaps subjunctive. 'So that our hymn wins'.

(5) *Tr.* May Ṛbhu fashion gain for the battle. May Vāja, conquerer of the enemies, make friends with us. May Mitra and Varuṇa, Sindhu, Aditi, Pṛithvī and Dyauḥ grant this to us.

I 161

(1) *Tr.* (The Ṛbhus ask:) Why has the excellent, why has the youngest come to us ? What is the message, for which he comes ? What have we said ? We have not blamed the cup of high origin. We have spoken about the quality of the wood.

Notes—The explanation of Sāyaṇa rests on a contradiction. Agni appearing as the fourth of the Ṛbhus etc. The explanation is cumbersome and improbable. What is said is *śreṣṭha* and not *jyeṣṭha* and there is no contradiction with *yaviṣṭha*. On the contary both are meant as expressing excellence. The poet has perhaps chosen *śreṣṭha* as a counterpoise to yaviṣṭha. Bhūti-excellence. The suspicion that the Ṛbhus had not recognised the newcomer is refuted in the most effective way through the address 'Agne bhrātar'.

(2) *Tr.* (Agni speaks:) 'Make one bowl into four.' This the gods want me to say. For that have I come. O Saudhanvanas, if you do this, you will be entitled to sacrifice with the gods.

Notes—On the symbolism used here we have already spoken on repeated times.

(3) *Tr.* (The Ṛbhus to the gods) What you have spoken to Agni (and what thus) means is:) a horse must be fashioned, a chariot must be fabricated here. A cow is to be created and the two are to be made young (again). O brother (Agni and the gods), after we have accomplished this, we will follow you here.

Notes—This is in conformity with what concerns the claimed performance, not with stz. 2.

(4) *Tr.* O Ṛbhus, when you had accomplished (your works) you said, 'Where has this messenger of ours gone now?' (Likewise) when Tvaṣṭṛ saw the cup divided fourfold, he has disappeared among his wives.

Notes—Disappearing—the beginning of the rainy season? *nyānaje*—TS VI. 5.8.4. *Devā vai Tvaṣṭāram ajighāṁsanta sa patnīḥ prāpadyata taṁ na prati prāyachan* (*patnīḥ śaraṇaṁ gataḥ*). What is meant is that Tvaṣṭṛ was ashamed when he saw his own work being surpassed.

(5) *Tr.* Because Tvaṣṭṛ said, 'Let us kill them, who have censured the cup, out of which the gods drink', they change their names in the sacrifice (in Ṛbhu, Vibhvan,

Vāja). Under these new names must the daughter (of Tvaṣṭṛ) receive you in a friendly manner.

Notes—anyā nāmāni—in the names of the ṛtus. *kanyā*—The Ṛbhus came to Tvaṣṭṛ and are received by his daughter, otherwise unknown. (the first dawn of the year ?)

(6) *Tr*. Indra has yoked for himself the two bay-horses, the Aśvins their chariot. Bṛhaspati leads away the cow Viśvarūpā for himself. When Ṛbhu, Vibhvan, Vāja, you went amidst the gods, as artists you came to the sacrificial share.

(7) *Tr*. Through your invention you made a cow come out of a (mere) hide. You made the two old ones young. O Saudhanvnas, you created from one horse another. You yoked the chariot and went to the gods.

Notes—The renewal of the world in the development of the seasons.

(8) *Tr*. 'Drink this water' you said, 'Or drink this cast from Muñja'. Saudhanvanas, if you do not accept this also, you must delight yourselves with Soma in the third libation.

Notes—It seems that the Ṛbhus were deceived in the matter of Soma. The Soma of the morning libations was water for the Ṛbhus, of the midday libation it was the cast of Muñja. So they chose the third libation.

(9) *Tr*. 'The waters are the main things,' so has one of you said. Agni is the chief thing,' the other one has named vadharyantī the lightining or the lightining-striking cloud ?) as such among many. You all, speaking truth, have formed the cup.

Notes—Vadharyantī—cf. the names of *Kṛttikāḥ, ambā, dūtā* etc, in TS.

(10) *Tr*. One leads away the lame cow (or the red ?) to the water. The other forms flesh, which has been brought from the slaughter-houses. On the hind the other brought

the refuge. Have the parents helped the children in any way ?

Notes—the rejuvenating process of the world has been depicted as a rotation of the ordinary process of the old and the mortals. The old ones, who themselves grew old and were exhausted could not be helpful in the process of their rejuvenation.

(11) *Tr.* You have creared grass on high places for this (mortal ?) and in the low lands you have created water through your artistic sense. O men, O Ṛbhus, do not repeat today that act of yours, that you slept in the house of the unconcealable one.

(12) *Tr.* As together you went around the worlds, where, then, were your paternal old ones ? You cursed him, who held your arm. You spoke back to him, who spoke to you.

(13) *Tr.* When you had (over) slept (in the house of Savitṛ) then you asked *Agohya*, 'who has awakened us now ?' *basta* (one from the sun-god's rams) named the dog as your awakener. In the year you opened the eyes for the first time.

Notes—Quotation from Grassmann—"Peculiar is the narration of the sleep of the Ṛbhus, lasting for a year, in the house of *Agohya*, during which they, though asleep, accomplished excellent works." The fact that we are right comes out also from the *tyāga* of the offerings for the Ṛbhus in the third libation, which is worded : Saudhanvanebhya ṛtubhya idam.

(14) *Tr.* The Maruts go in the heaven, Agni on the earth, the wind goes through the mid-region. Varuṇa goes in the waters of the ocean, all of them searching for you, O Children of strength.

III 60

(1) *Tr.* Here is your mental relationship. May you come to these works eagerly with treasure, with the magic-powers,

through which you, always having self-impelling forms, obtained a share in worthiness of sacrifice.

Notes—iheha—cf. Tāṇ. Mah. B XIII. 10.9—emphatic 'here' 'vedasā' does not mean 'with wisdom' and '*abhijagmuḥ*' does not mean 'learnt'; because generally one does not learn 'with wisdom'. They did not come to the sacrifice with empty hands. The sentence : *uśijaḥ......vedasā*—can be taken parenthetically, which is of course difficult. Or one must take '*jagmuḥ*' in the sense of '*jagma,*' which has sufficient analogies. It is moreover doubtful whether the uśijaḥ are the Ṛbhus. It can even denote 'the gods'. 'Iheha' is to be taken as referring to the *devayajana.* 'Here, where he gods enjoy honour'. It is the question of 'relationship' with these, not with human beings. For the gods have come eagerly through that what you have been able to do, accomplishing it by means of the magical powers, precisely the powers, by dint of which you have secured the right to participate in the sacrifice, being furnished with every new form corresponsing to every new undertaking. The instrumental '*vedasā*' (causal-motivated) is explained through '*māyābhiḥ*' which has been taken in a relative clause, just according to the common practice in Sanskrit. The identification *Vedasā-māyābhiḥ* is clearly brought out, since '*māyābhiḥ*' taken separately in the relative clause, does not belong to that place (i.e. the principal clause). *vedaḥ* Sā.—ŚB XII. 8.2.1—'*vittam vedaḥ*' *pratijūtivarpasaḥ—jūti* motive ? The motive, with which their form changes every time lies in the change of times. *ānaśa*—noteworthy. cf. Lāṭ Ś.S. II. 3.8. *Somasya pītimānaśadhve*—clearly derived from the active.

(2) *Tr.* The mights through which you fashioned the cup, the inventions through which you created the cow out of the hide, the intelligence, through which you produced the two bay-horses, through (all) these, O Ṛbhus, you have obtained god-head.

Notes—carmaṇaḥ—out of the peeled hide. The fact that the cow has not lost her hide in that act (of peeling) is certain. To the countrary is the wellknown apologue of the ŚB and AB, according to which the men might have been concealed beforehand in the hide of the cow, but might have bean robbed away by the gods for favour of the cow.

(3) *Tr.* The Ṛbhus have attained the friendship of Indra. The grandsons of Manu, the dexterious ones, expedited the work. The Saudhanvanas have secured for themselves immortality, because they, the good ones through good works, had served with sacrifice.

(4) *Tr.* Together with Indra go for the juice. Then be with the glory of your desires. O Priests, O Saudhanvanas, O Ṛbhus, your good deeds have no comparison, nor your heroic deeds.

(5) *Tr.* O Indra. in company of the mighty Ṛbhus, pour forth with both hands amply for yourself the Soma, that is gushing forth together, the Soma that is pressed. O Maghavan, praised with a hymn, drink in the house of the donor, together with the Saudhanvanas, with the heroic (sons).

Notes—āvṛṣ—cf. Āśv ŚS II. 7. *mādayadhvam-āvṛṣayadhvam*.

(6) *Tr.* O Indra, accompanied by Ṛbhu and Vāja intoxicate yourself in this libation of ours with Śacī. you much-praised one. These homes have, of themselves, shown interest in you, according to the laws of gods and customs of men.

Notes—vrata—cf. IV. 33.10.

(7) *Tr.* O Indra, come here along with the mighty Ṛbhus, strengthening the holy song of the singer. Come on hundred pressing invitations, for the living being, you, having thousand ways for the offering of sacrifice.

IV 33

(1) *Tr.* I send forth to the Ṛbhus the speech like a messenger. I entreat (them for the Śvaitarī cow for covering of the Soma. In their quick ways the skilful ones have gone around the heaven in a moment.

Notes—upastire-somopastaraṇāya—Generally closely connected with. '*abhidhāraṇa*' 'for pouring forth.' (vol III p. 379). But what is the cow *Śvaitaī* ?

The cow *Śvitrī* is named in I. 33.15. (cf. vol. III p. 147); doubtlessly with reference to a historical personality. At this place Śvaitarīm is freely explained by Sāyaṇa as '*payoyuktām śvetatarām vā*,' which recalls to the mind '*vāsarī*' 'shining' of the Brāhmaṇas (explained as *bahukṣīrā*—ṚVI. 137.3; VIII. 6.30; VIII. 48.7). It can be placed together with 'svetley' of the Slavonic. There lies only a great difficulty in finding a simple adjectival form in it. On the other hand if 'dhenu' denotes 'milk' here, then '*Śvaitarī* will not mean 'milk-rich'. For the other meaning (white) such an uncommon word will hardly be used. Thus through the adjective the meaning 'milk' of '*dhenu*' is highly improbable. Also one would not like to translate 'milchcow' (for milk) of (the cow) *Śvaitarā* (*as the original form might have read*). *Thus it is rather certain that* '*dhenu*' here means 'cow' and further that *Śvaitarī* is her own name. The fact that the cows were named and that their names were pronounced at the sacrifice is proved from the procedure of milking the three cows in the new-moon and Full-moon sacrifices. VS I. 3; TB III. 2.3 : *Gāṁ dugdhvā kumbhīm prati kṣīram ānayantam dogdhāraṁ* (*Adhvaryum*) *pṛcchet Kām adhukṣāḥ* ? "*Amūm*" *iti nāma gṛhṇāti.* Similarly SB I. 7.1.17 : *Amūmityāha-sā viśvayuh.*' By the second. '*sā viśvavyacaḥ.*' By the third '*sā viśvakarmā*' (standing for earth, the atmosphere, the heaven). Here '*amūm*' respresents the name. Here of course the mention is made which fully differs from the solemn forms of the Brāhmaṇas. It must have another connection also.

(2) *Tr.* When the Ṛbhus had made the two old parents perfect with attendance and with wonder-working of their (gift) of services, they secured the friendship of gods. The foresighted ones brought nourishment to their aim.

Notes—pariviṣṭī veṣaṇā cf. ŚB I. 1.2.1 *Karmaṇe tvā veṣāya tvā* (*veveṣṭīva hi yajñam*—cf. *Pariveṣaṇaṁ karoti*—With regard to '*manāyai* cf. ŚB III. 2.4.16. *Cidasi manāsi dhīraṣi dakṣiṇā.* Sā. explains the strange expression rightly as '*manase prakṛṣṭa-*

manasvāya' 'for their hlgh-soaring plan.' Yasna XL II. 9 *asahyāmanāyai.* Sā. explains *puṣṭim* as '*saviṣayām*' material nourishment.

(3) *Tr.* They, who rejuvenated their parents, that lay old as rotten pillars, may these Vāja, Vibhvan, Ṛbhu, resembling Indra, of the sort of Madhu, promote our sacrifice.

Notes—'*sanā*' could be adverb 'in old times.' In ŚB VIII. 7.1.9 it is explained as 'agre' in the text). Then *jaraṇā*, with greater probability, could belong to '*pitarā*.' The mention of *yūpa* might have been made, because near the standing sacrificial post, another lying on the floor also was brought. Upacaya—TB VI. 6.4.4.—ŚB III. 7.2.1. *yūpaikadeśinī bhavati yadvāsya upacayo bhavati.* cf. Kāt ŚS VIII. 8.9. commentary at the end and on sū 23.

(4) *Tr.* When the Ṛbhus fabricated the cow, together with the calf, when togather with the calf they formed her flesh, when together with the calf they brought mire (in the abdomen), then they obtained immortality through these works.

Notes—Grass—'*arakṣan*'—May be a more favourite word. We presume '*atakṣan*'—*māh*—In TS IV. 10.3 comes the noteworthy form '*masmasākuru*' for which VS has '*bhasmasākuru*,' clearly a corrupt form, *bhāsaḥ*—nourishment from *babhasti* : Sā.—'*dīptiravayavaśobhā*.'

(5) *Tr.* The oldest said, 'Let us make two cups.' The younger one said, 'We make three.' The youngest said, 'We make four.' O Ṛbhus Tvaṣṭṛ praised this speech of yours.

Notes—Here the characteristic infinitive form '*kara*'—already repeated by us fully twice, co-ordinated with '*kṛṇavāma*.' panayat–sā.—astaut.

(6) *Tr.* The men spoke truth. For so have they done. These Ṛbhus followed their divine way. When Tvaṣṭṛ saw these four cups, shining like days, he liked them.

Notes—*avenat*—Sa.—'*akāmayat*'. Grass 'became envious'—not provable. Construction with participle—TB III. 7.13.1.—

yatte grāvā bahucyuto acucyavuh......tvayā tat soma guptamastu naḥ, Sā naḥ sandhā asat parame vyoman. cf. IV. 24.9.—'*Avikṛto kāniṣam.*

(7) *Tr.* When the Ṛbhus, reposing, enjoyed for themselves the hospitality for 12 days, of him who is not to be hidden, they made the fields excellent. They brought the rivers. Plants spread themselves over the deserts and the waters (spread) in low lands.

Notes—In order to avoid the inference that we have drawn from this noteworthy place, Gras. lets the Ṛbhus perform their miracles during the period when they enjoyed themselves, reposing cheerfully. cf. I. 110.6 : They enjoyed the hospitality of god Savitṛ for 12 days. Also see vol. III p. 187.

(8) *Tr.* The Ṛbhus, who fashioned the lightly-moving chariot, occupied by men, who (fashioned) the all-urging, all-formed cow, may these Ṛbhus, fashion for us wealth also, with grace, with good skill and with good hand.

(9) *Tr.* Since the gods, thinking with insight and spirit were pleased with their work, Vāja became the skilled artisan of the gods, Ṛbhukṣan of Indra, Vibhvan of Varuṇa.

Notes—sā. holds that the youngest Vāja belonged to all the gods, Ṛbhukṣan to Indra and Vibhvan to Varuṇa; but perhaps this division was not seriously intended by the poet.

(10) *Tr.* They, who fashioned for Indra the two bay-horses, taking delight in medhā and uktha; the two horses that are easy to be yoked, O Ṛbhus, such as you are, give us nourishment of wealth, fashioning wellbeing like a friend.

Notes—*medhayokthā*—cf. 306.6 also III. 60.6. *vratā-dharmabhiḥ*—evident. cf. IV. 34.1. *ratnadheyā*, VI. 15.14 ṛta VII 1, 14 etc. *kṣemayanto na mitram*—cf. Ās. ŚS I. 7.7. *idopahvānam ......kṣemayantaḥ*—better 'who find (yourselves) in sure prosperity, prosperity as a friend.'

(11) *Tr.* They have brought forth for you this drink, this exhilarating drink, for you, at this time of the day. One

cannot have the gods as friends without exertion. Therefore O Ṛbhus, bestow on us excellent riches at this third libation.

Notes—Not without exertion etc. This proverb is often alluded to in the Brāhmaṇas.

IV 34

(1) *Tr.* Ṛbhu, Vibhvan, Vāja, Indra come here to this sacrifice with present of joy. At this time of the day the divine Dhiṣaṇā (longing) has fixed this exhilarating drink for you. The exhilarating drink has come to you.

Notes—ratnadheyā—evidently instrumental. Grass.—accusative-far from truth. It is to be marked against this that ratnadhā (with the exception of I. 20 *ratnadhātamaṁ stomam*) and ratnadheya are almost invariably used for the gods, especially in the hymns here viz. IV. 34.4, 6, 7, 8, 11; IV. 35.1; referred to Indra by Sā. That the Savana is ratnadheya, because it is prepared by them is unmistakably explained through stz 2 and also stz 9. Thus there can be no doubt that it is instrumental. Otherwise *yajñaṁ ratnadheyam* would be read as *savanaṁ ratnadheyam* in 35.9. Dhiṣaṇā—See Vol. III p. 378.; VII 38, 5; V 69, 20.

(2) *Tr.* Knowing the birth, you who have your strength for joy, enjoy yourselves O Ṛbhus, with the Ṛtus. Intoxication and abundance have come to you. Bring forth to us wealth along with good heroes.

Notes—Since the Ṛbhus represent the seasons, their connection with the Ṛtus here is understandable, *Ṛtubhiḥ* belongs to '*vidānāso janmanaḥ*' as well as to '*mādayadhvam*'. '*vidānāso janmanaḥ* could even be translated as 'You, who have obtained your (perpetual) birth.'

(3) *Tr.* Here is this sacrifice ready for you, which long since you have acquired for you in human manner. Those, who are found to be pleased with you, have themselves proceeded towards you. You were all (also the two elders) Vājas.

Notes—manuṣvat—instead of 'as a man' it would be better taken as 'like men' in human manner.' i.e. through this that they had served the gods quite like men through artistic handicraft activity. dadhidhve—old form.; *Abhūta Vājāh*—Gras. leaves the emphatic '*uta*' untranslated. The meaning cannot be doubtful : 'You were all Vājāḥ, though only the youngest is clearly called Vāja, it will not be that the remaining were not justified to have that name, if they themselves had carried it. Hence all together are shortly called Vājāḥ in stz. 4, 5. cf. IV. 33.9.

(4) *Tr.* O men, the present with joy was for him, who adores you, also now for the mortal donor. O Vājas, O Ṛbhus drink of this. This third libation is given to you in order that you get the joy of the drink.

Notes—idā 'tṛtīye savane'—Sā.

(5) *Tr.* O Vājas, Ṛbhukṣans, come to us, being sung on account of big treasure. At the close of the day the draughts have come to you, just as the cows delivering for the first time come to their dwelling.

Notes—Ṛbhukṣāḥ—pl.; *abhipitve* '*samāptau*' Sā. '*navasvaḥ-navaprasvāḥ gāvaḥ*'—Sā.

(6) *Tr.* O sons of Strength, come to this sacrifice, being invited with adoration. O Sūris, drink of this madhu, producing joy, you being accompanied by Indra, with whom you are of one mind.

Notes—yasya—Sā. rightly referring it to Indra' and he with whom you are of one mind.' ca—'*prasidhau*'—Sā.

(7) *Tr.* O Indra, drink the Soma, being of one mind with Varuṇa. O you, rejoicing in hymns, (drink this) being of one mind with the Maruts, one mind with those who drink first and with those who drink at the Ṛtus, of one mind with Gnāspatnīs, producing joy.

Notes—Gnāspatnībhiḥ is instrumental. TS I. 2.5.2 names the *Gnāhaspatnīḥ* as 'Tvaṣṭṛmatīḥ. cf. also VI. 52.4.

(8) *Tr.* O Ṛbhus, intoxicate yourselves being of one mind with the Ādityas, of one mind with the Parvatas, of one mind with the divine Savitṛ, of one mind with the rivers, giving delight.

Notes—Parvatebhiḥ 'the particular gods praised on the Full-moon and the New-moon *parvans*'—Sā.; but then what about the rivers ?

(9) and (10) *Tr.* (9)—The Ṛbhus, who have helped the Aśvins, who have helped the two old-ones, who have formed the cow, the two steeds, who have fasioned the armours that move on both sides, who have fashioned the two world-halves, the widely-working heroes, who have fashioned freedom, self reliance (good progeny ?), (10)—(being like that) O Ṛbhus, you who have fashioned treasures in cows, in strength, (treasure) having good heroes, much nourishment, who as such are the first-drinking ones, intoxicating yourselves, give us that treasure and give it to those, who sing of the gift.

N*otes*—(9)—See Vol. III p. 254, 284 and XXXVI. *svapatyāni*—The fact that the idea of freedom, self-reliance many times occupied their minds is seen in the Brāhmaṇas. TB generally (e.g. II, 5.2; II. 4. 1. 9; III. 8.3.6) explains *svagā* as *svādhīnam.* A V IX. 2.3.—speaks of '*asvagatā—aṁsatrā-'kavacāni*' —Sā.

(10) *gṛṇanti* is here to promise (the priests ?). cf. saṇgir-saṇgara. 'ca' throws light that 'tebhyām ye' is to be constructed as Gras. has done it.

(11) *Tr.* Do not stay away, O blameless ones, (therefore) we have not left you going thirsty at this sacrifice. O gods, rejoice yourselves together with Indra and Maruts, with the kings, in order to create joy.

Notes—aniśastāh-aninditāḥ—Sā. *atitṛṣaṁa*—TS III. 2.5.3 *Gaṇam me mā vititṛṣaḥ.*

IV 35

(1) *Tr.* Come here, sons of Strength, Saudhanvanas, Ṛbhus. Do not stay away. In this libation is your joy. Your intoxicating drink follows that of Indra.

Notes—That of Indra—'*Indram yuṣmāñcānvāgacchantu*'—Sā.; but Indra's Savana comes beforehand. cf. stz. 7.

(2) *Tr.* Joy of the Ṛbhus has come here. Here was the drinking of the well-pressed Soma, when, with your skill, with your craftsmanship, you made one cup fourfold.

(3) *Tr.* You divided the cup fourfold. You said, 'Friend, help us'. Then O Vājas, O deft-handed Ṛbhus, you went on the way of immortality, to the group of the gods.

(4) *Tr.* Out of what (i.e. out of which material) was the cup made, which, through widsom, you have made fourfold ? Then O Ṛbhus, you pressed the libation for intoxication and drank of the soma-mead.

Notes—sunudhvam—Thus they pressed the Soma for themselves. cf. stz. 2.

(5) *Tr.* Through your competence you made the old (parents) young. Through your competence you fashioned the cup, through which the gods drink. Through your skill you fashioned the two bayhorses, the coursers that carry Indra, whose strength delights you.

(6) *Tr.* O Vājas, he, who, at the close of the day presses the sharp libation in order to intoxicate you, o bulls, delighting yourselves, you have fashioned for such a man wealth with full group of heroes.

Notes—'*tīvram*'—*rasavattaram*—Sā.

(7) *Tr.* O Indra with bay-horses you drank the juice in the morning. The mid-day libation is fully yours. (In the third libation) drink together with the joy-creating Ṛbhus, whom, O Indra, you have made your friends on account of their skill.

Notes—sukṛtyayā—cf. stz. 2 *sukṛtyayā, svapasyayā.*

(8) *Tr.* You, who became gods through your skill, sat high in the heaven like a hawk. Hence fashion joy for us, O Sons of strength, Saudhanvans, you have become immortal.

(9) *Tr.* The third libation, which, through your skill, you fashioned for yourselves for your joy, O deft-handed ones, that libation has been sprinkled over for you here. Drink of it with intoxication, as Indra (drinks it).

IV 36

(1) *Tr.* The chariot, which, according to its origin, is not disposed towards (an ordinary) horse, which is without reins, which is rich in praise, which has three wheels, turns round the space. O Ṛbhus, that is the great skill of your godhead that you nourish heaven and earth.

Notes—Not for ordinary—Sā. *'vāhanāśvanirapekṣaḥ.'* So also *anabhiṣuḥ, tricakraḥ*—The chariot of the Aśvins is just fashioned by the Ṛbhus. A pun on he word also might be intended, 'the wheel (rolling) for the triad.' *puṣyatha—'puṣṭim kurutha,'*—Sā. Grassman—almost 'pardepit' 'you bring to flower.'

(2) *Tr.* O Ṛbhus, the intelligent ones, who, out of your mind, with inventive power, fashioned the smoothly-rolling chariot, that does not overturn (from the traversed track), O Vājas, O Ṛbhus, you who have done this, we invite you for the enjoyment of this libation.

Notes—avihvarantam. Sā. *'akuṭilam'*—which follows the track; *dhyayā* cf. *dhayāyate.* This might have given *'dhiyas'* which would have become dhīḥ whose 's' might have been seen as nom. sing. *āvedayāmasi*—free terminology *'nivedayāmasi'* would be expected. Avesta—*'āvaedayemi,* in the sense of *nivaedayāmi'*—was expected.

(3) *Tr.* O Vājas, O Ṛbhus, O Wide-working ones, that was the greatness of yours, already proclaimed among the gods,

that you made the long-decaying old parents once again young for agileness.

Notes—sanājur—cf. *amājur.*

(4) *Tr.* You have made one cup into four. Through your inventive mental power you have brought forth a cow out of a hide. O Vājas, O Ṛbhus, you have at once attained immortality amongst the gods. This (fact) about you is to be praised in Ukthas.

Notes—Āś. ŚS II. 10. 16. *śṛṣṭī—no Indra haviṣā mṛḷāti.*

(5) *Tr.* The wealth, orginating from the Ṛbhus, the one that the heroes wellknown for their strength have produced, is of excellent renown. That which is produced by Vibhvan is to be proclaimed in the assemblies. O Gods, he whom you protect, is excellent among men.

Notes—It is questionable whether along with '*ravih*' the chariot and perhaps even the cup (so Sāyaṇa) are not meant.

(6) *Tr.* The horse is vigorous. He is a Ṛṣi by eloquence, a hero in shooting, invincible in battles. He, whom Vāja and Vibhvan, he whom the Ṛbhus have taken under protection, has attained nourishment of wealth, has attained heroism.

Notes—Sā. explains—(see earlier)—'*Bhūmā vai rāyaspoṣah.*' *āviṣuḥ*—better 'have taken under your protection.

(7) *Tr.* For you was placed an excellent worthseeing form viz. a song of praise. O Vājas, O Ṛbhus, have pleasure in it. You are judicious, wise, poetic. As such we invite you here with this 'Brahma.'

Notes—peśah—Sā. '*rūpam*'—'you have been just depicted in the hymn'.

(8) *Tr.* O Ṛbhus, knowing all human needs, following our desires, fashion for us as vitality, marvellous, highest treasure, that is strong as a bull.

Notes—According to Grassmann *dhiṣaṇāḥ* are quite appropriate to the cups of the Ṛbhus. However it is not difficult to see that the poet could not say '*yūyaṁ dhiṣaṇābhyaḥ pari vājam rayim vayastakṣata.*' Sā., against this with reference to the ablative directly preceding '*stutibhyaḥ,*' which even lends expression to the wishes, is pertinent. Grassmann's translation does not suit 'parī' which means 'following' here and which generally means 'succession.'

(9) *Tr.* Giving progeny here and treasure there, fashion for us heroic renown, through which we shall surpass others. O Ṛbhus give us manly vigour.

Notes—citayāmāti—atikramya *jñāyemahi*—Sā. *dada*—infiinitive in Veda. cf. TB II. 4.4.9. *Bhūtam mā tasmād bhavyaṁ ca drupadādiva mucatua* (*mucatu* ?) also III. 7.13.3 and 4. *vida*—imperative. R V II. 31.6—*Trita Ṛbhukṣā savitā ca no dadhe.* TS V. 7.7.1.*jānitāt—vida rūpamasya*; ŚB II. 30.6. Hotāsa (hatāsi ?) Ṣaḍ B I. 5 *Āha vadedityarthah.*

IV 37

(1) *Tr.* O Vājas, O Ṛbhukṣans, O gods, come to our sacrifice by the paths, trodden by gods, so that you, O Cheerful ones, accomplish sacrifice in these tribes of Manu, on auspicious days.

Notes—'*dadhidhve*' one can translate more exactly as 'to accept.' Sā. alone knows about '*Sudinatve ahnām*' as modalistic tense. If the hymn belongs to a sacrifice, claiming more days, the mention of good weather is not useless. The rains (the tropical downpour of rains must be taken into account) must be disturbing the sacrifice basically.

(2) *Tr.* May these sacrifices be pleasing to your heart and mind. May they come ghṛta-covered. May the filtered juices go forth to you. When drunk, may they delight you for excellent strength and efficiency.

Notes—'juṣṭāsaḥ, can also be connected to 'guḥ.' 'May the offerings be agreeable to your mind'. *ghṛta*—covered—the Somas —sā. *praharayanta*—May they delight or may they persuade you to accept (for enjoyment).

(3) *Tr.* O Vājas, O Ṛbhukṣans, all welfare of the gods comes from your threefold ascent. So this Stoma is given to you. Therefore with you, who are high up in heaven I offer Soma as a human being among the younger tribes.

Notes—tṛyudāyam—It is difficult to understand that it should mean 'thrice.' It can only mean 'with three times commencement.' Whether Stomaḥ is not to be changed to Somaḥ can be thought about. It is unrefutable that the number three is to be connected with the number three of the Ṛbhus. Through the three Savanas the three seasons could be denoted. In the text '*yathā*' is connected with '*dade*' (accented); but it is not possible to join Stoma and 'devahitam.' Therefore we understand '*dade*' as the subordinate clause. It is doubtful whether '*devahitam*' as an abstract noun, cannot denote institution for godhead.' 'As your institution for gods is followed in the threefold commencement, so with it the Stoma is offered to you in order to indicate your godhead.' As you (IV 35,4) press Soma to be offered to yourselves and to the gods, so simultaneously I offer Soma as a human being among the human beings.' *bṛhaddiveṣu*—Sā—'the gods' which is scarcely just. Moreover it can be understood by itself.

(4) *Tr.* You have stout horses, shining chariot and iron-jaws. You are storng with gold ornament. You, sons of Indra, sons of strength, for you was intended the excellent one, in order to give you the joy of a drink.

Notes—Sūno—noteworthy word in singular. Stz. s 5 to 8 begin a new section.

(5) *Tr.* O Ṛbhus, we invoke excellent wealth; (we invoke) the strongest companion in battle, like Indra; ever rich in booty, rich in horses.

(6) *Tr.* O Ṛbhus, the mortal, whom you and Indra help, may he, through his inventive powers, be the winner in sacrifice and (a winner in battle) through a horse.

Notes—'May he be' more correct will be 'He must be'. cf. Grassmann-Antithesis with *dhībhiḥ* and *arvatā*. The two are meant separately, the priest—*dhībhih* the noble warrior—*arvatā*. cf. vol. III p. 221.

(7) *Tr.* O Vājas, O Ṛbhukṣans, make the ways free for us, so that we can sacrifice, for us, O Sūris, the praised ones, so that we shall cross all regions of the world.

Notes—yaṣṭave tariṣaṇi,—For the safety of yajana the prayer is put forth. The undistrubed conducing of the sacrifice resulted in the warrior, fighting victoriously in all regions of the world. (Digvijaya).

(8) *Tr.* O Vājas, O Ṛbhukṣans, O Indra, O Nāsatyas, bless this treasure and this horse, before that of other men, in order that we acquire greater treasures.

Notes—Is '*tam*' to be written for '*sam*' ? Here the speech is about the sacrificial horse.

VII 48

(1) *Tr.* O Ṛbhukṣans, O Vājas, rich men, take delight in this juice of ours. O Vibhus, may your sympathetic powers turn the man-loving chariot of yours, who are proceeding towards us, hitherwards.

Notes—'*arvācaḥ* is striking. Noted by Sā. and explained by him as '*arvāñcaḥ*''.

(2) *Tr.* May we, ourselves, Ṛbhus, be victorious with you, the Ṛbhus. Ourselves like Vibhu (may we be) strong over others strength with Vibhu. May Vāja help us there, where booty is won. With Indra as the companion, may we conquer Vṛtra.

Notes—Grassmann is in the highest distress on account of *Ṛbhuḥ*—We have taken '*vaḥ*' in that illogical way in which the genitive part is often found used in the *Veda.*, and not found as barely used by itself. Perhaps it stands directly for '*yuṣmābhiḥ*'. The meaning of this stz. obviously interpreted in a clumsy way is :—'We ourselves may possess your victorious strength as Ṛbhu, Vibhvan, Vāja'. We should have better given the passage as follows :—In the company of yours, who are Ṛbhus in the true sense of the word—(This on account of the plays on the etymological denotations of the words) – would like to be as the Ṛbhus. In so far as you are Vibhus we would like to be victorious like the Vibhus and so on. It is one and the same whether one says 'we would like to be the Ṛbhus' or 'we would like to be Ṛbhu'; but unfortunately grammar lays down that the subject and the predicate must agree in number.

(3) *Tr.* With their dominating power they are above many (tribes). They fight against all enemies in the neighbourhood. Indra, Vibhvan, Ṛbhukṣan, Vāja render futile the manly vigour of the wicked enemy in the contest.

Notes—śāsā 'svakīyayā ājñayā'—Sā.—good—'in the neighbourhood. They do not avoid coming to blows i.e. *uparatāti 'saptamyāh luk'*. Sā.

(4) *Tr.* O Gods, show love towards us. May all of you, of one mind, be helpful to us. May Vasus bestow strength on us. You always protect us with blessings.

VII

R.T.H. Griffith

I 20

(1) *Tr.* For the Celestial Race this song of praise which gives wealth lavishly, was made by singers with their lips.

Note—For the Celestial Race—*devāya janmane*, the divine class or race of the Ṛbhus, the three sons of Sudhanvan who is said to have been a descendant of Aṅgiras. They were named severally Ṛbhu, Vibhvan, and Vāja and styled collectively. Ṛbhus from the name of the eldest. "Through their assiduous performance of good works they obtained divinity and became entitled to receive praise and adoration. They are supposed to dwell in the solar sphere, and there is an indistinct identification of them with the rays of the sun : but, whether typical or not, they prove the admission, at an early date of the doctrine that men might become divinities". Wilson.

(2) *Tr.* They who for Indra, with their mind, formed horses harnessed by a word, attained by works to sacrifice.

(3) *Tr.* They for the two Nāsatyas wrought a light car moving every way : they formed a nectar-yielding cow.

Note—The two Nāsatyas :—The Aśvins. See I. 3,3. The Ṛbhus may have been the first to attempt the bodily representation of the horses of Indra and the chariot of the Aśvins.

(4) *Tr.* The Ṛbhus with effectual Prayers, honest, with constant labour, made their Sire and Mother young again.

Notes—Sire and Mother—Heaven and Earth, which they as deities of the seasons, refresh and restore to youth.

(5) *Tr.* Together came your gladdening drops with Indra by the Maruts girt, with the Ādityas, with the Kings.

Note—'According to Āśvalāyana, as quoted by Sāyaṇa, the libations offered at the daily (or evening) sacrifice are presented to Indra along with the Ādityas, together with Ṛbhu, Vibhvan and Vāja with Bṛhaspati and the Viśvedevas'. Wilson.

(6) *Tr.* The sacrificial ladle, wrought newly by the God Tvaṣṭṛ's, hand, four ladles have ye made thereof.

Note—"Tvaṣṭṛ, in the Paurāṇik mythology, is the carpenter or artisan of the Gods : so Sāyaṇa says of him, he is a divinity whose duty, with relation to the Gods, is carpentry...Sāyaṇa also calls the Ṛbhus the disciples of Tvaṣṭṛ...The act ascribed to them in the text, of making one ladle four, has probably, rather reference to some innovation in the objects of libation than to the mere multiplication of the wooden spoons used to pour out the Soma juice. The Nītimañjarī says that Agni, coming to a sacrifice which the Ṛbhus celebrated, became as one of them, and, therefore, they made the ladle fourfold, that each might have his share" Wilson.

(7) *Tr.* Vouchasafe us wealth, to him who pours thrice seven libations, yea, to each give wealth, pleased with our eulogies.

Note—Or the 'thrice seven' may refer to ratnāni, grant thrice seven rich treasures.

(8) *Tr.* As ministering Priests they held, by pious acts they won themselves, a share in sacrifice with Gods.

I 110

(1) *Tr.* The holy work I wrought is wrought again : my sweetest hymn is sung to celebrate your praise. Here, O

ye Ṛbhus, is this sea for all the Gods : sate you with Soma offered with hallowing word.

Note—This sea for all the Gods : this vessel containing Soma juice for all the Gods, or for the particular class of Gods called *Viśvedevāḥ* or Viśvedevas. The hallowing word : *Svāhā* (Ave. Hail.); an exclamation used in making oblations to gods.

(2) *Tr.* When, seeking ycur enjoyment onward from afar, ye certain of my kinsmen, wandered on your way, Sons of Sudanvan, after your long journeying, ye came unto the home of liberal Savitṛ.

Note—Seeking your enjoyment desirous of enjoying libations of Soma juice. My kinsmen—Sudhanvan, father of the Ṛbhus, was a descendant to Aṅgiras, as was also Kutsa the *ṛśi* of the hymn.

(3) *Tr.* Savitṛ therefore gave you immortality, because ye came pro-claiming him whom naught can hide; and this the drinking-chalice of the Asura, which till that time was one, ye made it to be fourfold.

Note—Him whom naught can hide—or, from whom nothing can be hidden, that is, Savitṛ as the Sun. The drinking-chalice of the Asura—the cup that had been made by the *Asura* or immortal God Tvaṣṭṛ. See I. 20.6. This chalice appears to be the moon which contains the *amṛta* or nectar of the Gods. The legend seems to mean that Tvaṣṭṛ as God of the year created it uniformly bright, and that the Ṛbhus, as Gods of the seasons, made it fourfold or diversified with four phases. See Hillebrandt, Vedische Mythologie, I. p. 515.

(4) *Tr.* When they had served with zeal at sacrifice as priests, they, mortal as they were, gained immortality. The Ṛbhus, children of Sudhanvan, bright as sun, were in a year's course made associate with prayers.

Note—Associate with prayers—"connected with ceremonies (appropriated to the different seasons) of the year" Wilson.

(5) *Tr.* The Ṛbhus with a rod measured, as it were a field, the single sacrificial chalice wide of mouth, lauded of all

who saw, praying for what is best, desiring glorious fame among Immortal Gods.

Note—Measured—in order to divide it into four, as is said in verse 3.

(6) *Tr.* As oil in ladles, we through knowledge will present unto the Heroes of the firmament our hymn, the Ṛbhus who came near with this great Father's, speed, and rose to heaven's high sphere to eat the strengthening food.

Note—This great Father—Savitṛ as the Sun, the source of all life. Strengthening food—Soma.

(7) *Tr.* Ṛbhu to us is Indra freshest in his might, Ṛbhu with powers and wealth is giver of rich gifts. Gods, through your favour may we on the happy day quell the qttacks of those who pour no offerings forth.

(8) *Tr.* Out of a skin, O Ṛbhus, once ye formed a cow, and brought the mother close unto her calf again. Sons of Sudhanvan, Heroes, with surpassing skill ye made your aged Parents youthful as before.

Note—A skin-perhaps the dried-up earth. A cow—the earth refreshed by the Rains. The mother—the earth; her calf—the autumn—Sun; parents—Heaven and Earth.

(9) *Tr.* Help us with strength where spoil is won, O Indra; joined with the Ṛbhus give us varied bounty. This prayer of ours may Varuṇa grant, and Mitra, and Aditi and Sindhu, Earth and Heaven.

I 111

(1) *Tr.* Working with skill they wrought the lightly rolling car: they wrought the Bays who bear Indra and bring great gifts. The Ṛbhus for their Parents made life young again; and fashioned for the calf a mother by its side.

(2) *Tr.* For sacrifice make for us active vital power; for skill and wisdom food with noble progeny. Grant to our company this power most excellent, that with a family all-heroic we may dwell.

(3) *Tr.* Do ye, O Rbhus, make prosperity for us, prosperity for car, ye Heroes, and for steed. Grant us prosperity

victorious evermore, conquering foes in battle, strangers or akin.

(4) *Tr.* Indra, the Ṛbhus' Lord, I invocate for aid, the Ṛbhus, Vājas, Maruts to the Soma draught. Varuṇa, Mitra, both, yea, and the Aśvins Twain : let them speed us to wealth, wisdom and victory.

Note—Vājas–this is Vāja and his two brothers Ṛbhu and Vibhvan, more usully called collectively the Ṛbhavaḥ or Ṛbhus. Similarly, in this line the Ṛbhu and his brothers.

(5) *Tr.* May Ṛbhu send prosperity for battle, may Vāja conquering in the fight protect us. This prayer of ours may Varuṇa grant, and Mitra and Aditi and Sindhu, Earth and Heaven.

I 161

(1) *Tr.* Why hath the Best, why hath the Youngest come to us ? Upon what embassy comes he ? What have we said ? We have not blamed the chalice of illustrious birth. We, Brother Agni, praised the goodness of the wood.

Note–The Ṛbhus ask Agni why he comes to them. The chalice—see : I. 20.6.

(2) *Tr.* The chalice that is single make ye into four : thus have the Gods commanded; therefore am I come; If, O Sudhanvan's Children, ye will do this thing ye shall participate in sacrifice with Gods.

(3) *Tr.* What to the envoy Agni in reply ye spake, A courser must be made, a chariot fashioned here, a cow must be created, and the Twain made young. When we have done these things, Brother, we turn to you.

Note—A courser must be made, etc : see I. 20.2, 3, 4 and I. 110 and 111.

(4) *Tt.* When thus, O Ṛbhus, ye had done ye questioned thus, Whither went he who came to us a messenger ? Then Tvaṣṭṛ, when he viewed the four wrought chalices, concealed himself among the Consorts of the Gods.

Note—Then Tvaśṭṛ—represented as hiding for shame among the Goddesses-probably the Celestial Waters—when he saw this alteration of his work, and in anger proposing to slay the Ṛbhus who had thus disgraced him.

(5) *Tr.* As Tvaṣṭṛ thus had spoken, 'Let us slay these men who have reviled the chalice, drinking cup of Gods', they gave themselves new names when Soma juice was shed, and under these new names the Maiden welcomed them.

Note—New names—Probably Ṛtus, Seasons, in place of Ṛbhus-Ludwig. The Maiden : apparently the daughter of Tvaṣṭṛ, meaning, perhaps as Ludwig suggests, the first Dawn of the Year, of which Tvaṣṭṛ is God.

(6) *Ta.* Indra hath yoked his Bays, the Aśvins', car is horsed, Bṛhaspati hath brought the Cow of every hue. Ye went as Ṛbhu, Vibhvan, Vāja to the Gods, and skilled in war, obtained your share in sacrifice.

Note—The cow of every hue—the fruitful earth restored to youth by the Gods of the Seasons.

(7) *Tr.* Ye by your wisdom brought a cow from out a hide; unto that ancient Pair ye gave again their youth. Out of a horse, Sudhanvan's Sons, ye formed a horse : a chairot ye equipped, and went unto the Gods.

(8) *Tr.* Drink ye this water, were the words ye spake to them; or drink ye this, rinsing of the Muñja-grass-or Soma juice which has been filtered through a strainer made of that grass. *Note*—"The two first alternatives intimate that the Ṛbhus may be participant of the libations offered at dawn or at noon; the third applies to the evening sacrifice; the right of Ṛbhus to share in this being elsewhere acknowledged"—Wilson.

(9) *Tr.* Most excellent are waters, thus said one of you; most excellent is Agni, thus another said. Another praised to many a one the lightning cloud. Then did ye shape the cups, speaking the words of truth.

Note—The meaning of these sayings in this place is not clear.

(10) *Tr.* One downward to the water drives the crippled cow, another trims the flesh brought on the carving-board. One carries off the refuse at the set of sun. How did the Parents aid their children in their task ?

Note—The restoration to youth of the aged Parents, Heaven and Earth, appears to be symbolically described under the figure of a scrifice. How did the Parents aid ? : weak and exhausted with age they were unable to give any assistance.

(11) *Tr.* On the high places ye have made the grass for man, and water in the valleys, by your skill, O Men. Ṛbhus, ye iterate not today that act of yours, your sleeping in the house of him whom naught can hide.

Note—In the house of him whom naught can hide—in the mansion of the Sun, to whom the Ṛbhus went to obtain immortality. In this and the remaining stanza, according to Sāyaṇa, the Ṛbhus are identified with the rays of the sun.

(12) *Tr.* As, compassing them round, ye glided through the world, where had the venerable Parents their abode ? Ye laid a curse on him who raised his arm at you : to him who spake aloud to you ye spake again.

(13) *Tr.* When ye had slept your fill, ye Ṛbhus, thus ye asked, O thou whom naught may hide, who now hath wakened us ? The goat declared the hound to be your wakener. That day, in a full year, ye first unclosed your eyes.

Note—When ye had slept—in the mansion of the sun. The goat declared the hound to be your wakener—the meaning is obscure. Sāyaṇa's rendering is 'the Sun replied that the awakener was the wind'. That day—Wilson following Sāyaṇa, explains, 'you have made this world today luminous, after the year has expired; that is, the rainy season being past, the rays of the sun and moon are again visible'.

(14) *Tr.* The Maruts move in heaven, on earth this Agni; through the mid-firmament the Wind approaches. Varuṇa

comes in the sea's gathered waters, O Sons of Strength, desirous of your presence.

Note—Sons of Strength-ye powerful Ṛbhus.

III 60

(1) *Tr.* Here is your ghostly kinship, here, O Men, they came desirous to these holy rites with store of wealth, with wondrous arts, whereby, with schemes to meet each need, Ye gained, Sudhanvan's Sons, your share in sacrifice.

Note—Here is your ghostly kinship-here, in the sacrificial chamber where the deities are worshipped, ye Ṛbhus, originally men, are spiritually connected with the Gods as partakers of sacrificial offerings. They-the Ṛbhus. With store of wealth-their great skill, 'the wondrous arts' of the following line.

(2) *Tr.* The mighty powers wherewith ye formed the chalices, thought by which ye drew the cow from out the hide, the intellect wherewith ye wrought the two Bay Steeds, through these, O Ṛbhus, ye attained divinity.

Note—See-I. 20.2, 3, 6.

(3) *Tr.* Friendship with Indra have the Ṛbhus fully gained, grandsons of Manu, they skillfully urged the work. Sudhanvan's Children won them everlasting life, serving with holy rites, pious with noble acts.

(4) *Tr.* In company with Indra come ye to to the juice, then gloriously shall your wishes be fulfulled. Not to be paragoned, ye Priests, are your good deeds, nor your heroic acts, Ṛbhus, Sudhanvan's Sons.

(5) *Tr.* O Indra, with the Ṛbhus, Mighty Ones, pour down the Soma juice effused, well-blent, from both they hands. Maghavaṇ, urged by song, in the drink-offerer's house rejoice thee with the Heroes, with Sudhanvan's Sons.

(6) *Tr.* With Ṛbhu near, and Vāja, Indra, here exult, with Śacī, praised of many, in the juice we pour. These

homes wherein we dwell have turned themselves to thee, devotions to the Gods, as laws of men ordain.

Note—*Śacī*—Might, personified, the Consort of Indra.

(7) *Tr.* Come with the mighty Ṛbhus, Indra, come to us, strengthening with they help the singer's holy praise; at hundred eager calls come to the living man, with thousand arts attend the act of sacrifice.

Note—The living man—the worshipper.

IV 33

(1) *Tr.* I send my voice as herald to the Ṛbhus; I crave the white cow for the overspreading. Wind-sped, the Skilful Ones in rapid motion have in an instant compassed round the heaven.

Note—For the overspreading—a technical expresstion for pouring the milk into or over the Soma juice. "For the dilution (of the Soma libation)"—Wilson. For the Ṛbhus, see Index.

(2) *Tr.* What time the Ṛbhus had with care and marvels done proper service to assist their Parents, they won the friendship of the Gods; the Sages carried away the fruit of their devotion.

(3) *Tr.* May they who made their Parents, who were lying like posts that moulder, young again for ever, may Vāja, Vibhvan, Ṛbhu, joined with Indra, protect our sacrifice, the Soma-lovers.

(4) *Tr.* As for a year the Ṛbhus kept the Milch-cow, throughout a year fashioned and formed her body, and through a year's space still sustained her brightness, through these their labours they were made immortal.

(5) *Tr.* Two beakers let us make, thus said the eldest. Let us make three, this was the younger's sentence. Four

beakers let us make, thus spoke the youngest. Tvaṣṭṛ approved this rede of yours, O Ṛbhus.

Note—Two beakers—or sacrificial ladles. See I. 20.6.

(6) *Tr.* The men spake truth and even so they acted, this Godlike way of theirs the Ṛbhus followed. And Tvaṣṭṛ, when he looked on the four beakers resplendent as the day, was moved with envy.

(7) *Tr.* When for twelve days the Ṛbhus joyed reposing as guests of him who never may be hidden, they made fair fertile fields, they brought the rivers. Plants spread over deserts, waters filled the hollows.

Note—Him who never may be hidden—the Sun; Savitṛ.

(8) *Tr.* May they who formed the swift car, bearing Heroes, and the Cow omniform and all-impelling, even may they form wealth for us, the Ṛbhus, dexterous-handed, deft in work and gracious.

Note—The swift car—the three-wheeled, chariot which bears the Aśvins. The cow omniform—or of every hue. 'Indra hath yoked his Bays, the Aśvins' car is horsed, Bṛhaspati hat brought the cow of every hue'—I. 161.6.

(9) *Tr.* So in their work the Gods had satisfaction, pondering it with thought and mental insight. The gods' expert artificer was Vāja, Indra's Ṛbhukṣan, Varuṇa's was Vibhvan.

(10) *Tr.* They who, made glad with sacrifice and praises, wrought the two Bays, his docile Steeds, for Indra, Ṛbhus, as those who wish a friend to prosper, bestow upon us gear and growth of riches.

(11) *Tr.* This day have they set gladdening drink before you. Not without toil are Gods inclined to friendship. Therefore do ye who are so great, O Ṛbhus, vouchsafe us treasures at this third libation.

Note—At this third libation—in the evening, the proper time for drink-offerings to the Ṛbhus. The myth of the Ṛbhus is exceedingly obscure. They are regarded as ancient sacrificers who attained immortality as the reward of their pious labours. The parents whom they restored to youth appear to be universal parents, heaven and earth, rejuvenated each morning and especially in the spring. The milchcow (stanza 4) is perhaps the Earth, regarded as the productive soil. The twelve days (stanza 7) are perhaps as Ludwig suggests, the twelve nights *vratyāh prajāpateḥ*, or 'holy to Prajāati'. See Hymns of the Atharaveda, IV. 11.11. For careful study and ingenious interpretations of the myth, see F. Nève, Essai sur le mythe des Ṛibhavas, Paris, 1847, and M. Bergaigne, La Religion Vedique, II. 403-413; III. 51-55.

IV 34

(1) *Tr.* To this our sacrifice come Ṛbhu, Vibhvan, Vāja and Indra with the gift of riches, because this day hath Dhiṣaṇā the Goddess set drink for you; the gladdening draughts have reached you.

*Note—Dhiṣaṇā—*a divinity closely connected with Soma and presiding over prosperity.

(2) *Tr.* Knowing your birth and rich in gathered treasure, Ṛbhus, rejoice together with the Ṛtus. The gladdening draughts and wisdom have approached you, send ye us riches with good store of heroes.

Note—Knowing your birth—knowing how you have attained immortality and deification. The Ṛtus—the seasons personified and honoured as deities. Ṛbhus as cosmic powers are closely connected with them.

(3) *Tr.* For you was made this sacrifice, O Ṛbhus, which ye, like men, won for yourselves aforetime. To you come all who find in you their pleasure, ye all were-even the two elder—Vājas.

Note—Vājas—that is, although Vāja is stricly the name of the youngest of the three only, you are all entitled to that appellation which means active, strong, or spirited. Professor

Grassmann translates 'ihr alle seid die ersten hier, O Vaescha's; "ye are all the first (entitled to precedence) here, O Vājas" but the word *uta* is then left untranslated.

(4) *Tr.* Now for the motal worshipper, O Heroes, for him who served you, was the gift of riches. Drink, Vājas, Ṛbhus, unto you is offered, to gladden you, the third and great libation.

Note—The third and great libation—See the preceding hymn, stanza 11.

(5) *Tr.* Come to us, Heroes, Vājas and Ṛbhukṣans, glorified for the sake of mighty treasure. These draughts approach you as the day is closing, as cows, whose calves are newly-born, their stable.

Note—Ṛbhukṣans-Ṛbhukṣan is anothar name of Ṛbhu, the the eldest of the three.

(6) *Tr.* Come to this sacrifice of ours, ye Children of Strength, invoked with humble adoration. Drink of this meath, Wealth-givers, joined with Indra with whom ye are in full accord, ye Princes.

(7) *Tr.* Closeknit with Varuṇa drink the Soma, Indra; close-knit, Hymn-lover, with the Maruts drink it. Close-knit with drinkers first, who drink in season; close-knit with heavenly Dames who give us treasures.

Note—Drinkers first—those who claim and receive the libation first; here, apparently, the Rtus or Seasons.

(8) *Tr.* Rejoice in full accord with the Ādityas, in concord with the Parvatas, O Ṛbhus; In full accord with Savitṛ, Divine One; in full accord with floods that pour forth riches.

Note—Parvatas-Gods presiding over mountains and clouds.

(9) *Tr.* Ṛbhus, who helped their Parents and the Aśvins, who formed the milch-cow and the pair of horses, made armour, set the heaven and earth asunder-far-reaching Heoes, they have made good offspring.

Note—Made armour : for the Gods.

(10) *Tr.* Ye who have wealth in cattle and in booty, in heroes, in rich sustenance and treasure, such, O ye Ṛbhus, first to drink, rejoicing, give unto us and those who laud our present.

Note—Those who laud our present—who accompany with hymns, and so recommend to the Gods, our oblation.

(11) *Tr.* Ye were not far, we have not left you thirsting, blameless in this our sacrifice, O Ṛbhus. Rejoice you with the Maruts and with Indra, with the Kings, Gods, that ye may give us riches.

Note—The Kings—the other Gods, or the Gods in general.

IV 35

(1) *Tr.* Come hither, O ye Sons of Strength, ye Ṛbhus, stay not afar ye Children of Sudhanvan. At this libation is your gift of treasure. Let gladdening draughts approach you after Indra's

Note—After Indra's—libations having been offered to Indra at dawn and at noon day. See stanza 7.

(2) *Tr.* Hither is come the Ṛbhus' gift of riches; here was the drinking of the well-pressed Soma, since by dexterity and skill as craftsmen ye made the single chalice to be fourfold.

(3) *Tr.* Ye made fourfold the chalice that was single, ye spake these word and said, O Friend, assist us; Then, Vājas, gained the path of life eternal, deft-handed Ṛbhus, to the Gods' assembly.

Note—O Friend—Agni.

(4) *Tr.* Out of what substance was chalice fashioned which ye made fourfold by your art and wisdom ? Now for the gladdening draught press out the liquor, and drink, O Ṛbhus, of the meath of Soma.

(5) *Tr.* Ye with your cunning made your Parents youthful, the cup, for Gods to drink, ye formed with cunning; with cunning Ṛbhus, rich in treasure fashioned the two swift Tawny Steeds who carry Indra.

Note—Cunning—power and skill as craftsmen; *śacyā.*

(6) *Tr.* Whoso pours out for you, when days are closing, the sharp libation for your joy, O Vājas, for him, O mighty Rbhus, ye, rejoicing, have fashioned wealth with plenteous store of heroes.

Note—Fashioned wealth—made or fabricated as craftsmen.

(7) *Tr.* Lord of Bay Steeds, at dawn the juice thou drankest, thine, only thine, is the noonday libation. Now drink thou with the wealth-bestowing Ṛbhus, whom for their skill thou madest friends, O Indra.

(8) *Tr.* Ye whom your artist skill—hath raised to Godhead have sat you down above in heaven like falcons. So give us riches, Children of Sudhanvan, O Sons of Strength, ye have become immortal.

(9) *Tr* The third libation, that bestoweth treasure, which ye have won by skill, ye dexterous-handed, this drink hath been effused for you, O Ṛbhus, drink it with high delight, with joy like Indra's.

IV 36

(1) *Tr.* The car that was not made for horses or for reins, three-wheeled, worthy of lauds, rolls round the firmament. That is the great announcement of your Deity, that O ye Ṛbhus, ye sustain the earth and heaven.

Note—The car—the three-wheeled charot of the Aśvins, drawn by assess, i.e. the grey clouds of morning twilight.

(2) *Tr.* Ye Sapient ones who made the lightly-rolling car out of your mind, by thought, the car that never errs, you, being such, to drink of this drink-offering, you, O ye Vājas, and ye Ṛbhus, we invoke.

(3) *Tr.* O Vājas, Ṛbhus, reaching far, among the Gods this was your exaltion gloriously declared, in that your aged Parents, worn with length of days, ye wrought again to youth so that they moved at will.

Note—Ye wrought again to youth-forms of the verb *takṣ*, to form, fabricate, fashion, as a carpenter does with wood, are used in this and other hymns to the Ṛbhus, the artificers, instead of words signifying restoring, giving, producing, and the like.

(4) *Tr.* The chalice that was single ye have made fourfold, and by your wisdom brought the Cow forth the hide. So quickly, mid the Gods ye gained immortal life. Vāja and Ṛbhus, your great work must be extolled.

(5) *Tr.* Wealth from the Ṛbhus is most glorous in renown, that which the Heroes, famed for vigour, have produced. In synods must be sung the car which Vibhvan wrought, that which ye favour, Gods, is famed among mankind.

Note—The car which Vibhvan wrought—or the sacrifical cup; the text has only *vibhvataṣṭaḥ*, that which was fabricated by Vibhvan, or as Sāyaṇa says, by the Ṛbhus.

(6) *Tr.* Strong is the steed, the man a sage in eloquence, the bowman is a hero hard to beat in fight, great store of wealth and manly power hath he obtained whom Vāja, Vibhvan, Ṛbhus have looked kindly on.

(7) *Tr.* To you hath been assigned the fairest ornament, the hymn of praise, Vājas and Ṛbhus, joy therein; for ye have lore and wisdom and poetic skill, as such, with this our prayer we call on you to come.

(8) *Tr.* According to the wishes of our hearts may ye, who have full knowledge of all the delights of men, fashion for us, O Ṛbhus, power and splendid wealth, rich in high courage, excellent, and vital strength.

Note—According to the wishes of our hearts—or, according to Sāyaṇa, on account of the praises which we have offered to you.

(9) *Tr.* Bestowing on us here riches and offspring, here fashion fame for us befitting heroes. Vouchsafe us wealth of splendid sort, O Ṛbhus, that we may make us more renowned than others.

IV 37

(1) *Tr.* Come to our sacrifice, Vājas, Ṛbhukṣans, Gods, by the paths which Gods are wont to travel, as ye, gay Gods, accept in splendid weather the sacrifice among these folk of Manus.

Note—In splendid weather—after the rains, when protracted sacrifices are not interrupted by storms. These folk of Manus-Aryan men.

(2) *Tr.* May these rites please you in your heart and spirit may the drops clothed in oil this day approach you. May the abundant juices bear you onward to power and strength, and when imbibed, delight you.

(3) *Tr.* Your threefold going near is God-appointed, so priase is given you, Vājas and Ṛbhukṣans. So, Manus-like, mid younger folk I offer, to you who are aloft in heaven, the Soma.

Note—Threefold going near-coming to the altar at the three daily sacrifices.

(4) *Tr.* Strong with fair chains of gold and jaws of iron, ye have a splendid car and well-fed horses. Ye Sons of Strength, ye progeny of Indra, to you the best is offered to delight you.

(5) *Tr.* Ṛbhukṣans, him, for handy wealth, the mightiest comrade in the fight, Him, Indra's, equal, we invoke, most bounteous ever, rich in steeds.

Note—Him—Ṛbhu, as representing his brothers also.

(6) *Tr.* The mortal man whom, Ṛbhus, ye and Indra favour with your help, must be successful, by this thoughts, at sacrifice and with the steed.

Note—By his thoughts—referring to the worshipper who by his devout thoughts and acts will obtain success in sacrifice. With the steed—referring to the warrior who will be victorious in battle with his war-chariot.

(7) *Tr.* O Vājas and Ṛbhukṣans, free for us the paths to sacrifice, Ye Princes, lauded, that we may press forward to each point of heaven.

Note—Press onward to each point of heaven—this is, be everywhere victorious, achieve, what was in later times the object of great king's, highest ambition, the *digvijaya* or conquest of lands in every direction.

(8) *Tr.* O Vājas and Ṛbhukṣans, ye Nāsatyas, Indra, bless this wealth, and, before other means, the steed, that ample riches may be won.

Note—Nāsatyas-Aśvins. The steeds-either the war-horses in general, or, as Professor Ludwig suggests, a particular horse that is to be sacrificed.

VII 48

(1) *Tr.* Ye liberal heroes, Vājas and Ṛbhukṣans, come and delight you with Soma. May your strength, Vibhus, as ye come to meet us, turn hitherward your car that brings men profit.

Note—Vājas and Ṛbhuṣans—ye three, Ṛbhu, Vibhvan and Vāja.

(2) *Tr.* May we as Ṛbhus with you Ṛbhus conquer strength with strength, as Vibhus with the Vibhus. May Vāja aid us in the fight for booty, and helped by Indra, may we quell the foemen.

Notes—The meaning is, may we be as powerful as Rbhus, as mighty as the company of Vibhus, (another name of the Ṛbhus). Sāyaṇa explains *ṛbhus* as great and *vibhvah* as powerful. In the fight for booty—Vājasātau; a play on the word and name Vāja.

(3) *Tr.* For they rule many tribes with high dominion, and conguer all their foes in close encounter.

(4) *Tr.* Now, Deities, give us ample room and freedom, be all of you one-minded our protector. So let the Vasus grant us strength and vigour. Preserve us evermore, ye Gods, with blessings.

Note – The Vasus—according to Sāyaṇa, *vasavaḥ* here is an epithet of Ṛbhavaḥ, understood 'the exalted (Ṛbhus)'—Wilson.

VIII

Rgveda Notes
Hermann Oldenberg

I 20

(8) They had spent their life as travelling (?) priests.—To me it is clear that '*bhāgam*' is the object of '*adhārayanta*' as it is of '*abhajanta*'. cf. VIII. 36.1; VIII. 100.

I 110

Whitney (212 d) ? cf also under 113, 5.
Roth not convincing ZDMG 48, 118.

(2) '*ābhogaya*' formed like *gavyaya, avyaya* etc.

(6) The accent on *vā* in '*vājam aruhan*' is correct. IX 83; IX 86, 40. There is no ground to stress ā, (Lud) Relative sentence only upto saścire.

I 111

(3) '*maheta*' to be understood as 2nd per. pl. with Ludwig.

I 161

(4) Like Bergaigne (Etudes sur le lexique) I doubt that '*nyānaje*' means 'He concealed himself'. What Neisser

(Probe eines ai wurzel—wörter-buch 5) puts forth does not appear to me as supplying sufficient ground for accepting it. In order to get the concerned idea one could think about '*nyānace*'. He bent stood low'. cf. V. 54.12. But with our insufficient knowledge we are not right in finding fault with the tradition and then with the explanation given by it. viz. 'He annointed himself'. Did Tvaṣṭṛ desire to make himself unknown by dressing himself as one of the *gnāḥ*—perhaps in order to assault the Ṛbhus ? cf. stz. 5.

(6)-(7) These stanzas would appear better if transposed; but that does not prove anything.

(8) '*idamudakam*' with slur on m. cf. Wackernagel I 333.—water to expiate (Bartholomae Studien I 105) difficult. One has the impression that this is the description of how the Ṛbhus approach the gods. At first the gods try to satisfy the Ṛbhus with inferior drink; but at last they have to offer them the promised Soma. With this '*abravitana*' does not suit well, as it seems to have 'the Rbhus' as the subject. However are 'the gods' the subject, so that the poet, once in the train with the 2nd per. pl. ; would have used this person wrongly here ?

III 60

(1) Perhaps this is to be understood as follows—"You men through your intellectual power (*manasā*), have connection (*bandhutā*) here and there. (with gods and men)—*iheha*-about the conditions of their origin. cf. I. 181.4; VI.59.2). The Uśijs, with their knowledge (vedasā) have turned to these (things), through what sort of artifices etc. Nevertheless parallel places make it probable that '*manasā*' is rather to be connected with '*abhijagmuḥ*'. "O Men, here and there (i.e. in every individual case), the Uśijs, with their intellect, with the help of their relationship (with you as human beings), through their knowledge, have come to know of these works of yours etc. Probably Geldner so-Rel. Lesebuch 101.

(6) To me it appears quite uncertain that *'vratā'* can be instrumental. One should be careful about accepting such instrumentals, except in certain cases particularly as in the case of Neuter nouns in *'tva'* and *'tvana' vratā devānām* can be plural as in III. 7.7; III. 55.1; III. 56.1 (cf. VII. 76.5). Then certainly the construction, as often, is not clear. "These pastures are offering themselves to you, the divine ordinances and according to the precepts of Manu." That means probably—The ordinances of the gods, by means of which your claim on Soma is established are the particular pastures, to which you proceed in order to enjoy Soma.—One may follow the ideas which otherwise appear in connection with 'svasara.'—And also according to the precepts of Manu the *svasaras* of Soma stand at your disposal. To me Bergaigne (III 250) does not seem to be just to *'ca'* which points out the parallelism between the divine and the human precepts—quite different Geldner (Ved. Studien III 115).

(7) *Vājayan* ZDMG 55, 294.

IV 33

(3) *Vibhvāñ*—The nasalization on 'n' naturally artificial. The fact that the form ending in-an, whenever following ṛ (more over not at the end of the stz as Bartholome—KZ 29,541 A, 3 Opines) ends in a in all other cases should have made me sceptical about accepting *Vibhvān* as a Naminative form. Compare also Lanmann 529; on S 34, Under VI 34, 2.

(4) *arakṣan* is correct. (Ludwig thinks of atakṣan) of I 161,10 bhāsaḥ 'nourishment' (Ludwig IV 166. Geldner-Kaegi I. 175—translates 'dung'. Geldner-Gloss-'garbage'. In consideration of I: 161.10 it is obvious that *'bhāsaḥ'* here and *'śakṛt'* there are the same. Cf. Ṛbhus in the Ṛgveda' Ryder-34. I doubt about the *śleṣa* in this verse, which is shown there.

(5) The present-stem is extra-ordinarily rare in the RV, more seldom than what Neisser takes it, for the Vedic verbal-

learning-9 ff probability speaks for this that *'kareta'* has been dissolved into *'karā iti.'* So also Neisser B B 20,55, who only—I believe-allows *'karā'* to be substituted by *karāma*, without any ground.

(10) a *'medhayā ukthā madantaḥ'* who by virtue of their wisdom, intoxicating themselves with the hymn of praise.' On 'mad' with Accusative, of that by which 'one rejoices oneself, intoxicates oneself' see Gaediche 75 (fn. 1, p. 296). In *ukthā madanaḥ* lies the hint of the idea of *uktham madaśca, ukthamadā.* But I cannot understand how Grassmann's translation, 'spiringing at the speech' or Geldner's explanation 'who recite *ukthāmadas*' stands in accord with the usual usage, *'mada'* in 'uktham madaśca' is evidently inherent with the praise-receiving god, not with the praising priest. Just the next verse and many other verses speak about the *'mada'* of the Ṛbhus.

d—'as the people, who indulge in peaceful life, form a bond of friendship.' The same simile as in II. 4.3 : *'kṣemayanto na mitram.* In both cases the governing verb *'dhā'* from the preceding stanza is to be supplied to *'mitram.'* (cf. VI. 15.2; X. 108.3 and the use of 'sudhita'). The constant connection of this verb with *'mitram'* is misunderstood if *'mitram'* is made dependant upon *'kṣemayantaḥ.'* cf H.O. Rel. des Veda.

(11) *asmè*—not *pragṛhya* S. Prole. 455.

IV 34

(1) On *'ratnadheyā'* which I take as Acc. pl. and not as Dat. sg, see my article on 'The Dative in ā' ZDMG 63.

(2) *'janmanar'* as Abl. – difficult, if possible. "You became invented known as *'vājaratnaḥ'* on account of your birth." predicative vocative cf. Delbrück 'Alt, Synt'. 100. *janmanaḥ*—preferably Gen. dependant upon *'vid'* perhaps to be compared with *janmano vidvān* (IX. 18.2); *Nakirh-yeṣām janūṁṣi veda te aṅga vidre mitho janitram* (*VII. 56.2*). The apparent medium of *'vid'* to know in the last place

(also in VII. 99.1 and according to my oft-repeated opinion) has to give the direction to the explanation ; knowing of the birth (of ones own and of others). Further one would come in consideration of an interpretation, which stands in good harmony with the predominently passive use of *Vidānā* and *Vidānā*; but which is otherwise risky. i.e. "Your birth being invented (or known)"—Is there a mixture of the ideas that the Ṛbhus as such are '*vidānāḥ*' and that one knows of their birth ? I think yet I am not quite sure about the expression appearing similar to V. 80.5. The vocative *vājaratnāḥ* could point out as to what kind of essence the *janman* of the Ṛbhus implies. In short it would not be proper to ascribe to the idea of the ṛṣi a full-fledged sharp distinction between 'vid, to 'find' and 'vid' to know.' One can easily think of '*purandhīḥ*; but the singular is significant.

(3) *agriyota* could be *agriyāḥ uta-agriyam uta* is scarcely probable. (Roth ZDMG 48, 114, 684) Ludwig appears to see it correctly as agriyā uta retained. "You were all (also) both the two elder ones) Vājas", not only Vāja himself but even Ṛbhu and Vibhvan. For the Vocative see Delbrück—Alt. Synt 106.

(6) cd—I suggest "And drink of the honey-drink, by which you find joint delight (with Indra ?)."

fn,—'*yasya*' not referring to Indra contained in *Indra-vantaḥ*-'*yena*' would be expected.

(7) *gnāspatnībhiḥ*—finally Wackernagel II 247. To me the nom. sg. '*gnās patnīḥ* (cf. gnāḥ devapatnīḥ I. 61,8; V.46.8) seems to be confused together, so that this Inst. was formed jointly from it; (similarly Wackernagel II 47, 254) at the same time under the influence of *gnāspatatnīḥ*, *ratnadhābhiḥ*—an adjective characteristic of the circle of the ideas about the Ṛbhus, here belongs to *gnāspatnībhiḥ*, who naturally receive that epithet just in consideration of that circle of the ideas as in stz. '*sindhubhiḥ ratnadhābhiḥ*.'

(9) elliptical—The Ṛbhus, who (have provided) the Aśvins (with chariot) who (have rejuvenated) the parents, who

have created the milch-cow for prosperity and the two horses, who the armours ? (cf. Bergalgne II 410 A-3), who (have kept themselves hidden) aside, who (have made) the two worlds (thrive ? cf. IV. 36.1) etc. It appears strange that the miracle of the four cups is not mentioned : It is scarcely referred to in '*ye ṛdhak*.'

(4) '*sunudhvam*' can be noted. 'May you press for yourselves' cf. I.103.3; I.108.4.

(5) c—It is probable through the feminine dhanutṛ that the Agent noun '*dhanutar*' is present in '*dhanutarau*'. In the compound with '*tara*' accentuation would be expected.—comparative degree of an adjective '*dhanu*' (running) is little probable. Would it be written as '*dhanutārau*' ? The material for shortened vowel forms is scaree. (Lanmann 420, cf. I. 46.2) Lanman traces that '*a*' on metrical consideration; but the regular type of the metre rather accords with 'ā'. The corruption, if any, would arise from this that one could think of it as a comparative form or as a construction with '*tara*'.

IV 36

(2) definitely not *paridhyayā*. On the artificial nasalization of *Vibhvañ* see IV. 33.3.

IV 37

On the possible analysis of the hymn in two parts of four stanzas each see Prolog. 198.

(2) *pra-harayanta* to *haryati*.

(3) Ludwig unnecessarily thinks of '*soma*' for '*stoma*' cf. IV. 36.7 '*dade*' is perhaps to be written without an accent. The accent of '*yathā*' perhaps also in IV. 34.4 can be based upon misunderstanding. The authority of the subordinate clause can be dragged further, as our instinct would agree. The accentuation of the introductory clause also is to be thought about ZDMG 60, 734.

(4) *ayahśiprāsaḥ*—Grassmann, Lanmann 345.

(7) The infinitive *'yātave'* often stands near the word *'path'* (I.113.16; VIII. 7.8; VIII. 12.3; X. 75.2). One could guess it here also mainly because the opening of the paths for the sacrificial worship does not suit particuarly the character of the Ṛbhus (cf. certainly the material in Bergaigne II. 408, at the end); but the origin of the corruption remains dark and the idea of the paths on which the worship proceeds is itself not to be questioned. cf. *yajñapatha*—Grassmann on I 574 will definitely not be right in deriving *'yaṣṭave'* from *'yakṣ'* instead of *'yaj'*. The text of 'd' supported through V.10.6 is not made doubtful as Delbrück (Alt Syn 416.) means. Perhaps after the first sentence 'a' to 'c' 'd', an independant sentence has been joined. Nevertheless 'd' can also mean "in the crossing over"—(In every case the crossing ones are 'we' not the Ṛbhus' just as they are *sūrayaḥ* and not the gods in V. 10, 6). If we translate this here as in the crossing over but in V.10.6 as 'May they cross over' there lies a distinction only for us, not for the Indian interpretation. For the Indian interpretation the infinitive in-sani always denotes that itself.

(8) Ludwig thinks of *'tam'* for *'sam'* not rightly. In *'carṣaṇibhyaḥ ā*, lies the bringing together of the cherished good things out of all quarters of the world. (cf. I. 84.20; VI. 48.15—where it is said, *saṁ kariṣat*) I suggest : "O Vājas, carve together for us those possessions, a horse from various countries, carve together many things for the participation of your generousity) i.e. in order to participate in your genersority)—'Carve together means' 'Carve it in the right place (craftsmen that you are) and bring it together', Śasta from *śas* rather than from *śaṁs*.

VII 48

(1) *asme* doubtlessly Locative—Bolensen ZDMG 47, 593. I cannot see why *'arvācaḥ'* should be Nominative (J. Schmidt plural. abl. 394; Macdonell p. 182, A 6), or why it should be changed into *arvāñcaḥ* (Lanmann a.a.o.). I do not find any consideration against Accusative. cf. in particular

I. 168.1 then I.47.8 etc. On '*kratavo na yātām*' cf. IV. 28.3'. *yātām*' not 'of the living beings' (Pischel Ved, St. II. 72). In 'na' I do not find any ground for accepting it as a particle of emphasis. (Hillebrandt G G A 1889, 414). I understand; "May (they) direct yourselves (and your) manly chariot hitherwards like the will-powers of the travellers." Just as the travellers know how to turn their chariot, may the powers setting you in motion (your decision, our prayers etc) turn you hitherwards. Perhaps the interpretation proposed for IV.28.3 viz. "with his lance Indra has struck down thousands of the enemies (according to his sweet will) just as through the will-powers of the travellers (the chariots are turned according to their sweet will)."—is to be somewhat modified in order to suit here.

(2) Grassmann unnecessarily thinks of '*Ṛbho*' for '*Ṛbhu.*'

(3) As regards *śāsāh,* see Grass. Lanmann 495 and II. 23.12 earlier. *viśvān aryaḥ* (cf. VIII. 65.9) 'All miserly ones' not "all (also) the rich rivals," (Geldner—Ved. St. III. 87). just as *viśve devāḥ* does not mean 'all (also) the gods' still different—Vide St. I. 167—*uparatāti* is to be understood following II. 4.9, which place has '*van*' and '*abhi*' as common to this. cf. Geldner—Ved. St. III. 44. A 2—*Vibhvāñ* Refer to IV. 33.3.

IX

Alfred Hillebrandt

TO THE ṚBHUS

Introductory Note

The Ṛbhus are overseers, the artists among the gods, who, with their dexterity, fashion the bay-horses for Indra, a chariot for the Aśvins and because of that later attain a place among the gods in the sacrifice. Their number three corresponds to the three seasons and can be interpreted as that with some probability. The three brothers, according to A, are the gods of a clan, which specially looked after the building of carts (The carpenters lay down their fire according to the manner of the Ṛbhus) and which had raised the spirits of the seasons to their gods.

I 20

(1) Tr. This hymn, which brings much treasures, was recited by the singers to the divine race in front of it.

(2) *Tr.* (The Ṛbhus), who, by means of their mind, fashioned for Indra the two bay-horses, yoking themselves on word, have obtained (a share in) the sacrifice through their skill.

(3) Tr. They fashioned for the two sons of Nasati the lightly-travelling chariot. They created the nectar-milking cow.

(4) *Tr.* The Ṛbhus, possessing efficacious charm, having good intentions, made their parents young again by means of their works.

(5) Tr. The exhilarating drink for you has united itself with Indra, accompanied by the Maruts and with the princely Ādityas.

(6) Tr. You make fourfold again this new well-decorated cup of god Tvaṣṭṛ.

(7) Tr. Give us thrice seven treasures for him, who presses Soma, and one for our hymn.

(8) *Tr.* They maintained themselves as chariot-drivers. Through their skill they obtained a share among the gods in the sacrifice. *Note*—They wander about and come in the house of Savitṛ. (I 110, 2). If they are called '*vahnayaḥ*)', that refers to the travelling chariot of the Nomads (Cf 120, 3).

I 161

Preliminary note

The hymn is partially a variation of the same theme as the one just translated above and it depicts the Ṛbhus in a lively manner. It makes Agni approach them with an errand, whose execution must provide them immortality and reception among the gods. Some verses contain references to unknown sagas and are ambiguous.

(1) Tr. The Ṛbhus) "Why has our excellent, our youngest (brother) come to us ? Why such hurried course of the messenger ? What was it that we have said ? We have not blamed the cup, that is of a noble sort. We were speaking about the excellence of the wood".

(2) Tr. (Agni) 'Make four cups out of one' so have the gods told you. Therefore I have come to you. O Sons of Sudhanvan, if you do that, you will be honoured in the sacrifice together with the gods.

(3) *Tr.* (A person) So you replied to the messenger Agni: "Yet a horse is to be fashioned (first), a chariot is to be prepared, a cow is to be fashioned, the two are to be made young: When we have done all that, then O brother, shall we come to you".

(4) *Tr.* Then O Ṛbhus, after the work was over, you asked, "Where has he gone, the one that had come to us as messenger? And when Tvaṣṭṛ has seen the four ready cups, he conceled himself among his women. *Note*—Tvaṣṭṛ to the Ṛbhus, an opposition, which is probably based upon a different cult and a different circle of legends. Here is Tvaṣṭṛ with one cup on one hand and the Ṛbhus with four cups on the other.

(5) Tr. When Tvaṣṭṛ said, 'Let us kill those who have blamed the cup, in which the gods drink' then they assumed different names at the sacrificial drink. The young girl saved them under different names. *Notes*—They receive different sacred names suitable to their reception in the cult (See Stz 6). On such names in general see Ved. Myth I 486 ff; II 52 ff and 318 ff. There is a similar precedent as in a defection to another religion, when at times, the name is changed. *kanyā*—ambiguous.

(6) *Tr.* Indra yoked the two bay-horses for himself, Aśvins the chariot. Bṛhaspati drove home for himself the (speckled) cow. As Ṛbhu, Vibhvan, Vāja, you went to the gods, excellent workers, you received a share in the sacrifice.

(7) Tr. With skill you fashioned a cow out of a hide. You rejuvenated the two old ones. O Sons of Sudhanvan, you created one horse from another. You yoked the chariot and went to the gods.

(8) *Tr.* 'Drink this water here', so said (the gods) to you. 'Or this infusion, here of the Muñjareed'. 'O Sons of Sudhadanvan, if you do not like this, then exhilarate

yourselves in the third (evening) Soma—pressing'. *Note*—The gods negotiate with the Ṛbhus. First they offer them something inferior (to Soma) and at last grant them a share in the Soma. (See Oldenberg Ṛgveda Notenl—IV at this place).

(9) Tr. "Water is the most important", spoke one. "Fire is the most important", said another. The third one announced the flash of lightening (?) as standing above all. Keeping the word you divided the cup fourfold. *Note*—Reference to the three seasons. See Ved. Myth III 141, ff.

(10) *Tr.* One leads the lame cow to water. The other cuts up the flesh that is brought in a basket. At about the sunset one carried away the mire. What help did the parents give to their sons ? *Note d*—ambiguous.

(11) *Tr.* O men, when you slept in the house of Agohya, with your skill you created for him grass on high lands and water in the valleys. Therefore today do not fall short of it. *Note*—To others and to me Agohya seems to denote the Sun-god. They stay with him for 12 days. These 12 days or nights at the end of the year provide fertility for the whole year.

(12) *Tr.* When closing your eyes, you prawled around the world, where, indeed, were your dear parents ? You cursed him, who held your arm. You have spoken to him, who spoke. *Note*—The verse cannot be interpreted, because it refers to a saga, quite unknown otherwise.

(13) *Tr.* When your sleep was over, you asked, "Agohya who has awakened us here ?" Then the ram named a dog as the awakener. Today at the end of the year you have opened your eyes here. *Notes*—Ram and dog ambiguous. I guess constellations. About the Locative *saṁvatsare* See Delbrück Syn. Forsch V 117; but the Locative is also used to point out the point of time, after which something

takes place. See also Gaedi Accusative S 178—For the last twelve days they come in the house of *Agohya* (Savitṛ) sleep here and wake up again by the end of the year.

(14) Tr. The Maruts wander through the heaven, fire on the earth, wind wanders through the atmosphere. Varuṇa wanders in the waters of the sea. O Sons of Strength, they are searching for you.

X

Karl Friedrich Geldner

I 20

(Metre-Gāyati)

(1) *Tr.* This song of praise that brings much reward has been prepared for the divine race by those skilled in speech, with their lips (Lit.—mouth).

Notes ab—cf III 60, 2; *c* They have performed these different miracles under assignment of the gods and through theese they obtained the divine rank and a fixed share in the sacrifice.

(2) *Tr.* They, who, by means of intellect fashioned for Indra the two bay-horses yoking themselves on word, have obtained (the claim to) sacrifice through their excellent works.

Note b–cf VI 32, 1; VII 99, 7.

(3) *Tr.* They constructed for the Nāsatyas the chariot, moving around with ease. They created the cow Sabardughā.

Notes c—about the cow—The divine desire-yielding cow. (Cf. Bṛ. De III 85) or the cow of Bṛhaspati (I 161, 8).

(4) *Tr.* The Ṛbhus, truthful of words with honest efforts made their parents young again through their dutiful attendance.

Nates—The rejuvenation of the parents (I 161, 3 and 7; I 110, 8; I 111. 1, IV 35, 5; IV 36, 3) was connected with their certain dutiful services according to I 161, 10; IV 33, 2 and 4.

(5) *Tr.* Your joy of drink has united with Indra, in company of the Maruts and the Ādityas, the kings.

Notes—This means : They obtained a share of Soma in the Evening-libation together with *Marutvān* Indra and with the Ādityas—A more detailed explanation about 2C. IV 34, 1 and 2.

(6) *Tr.* And you have repeated fourfold that cup, the new work of god Tvaṣṭṛ.

(7) *Tr.* Bring to us the jewels thrice sevenfold for the Soma-presser, one each for the beautiful word of praise.

Notes b—to the sacrificers, *c*—to the singers.

(8) *Tr.* The conductors (of sacrifice) asserted themselves. They obtained a share in the sacrifice among the gods through their craftsmanship.

Notes ab—'Hysteron proteron'. While they themselves were primitive '*vahnayaḥ*' 'Directors of sacrifice' or 'Travelling singers' (I 110, 4; III 60, 4), finally they obtained a place in the cult and asserted themselves. Yet following Sāyaṇa '*adhārayanta*' '*Prāṇān dhāritavantaḥ*' could be translated as "They prolonged (their life) as travelling singers."

I 110

(Metre 5, 9—Triṣṭubh, rest—Jagati)

(1) *Tr.* My work was formely performed. It is performed again. The sweetest composition is recited for a poem of praise. Here is the sea (of Soma) destined for all-gods. Revel (in the drink) consecrated with '*Svāhā*'.

Nates a—The poet is trying in this field not for the fiast time. He had formerly spun the same threads. The picture is taken from weaving with which the composition, like the ritualistic work, is often compared. (II 3, 6; II 28, 5; IX 22, IX 69, 6;

X 130, 1) To '*taṭam*' Sāyaṇa analogously supplies 'formerly many times'. 'cf *tantuṁ pūrvyam* I 142, 1. The fact that poetry must be '*apas*' i.e. an artistic work is particularly stressed in the hymn, addressed to the artists Ṛbhus. *b* explains a—*c*. It refers to the third Savana, that belongs to All-gods. V.S. XIX 26; Ai. Br. VI 4,6; Śa. Br. IV 4, 2, 3.

(2) *Tr*. When you, seeking livelihood moved further westwards, eastwards, as certain acquaintances of mine, then O Sons of Sudhanvan, after a long wandering you reached the houses of savitṛ, the sacrificer.

Notes—At that time they were—what the poet himself is—travelling scholars or artists. cf. III 60, 3.

(3) *Tr*. Then Savitṛ granted you immortality, when you came calling Agohya. You have even made fourfold the cup, the drinking glass of Asura, which was one single.

Notes —Ait. Br. III 30; RVI 161, 11-13; IV 33, 7.

Notes b—Agohya is explained as Savitṛ. Unfortunately the myth is too fragmentary, *cd*—cf. IV 36, 4; I 20, 6; I 161, 1-2-4; III 60, 2; IV 33, 5, IV 36, 2; A V 47. 3. The Asura is Tvaṣṭṛ.

(4) *Tr*. After the travelling (?) singers had worked with correct diligence and punctuality, they, who were mortal, obtained immortality. The Ṛbhus, the Sons of Sudhanvan, the sun-eyed ones, saw their expectations fulfilled after the period of one year.

Notes c—'being sun-eyed' is a characteristic of the gods. *d* cf. X 95, 6 b.

(5) *Tr*. The Ṛbhus, the praised ones, praying for the highest (reward), seeking fame among the immortal ones, measured out the one gaping cup, like a piece of land, with a canestick.

Notes—In stzs 5 and 6 once again the cup of Tvaṣṭṛ; *b*—cf IV 33, 6 c; *c*—One can supply *śravaḥ* out of *d* (cf VIII 80, 5,

VIII 99, 2) or similar term to *upamam—nādhamānāḥ* cf I 109, 3 and I 126, 2—change of accent in I 181, 7 c.

(6) *Tr.* We, as well-informed, desire to bring to the heroes of the mid-region a poem as offering like ghee (offered) with a ladle., (to the Ṛbhus), who have reached the punctuality of its father and have ascended to the space of the heaven by way of reward.

Notes—asya—of the cup. Its father i.e. the fabricator is Tvaṣṭr. cf. II 17, 6 ab. *d*—IX 83, 5 C.

(7) *Tr.* On account of strength Ṛbhu is a new Indra to us. Ṛbhu with the Vājas and the Vasus is benevolent donor. O gods, with your help we would overcome, on an auspicious day, the hostilities of those who do not press Soma.

Notes b—VIII 24, 3C *c*—VIII 59, 20—The day is meant. '*priye*' according to Sāyaṇa *anukūle d*—cf V 4, 1 d.

(8) *Tr.* O Ṛbhus, you formed a cow out of the hide and made the mother join the calf. O Sons of Saudhanvan, O heroes, through your craftmanship you made the aging parents young again.

Notes—Of the dead cow only the hide was remaining. Out of it the Ṛbhus created a new mother-cow for the orphaned calf. cf I 111, 1; 161, 7; IV 36, 4; III 60, 2.

(9) *Tr.* Stand by us in the winning of reward along with the Vājas. O Indra, in company of the Ṛbhus, knock out for us a handsome honourable gift. Mitra, Varuṇa, Aditi, Sindhu, the Earth and the Heaven should grant that to us.

Notes a—Vāja is the name of one of the Ṛbhus, in plural disignation of the three Ṛbhus. Here at the same time a play on the word with the general meaning 'reward.' Stz 6 d just as already in stz 7 above. cf also VIII 46, 11 d.

I 111

(Metre 1-4 Jagatī 5 Triṣṭubh.)

(1) *Tr.* Working with knowledge they fabricated the smoothly-running chariot (of the Aśvins). They fashioned the bay-pair that carries Indra,......, For their parents they fashioned youthful age. They created for the calf an accompanying mother.

Notes—play with the verb *takṣ* to fabfricate,' the proper word of the work of the Ṛbhus. *b* vṛṣaṇvasū ? *d*—I 110, 8.

(2) *Tr.* Fashion for us masterly might, for the sacrifice i.e. in order to speak (of it) and to perform (it). (Give) ample blessings to children. Bestow Indra-like strength on our army-troop, so that we can dwell securely with our tribe, fully made up of heroes.

(3) *Tr.* O Ṛbhus, O Lords, grant us a prize for the chariot, a prize for the race-horse. You should always present (?) us victortous prize, (champions), surmounting in battles a relative as well as a stranger.

Notes c—'Saṁ maheta' is uncertain. 'Sarve janāḥ samyak, pūjayantu'—Sāyaṇa. *d Sakṣaṇim*—perhaps direct adjective of *'sātim.'*

(4) *Tr.* I call here Ṛbhukṣan Indra for help. I invite the Ṛbhus, the Vājas the Maruts for the Soma-draught, Mitra and Varuṇa, the pair, and the Aśvins now. They should incite us so that the poem wins the prize.

Notes d— I 27, 11 c.

(5) *Tr.* Ṛbhu should make (us) sharp, so that we can carry away the booty from there. Vāja, the victor in contest, should stand by us. May Mitra, Varuṇa, Aditi, Sindhu, the earth and the Heaven grant us that.

I 161

(Metre—Jagatī Stz 14 Triṣṭubh)

(1) *Tr.* (The Ṛbhus). "Has the first, has the youngest come to us ? Which message does he bring ? What was it that we have spoken ? We have not blamed the cup, which is of good descent. Brother Agni, we have spoken of the origin of the wood."

Notes—The exploits of the Ṛbhus in a dialogue, in which more often the wellknown poet himself is made the speaker. 1-5 specimen—The preparation of the four cups. cf I 20, 6; I 110, 3 and 5; III 60, 2 and 4; IV 33, 5; IV 35, 2 and 3; IV 36, 4 A V VI 47, 3. Stz. 1—The Ṛbhus reply to Agni, sent by the gods as a messenger. According to Sāyaṇa he had assumed the form of the Ṛbhus, all having similar forms and according to him the above—mentioned question is about him. 'Has the eldest or the youngest amongst us come ? It is Agni himself that is meant. cf I 44, 4. *d* is explained through stz. 9, cf IV 35, 4 a.

(2) *Tr.* (Agni) 'Make four cups out of the one' So have the gods said to you. That is why I have come to you. O Sons of Sudhanvan, when you would have done this, then you will be worthy of sacrifice together with the gods.

(3) *Tr.* This is what you replied to the messenger : "We must yet fashion a horse and must fabricate a chariot here. We must fashion a cow and must make the two young. When we have done this, then shall we follow you, O brother."

Notes a—belongs to the speaker. *b* to *d*—The additional tasks, which the Ṛbhus have undertaken......The horse i.e. the Harīs of Indra, the chariot of the Aśvins, the cow *Viśvarūpā* of Bṛhaspati. Cf Stz 6; IV 33, 8; Śān. Ś. Sū VIII 20, 1.

(4) *Tr.* O Ṛbhus, when you had done that you asked, "Where has he gone, he who had come to us as a messenger ?" When Tvaṣṭṛ had beheld the four ready cups he concealed himself among the wives of gods.

Notes d—Out of shame Tvaṣṭṛ concealed himself behind his attendants—Cf T.S. VI 5, 8, 4; Jai. Br. II 55, 2 (Oertel in Translation of the Connecticut Acct. 1909 S 181), where Tvaṣṭṛ seeks protection among the wives of gods. '*ni añj*' to mix with, to interfere, to mingle; Med. 'to meddle with, to cling to.' cf T. Br. I 2, 1, 9. ('*nigūḍham*' Sāyaṇa), II 5, 1, 3 ('*nilīnam*' Sāyaṇa).—'*nyakta*' is the trace, the residue remaining back. M.S. III. P. 23, 2; P. 101, 5; Kāṭh I p 85, 7—10; II p 1, 11; III 1—(near *śliṣṭam*). Therefore *nyañja* 'residue' Tai. Br. III 7, 6, 20 —'residue, similarity, substitution.' Ait. Br. II 39, 9; Śa. Br. IV 5, 10, 2 and 5; Lāty. Br. V 1, 8.

(5) *Tr.* When Tvaṣṭṛ said, 'Let us kill them who have censured the cup for the gods' drink,' then they assumed other names at the Soma (sacrifice). The young maiden brought them to safety under other names.

Notes c—The names in stz 'c while so far they were called Saudhanvanas. *d* It is not stated as to who the young maiden was. Sāyaṇa thinks of their mother, which is inconsistent with 'kanyā.'

(6) *Tr.* Indra yoked his bay-pair, the Aśvins their chariot. Bṛhaspati drove home the cow Viśvarūpā, As Ṛbhu, Vibhvan, Vāja, you went among the gods. As artists you came to the share of sacrifice.

Notes—The gods take for using the particular productions of the Ṛbhus and admit the Ṛbhus in the divine community. *d* I 20, 8; III 60, 1.

(7) *Tr.* Through your inventive faculty you made a cow out of a hide. You made two old ones (your parents) young. O Sons of Sudhanvan, out of one horse you created a (second) horse. You yoked the chariot and came to the gods.

Notes—From here onwards the composition of the hymn is loose.—Till now—a master piece. *a* IV 36, 46; cf III 60, 2; I 111, 1. "Out of the peeled hide of the dead cow you made a cow come out, i.e. you created another similar cow, clad in the same hide."–Sāyaṇa–*b* I 20, 4; I 110, 8; I 111; IV 33, 3; IV 35, 5; IV 36, 3. *c* Out of one horse they created two.–The *Harī* of Indra, or horses for their own need as in *d*.

(8) *Tr*. "Drink this water," so said you, "Or drink those reed-slops" "O Sons of Sudhanvan, if this does not suit you, then you must delight yourselves in the Soma-libation."

Notes ab–The Ṛbhus sarcastically reject the offered Soma —substitute–According to Sāyaṇa they reject the two Savanas as too thin and obtain a share in the third *Soma-savana*, promised to them. *ab* is precisely the speech of the Ṛbhus, not of the gods, as Sāyaṇa also believes. *cd*–The words of the gods.

(9) *Tr*. One of them said, "Water is the most important." "Fire is the most important," so said another. Still another gave superiority over many others to the tempest-time (?). Speaking truthful words you carved the cups.

Notes–Stz. 9 is specification of Stz. 1 *d. bhūti* there, *bhūyi ṣṭhāḥ* here). These words are spoken when they are manufacturing the cups. Each one of them expresaes a different opinion on the question as to what has contributed the most towards the origin of the wood, the fire (in the plants), water of the rain or 'the *vadharyantī*.' According to Sāyaṇa this is the row of clouds or the earth, as desiring for the lightning. In fact the earth will suit as the third element. If the meaning thunder-time, rainy season, is accepted then '*ṛtubhyaḥ*' or similar term is to be supplied to '*bahubhyaḥ*' The Ablative in *pra-bru* as in *pra-as*.

(10) *Tr*. One leads away the lame cow to water. One cuts the flesh that is brought in a basket. One carries away the dung till sunset. Have both the perents helped their sons in this ?

Notes–Further the Rbhus work in association with the *Agohya*–saga. Stzs 11 to 13. Cf IV 33, 7; I. 110, 2. *d* The question similar to one in stz 12, *b* i.e. a rhetoric question.

(11) *Tr.* O Men, when you had slept in the house of Agohya, you laid for him grass on high lands and with your craftsmanship you led water in low lands. O Ṛbhus do not imitate it today any more.

Notes b—That is you watered the low lands.

(12) *Tr.* When you prawled around the creatures with your eyes closed, where were your loving parents then ? You cursed him who held your arm. He, who spoke to you, you were in discussion with him.

Notes—An obscure legend. The acceptance among the gods seems to be preceded by a transitional period, a somnambular condition, similar to sleep. sammīlya–vyakhyata in 13 *d* are antonyms.

(13) *Tr.* O Ṛbhus, when you had slept your fill, you asked, "Agohya, who has awakened us ?" The goat named the dog as the awakener. After a year's interval you have today looked around in this (world).

Notes b—According to I 110, 3 *Agohya* is Savitṛ. But according to Ait. Br. III 30, 2 the Ṛbhus were the pupils of Savitṛ, in order to be trained at any rate, in the divine rank. *d*—cf. IV 1, 18. Śānkh. Śr. Sū VIII 20, 1. Or—Does the *pāda* belong to the speech in the Agohya legend ? *saṁvatsare* - (cf. I 110, 4) as in Tāṇḍ Mah. Br. IX 8, 13; Kāṭh I P 92, 1; Sat Br. X 1, 1, 4. Sāyaṇa—'When the year was full'. According to IV 33, 7 they slept for 12 days i.e. the last 12 days of the year at Agohya.

(14) *Tr.* The Maruts go in the heaven; Agni on the earth, wind in the mid-region. Varuṇa goes in the waters, in the sea., where they search for you. O Sons of Strength.

Notes—Stz. 13 ends this well. The gods searched for the Ṛbhus, newly taken in their league, when they kept themselves warped at *Agohyas.*'

III 60

To the Ṛbhus (and Indra)

(Metre—Jagatī)

(1) *Tr.* O Lords, here and just here, have the Uśijs, through musing, through family-relation, through knowledge, learnt these things of yours, the magic-arts, through which, you, O Sons of Sudhanvan, have obtained a share in the sacrifice, by assuming a different form according to the impulse.

Notes—The poet is reporting how his ancestors, the Uśijs, have come to get the information about the history of the Ṛbhus—through musing (*manasā*), through congenial relationship, thus, through family-tradition (*bandhutā*) and through the knowledge of the sagas (*vedasā*). *c*—To the uncertain '*pratijūtivarpasaḥ*' cf. I 161, 5 cd. *d*—I 20, 5 and 8; 161, 2 and 6.

(2) *Tr.* Through the arts with which you fashioned the cups, through the inventive genius with which you brought out a cow out of the hide, through the musing with which you have created both the bay-horses, through all these, O Ṛbhus, you have obtained divine rank.

Notes—a I 161, 2; *b* I 161, 7–*bc* IV 36, 4; IV 35, 5–*c* I 20, 2.

(3) *Tr.* The Ṛbhus obtained friendship of Indra. The Grandsons of Manu, have set out for journey as artists. The Sons of Sudhanvan, the craftsmen with craftsmanship, have gained immortality, after they had worked with real diligence.

Notes—b I 110, 2. The expression '*Manornapāthaḥ*' should characterise them as originally mortal. *apasaḥ*—also IV 33, 1. *d* IX 94, 2 *C*.

(4) *Tr.* Come with Indra in the same chariot for Soma. Now you are in the possession of the glory of (all) wishes, O Travelling (?) Singers, O Sons of Sudhanvan, O Ṛbhus,

your artistic works do not stand a comparison, nor your exploits.

Notes—To go with Indra for Soma was the high aim of their wishes. Now they have obtained that. *c. vāghataḥ* I 110, 4a f.n. on 'wishes'—immortailty and divine rank.

(5) *Tr.* O Indra, in company of the Ṛbhus associated with Vāja, pour in your hands, into yourself, the pressed out Soma mixed (with water). O bountiful one, urged with a hymn, rejoice yourself in the house of the sacrificer, together with the Sons of Sudhanvan, the Lords.

Notes a—stz 6 *a*, stz 7 *a samukṣitamas* as VII 4, 12 *c*—Sāyaṇa, "*samyak adbhiḥsiktam.*" *b gabhastyoḥ*—Sāyaṇa—"Drink Soma, holding the cup with both arms." Yet it is to be thought whether '*gabhastyoḥ*' could be connected with '*sutam*' related to the participle '*putam.*' Cf IX 71, 3; II 14, 8 c; IX 86, 34 c.

(6) *Tr.* O Indra, intoxicate yourself according to your capacities, in company of the Ṛbhus and the Vājas, here at ours in this drink-offering, O you much-praised one. These (Soma—) pastures have given themselves up to you alone, on the command of the gods and according to the laws of men.

Notes—'*śacyā*' connected with '*matsva*' or with '*puruṣṭuta*' Cf X 104, 3 a. According to Sāyaṇa with Śacī. *C* IV 35, 7 b. *d* '*vratā*' could also be Nom. pl. *yā* to be supplied—Cf. Oldenberg—notes to this stz.

(7) *Tr.* O Indra, along with the Ṛbhus associated with the Vājas, come here for the wager to this divine song of praise of the singer., (come) with hundred zealous desires for the *Āyu* son, you knowing thousand ways for the conducting of sacrifice.

Notes—a I 106, 4 a.—*Vājibhiḥ* evidently Vājavadbhiḥ in stz. 5, whereby, at any rate, appelative meaning of Vāja is suggested. *cd*—cf I 100, 12 ab.

IV 33

(Metre—Triṣṭubh)

(1) *Tr.* I send speech as a messenger to the Ṛbhus. I call the Śvaitarī cow for infusion, (I send speech to the Ṛbhus) who, as artists speedy like the wind, have instantly reached the heaven through their steadfast ardours.

Notes—a 173, 3 d. *b* IV 3, 9; IX 62, 28; IX 71, 1. *b*. Either the Milchcow is meant for the Soma-infusion as according to Sāyaṇa [f. n. In that case *a* and *b* would present the common connection of a hymn and *a* Soma-sacrifice] or the sacrificer himself drinks milk as support to his speech. In this case one has to compare II 31, 5 d; VIII 20, 8 a; Ait. Br. IV 7, 2; Āṣ Gṛ Sū I 24, 13. *Śvaitarī* is a particular species of cows. cf I 33, 14 d) *cd* suits well in their journey to the heaven (IV 35, 8) after which they were taken amongst the gods. Cf I 110, 6; I 161, 7; IV 35, 3 and 8; AV VI 47, 3. *Paribabhūvuḥ*–'*sarvato vyāpnuvanti*'—Sāyaṇa. (Cf paryabhavad divam AV X 2, 18). '*paribhū* is first to take something and then to catch hold of some thing, to take in something, to obtain something. AV XII 3. 31. To *tarṇibhirevaiḥ*. Cf *taraṇitvā* in I 110, 6. [f.n. According to Sāyaṇa 'with horses.']

(2) *Tr.* When the Ṛbhus had served their parents with attendance, care and artistic skill then first of all they obtained the friendship of gods. Skilled in work they brought expansion to poetry.

Notes—2 to 4 the works of the Ṛbhus for the parents. C IX 99, 5 a; *d* In so far as they are celebrated in the songs of the poets. *Puṣṭim vah*—also VI 36, 6.

(3) *Tr.* They, who rejuvenated the parents, that lay old like decayed pillars, these Vāja, Vibhvan, Ṛbhu, the enjoyers of honey, should show preferance to our sacrifice, along with Indra.

Notes—Rejuvenation of the parents–I 20, 4; a IV 35, 5 (and in another context) VS XV 53—Punaḥ kṛṇvānāḥ pitarā yuvānā. *c* The names of the Ṛbhus after their apotheosis. (cf 161, 5), in reverse order IV 34, 1; I 161, 6. *d* 'madhupsarsaḥ' Sāyaṇa—'the enjoyers of sweet Soma-juice' or 'of beautiful forms.'

(4) *Tr.* When the Ṛbhus had protected the cow for one year, when they had carved with flesh for one year, when one year long they had brought fodder (?) to her, through these services they obtained immortality.

Notes—According to I 161, 10 they perform all these works for the parents. *b*—so also Sāyaṇa. Cf. *piśita*. *c*—I 161, 10 C—different. *bhāsaḥ* (?)—Sāyaṇa 'when they prepared her brilliance, the beauty of her limbs.'

(5) *Tr.* The eldest said, "I shall make two cups." The younger said, "Let us make three." The youngest said, make four cups." O Ṛbhus, Tvaṣṭṛ took you by the word.

Notes—5—6 the cup of Tvaṣṭṛ I 20, 6; I 161, 1 to 5. and 9. *a* pp reads *kara*—Read *karā* conju. I. *d* '*panayadvacaḥ*' is uncertain. Sāyaṇa '*astaut, aṅgickāretyarthaḥ*.'

(6) *Tr.* The men had spoken truth, since they did so. They followed this their own way. When Tvaṣṭṛ saw the four cups, which were shining like (new) days he opened the eyes in surprise.

Notes—*b* Cf *svadhām anubhū* I 165, 5. *c* AV V 1, 1 c.

(7) *Tr.* When the Ṛbhus had made themselves comfortable, sleeping for twelve days in the hospitality of Agohya, then they brought the fields to good condition. They diverted the rivers. The plants grew in the desert. Water stood in low lands.

Notes—The *Agohya*—saga I 110, 2 and 3, I 161, 11 to 13.

(8) *Tr.* The Ṛbhus who fashioned the lightly-rolling chariot, that keeps the man steady, who (fashioned) the all-

impelling cow Viśvarūpā, who are skilled in helping, skilled in working, skilled with hands, should provide us with riches.

Notes—a for the Aśvins I 20, 3; IV 36, 2 *b* the cow for Bṛhaspati I 20, 3; I 161, 6; Śān Śrau Sū. VIII 20, 1 *c* I 111, 2 and 3; IV 35, 8—'*takṣ*' is the verb suitable for the Ṛbhus.

(9) *Tr.* Then the gods, who contemplated on their works with insight and discernment, were pleased with them. Vāja was the artificer of the gods, Ṛbhukṣan of Indra, Vibhvan of Varuṇa.

(10) *Tr.* They, delighting in a hymn of praise, who, with their inventive genius fashioned for Indra the two bay—horses, easy to be yoked, (they i.e.) you O Ṛbhus, (grant) us augmentation of riches, treasures. Contract friendship with us as those who desire for peace.

Notes—ab—ye—ye like *yam—yam* IV 36, 6 d to *ukthā madantaḥ* Cf *ukthā sadhamādyāni* IV 3, 4 and *pītvā madā ukthāni śaṁsati* X 44, 8. So also *madanto gīrbhiḥ* III 53, 16 and without *gīrbhiḥ* IV 50, 2. *b* IV 34, 9b *d* II 4, 3 b *kṣaya* in II 4, 3; I 58, 6; VI 15, 2 (masc—here); 96, 6; X 108, 3 (nt-here); *mitradhīti, mitradheya*.

(11) *Tr.* At this time of the day they have granted you the drink and the exhilaration. One cannot have gods for friendship without exertion. Therefore, O Ṛbhus, grant us treasures now in this third libation.

Notes—a—the gods. The time of evening libation is meant *d*—cf IV 34, 1 c and 5. The Ṛbhus have obtained from the gods the right to the evening--libation as a reward. 1 161, 8; IV 34, 4; IV 35, 9; Ait. Br. III 30, 2; VI 12, 3. Sāyaṇa—"The Soma—drink and the intoxication arising from it." *b* I 179, 3 a; IV 33, 2 c.

IV 34

(Metre—Triṣṭubh)

(1) *Tr.* Ṛbhu, Vibhvan, Vāja, Indra come to this sacrifice of

ours for reward, because at this time of the day the goddess Dhiṣaṇā has fixed the drink for you. Your intoxications are in community.

Notes—a— Nom. in stead of voc. *b ratnadheyopa* either for *ratnadheyāya* as in stz 11(cf *ratnam̐ dhāta* IV 35, 8) upa or for *ratnadheyam* in the same sense as in IV 35, 1—2 and 9; *ratnadheya* is a favourite word in these Ṛbhu-hymns. Ratna often denotes the reward that the singer expects through the help of the divinity. Clearly in X 78, 8. Thus *ratnadheya* receives the sense of a reward in general. The Ṛbhus are men vis-a-vis *ratnadhāḥ* (IV 34, 6; IV 35, 7) and have obtained the third Savana as their *ratnadheya* (IV 35, 9).

c IV 33, 11;

d I 20, 5 and IV 34, 2 c; IV 35, 1 d. The sense is:–You are *sadhamādaḥ* with one another and with other gods. cf. *sam-mad* in stz 31 *sam-pā* IV 35, 7 and 9; VII 37, 2 and Sāyaṇa's second explanation : *yad* vā *vo madā devaiḥ saṁgatāḥ*.

(2) *Tr.* O richly-rewarded Ṛbhus, keeping in mind your origin, exhilarate yourselves at your times—Your intoxications and Purandhī have found themselves together. Bring to us possessions and efficient men (i.e. sons).

Notes—a VII, 56, 2. As formerly mortals, they have a right only in the Evening-libation. *b* in ṛtu-turns Cf IV 35, 7 and ṛtvaḥ in I 15, page 15 of this (i.e. HOS 33) volume. *c* The sense is—In Soma—intoxication generosity comes over you. cf IV 26, 7. *d* explains c.

(3) T*r*. This sacrifice has been prepared for you, which you have received long since as at Manu. The favourite Soma-draughts have approached you and you all, O Vājas, have the first claim over them.

Notes—b IV 37, 1 C—To '*pradive dadhidhve*' III 38, 5 d; III 43, 1 b. '*dadhiṣye pradivi*' VII 98. 5. *c*—Sāyaṇa quite rightly supplies '*Somaḥ*.' Then *jujuṣāṇa* is equal to *juṣṭa* (IV 37, 2) and *pra-asthuḥ* stands to join with '*pra sutāso asthiran*' I 135, 1; *prasthitān* (somān) 1 23, 1; VII 98, 2. '*agriya*' for '*agriyaḥ*' and this with '*madhvo agram*' (IV 27, 5 and 6) or '*madhvo agriyām*' (VII 92, 2) respectively is connected to '*agriyam*' in IV 37, 4, thus essentially equal to *agrepāḥ* in stzs 7 and 10 of our hymn. Somewhat general according to Sāyaṇa—"*agrārhā agratvasampādino vā.*" On the position of '*uta*' Cf IX 1, 9. Ludwig's explanation is noteworthy "You were all (also the two elders) Vājas." '*agriya*' is certainly also equal to *agraja* Cf I 13, 10; IX 5, 9. The individual names of the Ṛbhus also are transferred to others, in which appelative designations also are included.

(4) *Tr.* O Lords, now has comc for your worshipper, for the mortal sacrificer, the time for your reward. Drink, you Vājas, you Ṛbhus. The third great Savana has been granted in order to intoxicate you.

Notes—ab is explained through IV 35, 2. The reward is just the Evening-libation. One could also think : Now you have a reward for worshipper. VI 65, 4 a would speak for this. *c*—IV 37, 3 b.

(5) *Tr.* O you Vājas. O thou Ṛbhukṣan, Lords of great wealth, being praised, come here to us. These draughts come to you, when the days come to close, just as the newly-delivered cows (go) to the house.

Notes—a IV 37, 1.

(6) *Tr.* O Sons of Strength, come to this sacrifice being invoked with reverence. Bringing rewards, accompanied by Indra, drink in accord of this mead, of which you are sacrificial lords.

Notes—c is explained through IV 35, 4. As is said there the Ṛbhus must press their Soma, hence they are designated '*sūrayaḥ*' of Soma; presuming that *sūrayaḥ* is predicative vocative here, certainly they are designated '*sūrayaḥ*' otherwise also in IV 37, 7. The real denotation of '*sūrī* is uncertain—Here probably an ellipsis 'whose (drinkers) you *sūryaḥ* are (cf also '*yasya stha*' AV II 24, 1). Sāyaṇa—Indra, to whom you belong. *d*—ratnadhāḥ and sūrayaḥ in *c* successively relate to each other—ratnadhāḥ is explained through VII 16, 6 a.

(7) *Tr.* O Indra, drink Soma in accord with Varuṇa, in accord with the Maruts, (O Indra), you desiring praise, (drink) in accord with those who drink first and with those who drink at their time (i.e. the Ṛbhus), in accord with the reward—bringing divine spouses.

Notes—*b*—VI 40, 5 d *c* These are the Ṛbhus according to stz II but according to Sāyaṇa '*ṛtuyājadevāḥ.*' *d* the *gnāspatnayaḥ* according to Sāyaṇa are the divinities who are the protective divinities of women.

(8) *Tr.* O Ṛbhus, intoxicate yourselves in accord with the Ādityas, in accora with the mountains, in accord with the divine Savitṛ, in accord with the reward-bringing rivers.

(9) *Tr.* The Ṛbhus, who (have looked after) the Aśvins, who (after) the parents, who, through their help have fashioned the cow and the two horses, who (fashioned) the armours, who, who (brought ?) the two worlds, the lords, the Vibhus, who have fashioned the means of good progeny.

Notes—*a* and *c* are zeugma. A verb suitable for 'takṣuḥ' is to be inserted. It is not probable that the Ṛbhus fabricated the Aśvins themselves and the parents themselves. (Bergaigne II 410 fn). Also it is not probable that the parents are the heaven and the earth (ibid 411). *b* '*dhenu*' is that of Bṛhaspati cf IV 33, 8 b. *c* The fabrication of the armours is otherwise unknown. For *ṛdhak* already Yāska (IV 25) has taken a double meaning—'*pṛthak*' and '*rudhnuvan*'. That difficult words is yet to be investigated more exactly. After that the meaning of the above-mentioned place will be determined better. With it IV 36, 1 d is to be specially considered again. *d* Better as 'the gods, who have produced good progeny.' Cf VII 91, 3 d; VIII 15, 10 C; I 72, 9. Procreation of children (cf I 111, 2; IV 36, 9; IV 34, 2; IV 35, 6.) is generally a part of their creative efficiency. Hopkins (JAOS XV 280) brings this trait together with the saga of the rejuvenation of the parents, who must not be necessarily their own parents. This last-mentioned is not at all probable. Probably it would also be—"who have rendered good services to children." With reference to places like IV 33, 2 and 4 Vibhu is Vibhvan, one of the Ṛbhus and from him it is transferred to others. cf IV 36, 3.

(10) *Tr.* They who produce wealth in cows, in prize, in good men, in good treasures, and in abundant cattle, (they i.e.) you, Ṛbhus, who drink first and intoxicate yourselves, give us these and to those who sanction (?) a gift.

Notes—b VI 68, 6 b; VII 84, 4 b *C* stz 7 c *d* doubtful. The subject of '*gṛṇanti*,' is the 'sacrificers,' as Sāyaṇa accepts in his second interpretation. Thus also Ludwig IV 168 P 16. "They, Who psomise a gift to the priests." To '*rātim gṛṇanti*' Cf VII 56, 18; IV 17, 5.

(11) *Tr.* You have not stayed away. We have not left you thirsty. O Ṛbhus, do not be exempted from the prize of praise in this sacrifice. You gods, intoxicate yourselves along with Indra, with the Maruts, the kings, in order to reward (us).

Notes—anihśastāḥ ? Sāyaṇa—'*aninditāḥ* (cf *niśasā* X 163, 3). Always remembrance of their non-divine origin. *d*—The kings are the Ādityas.

IV 35

Metre–Triṣṭubh

Close relationship of the hymn with 34 and 36

(1) *Tr.* Come here, O Sons of Strength, O Ṛbhus, O Sons of Sudhanvan, do not stay away; because in this libation is your reward. Your intoxications should come after Indra.

Notes b–IV 34, 11 a. *c* stz 2 and 9; IV 34, 1. *d* IV 34, 1, d.

(2) *Tr.* Now is the turn of the reward of the Ṛbhus. There is the drinking of the well-dressed Soma, since you have divided one cup four-fold, with your dexterity and craftsmanship.

Notes b–abhūt like IV 34, 4. *d* IV 36, 4 a. Cf I 161, 2.

(3) *Tr.* You have made the cup fourfold. "Friend, try"., so spoke you. Then O Vājas, O defthanded Ṛbhus, you went on the way of immortality amidst the assemblage of the gods.

Note b—Agni is addressed. So also Sāyaṇa. Cf I 161, 1. *c* 161, 7 d; III 60, 2 and 3; IV 33, 4.

(4) *Tr.* Out of which material was that cup made, which you with your wisdom, have divided fourfold ? Now press for yourselves the libation—drink—in order to intoxicate you. Drink O Ṛbhus, of the Soma-mead.

Notes a—I 161 , 1 d. *c* The Ṛbhus, skilled in work are depicted as pressers of their own Soma here. Cf IV 36, 6 c. Yet 'a *brevilo quenz*' also may be present. "Allow for yourselves, to press." So Oldenberg. Cf I 108, 4. Or "Then you pressed for yourselves, of course to inaugurate (?) the four cups."

(5) *Tr.* With skill you have made the parents young. With skill you have fashioned the cup out of which the gods drink. With skill you carved the two bay-horses, the best runners, the vehicle-animals of Indra, you richly rewarded Ṛbhus.

Notes a—IV 33, 3 a; *c dhanutara* formed like *sanutara* or for dhanutṛtara ?

(6) *Tr.* O Vājas, whosoever presses for you in order to intoxicate you, the sharp libation of drink at the close of the day, O Ṛbhus, O bulls, intoxicating yourselves, produce for him a treasure of heroic sons.

Notes cd—IV 36, 8 d.

(7 *Tr.* O Driver of bay-horses, you drank the pressed (Soma) in the morning. The Midday-libation belongs to you alone. Drink together with the reward-bringing Ṛbhus, whom O Indra, you have made your friends on account of their craftsmanship.

Notes c—ratnadhebhiḥ (Cf IV 34, 1 b) is explained through 6 cd.

(8) *Tr.* You who became gods through your craftsmanship and have seated yourselves in the heaven like an eagle (in the nest), you, O Ṛbhus, must bring rewards, you Sons of Strength. O Sons of Sudhanvan, you have become immortal.

Notes b—I 164, 39 b.

(9) *Tr.* O deft-handed ones, the third Soma-libation, which you have secured as a reward for yourselves through your dexterity, that O Ṛbhus, has been poured out for you. Drink together with the intoxications of Indra.

Notes a—stz 1 C, id i.e. intoxicate yourselves along with Indra. Cf IV 34, 11; I 20, 5.

IV 36

Metre 1-8 Jagatī 9—Triṣṭubh

(1) *Tr.* The praiseworthy chariot with three wheels, which is yoked with a horse, without reins, turns round the space. O Ṛbhus, that was a great proclamation of your divine nature that you bring the heaven and the earth to bloom.

Notes—The wonderful chariot of the Aśvins, which moves by itself. *a*—The first three words also in I 152, 5 a, there about the sun and more suitable. (b) Through this first deed they have made known their divine strength (c) and also made known that they are capable of bringing the whole world to prosperity (d) Cf Stz 3 a *d* Cf IV 34, 9 c.

(2) *Tr.* The intelligent ones, who, following (mere) thinking, with inventive skill, have fashioned the lightly-rolling non-toppling chariot, them, i.e. you O Vājas, O Ṛbhus, we now invite, in order to drink this Soma-libation.

Notes—a IV 33, 8 *b manasā paridhyayā* cf III 60, 2 bc.

(3) *Tr.* O Vājas, O Ṛbhus, O Vibhus, this greatness of yours has been well-recognised among the gods, through this that you have rejuvenated your aged parents, weakened by age and have made them capable of walking.

Notes d—almost identical with X 39, 4 b.

(4) *Tr.* You have changed the one cup into fourfold. Through your inventive skill you made a cow come out of a hide. And you have obtained immortality from the gods through your readiness to serve. That of yours is to be extolled in a hymn.

Notes a—I 10, 3 d; IV 35, 2 d; IV 35, 39. *b* I 161, 7 a. *c* The Locative '*deveṣu*' as in I 20, 8; I 73, 5; I 91, 1; II 14, 8; II 21, 5. *d śruṣṭī* or 'willingness'.

(5) *Tr.* From the Ṛbhus proceeds, the first most famous riches, which the lords (i.e. the Ṛbhus), wellknown through Vāja have created. That carved by Vibhvan is to be praised in wise discourses. He, whom the gods favour, distinguishes himself in front of many people.

Notes—Prathama—Vāja—Vibhvan in this composition there are at once allusicns to the eldest Ṛbhu, so also to Vaja and Vibhvan. Id stz 6. Cf 37, 6.

(6) *Tr.* He becomes a prize-wining steed, a *Ṛṣi* in eloquence, a valiant marksman, invincible in battles. He obtains growing treasure, he (obtains) mastery, he whom Vāja, Vibhvan, the Ṛbhus have favoured.

(7) *Tr.* The most beautiful worthseeing ornament, a hymn of praise, was attributed to you. O Vājas, O Ṛbhus, rejoice in it. Because you are wise seers, skilled in speech, we invite you with this benedictory word.

Notes—a Cf '*Śucipeśaṁ dhiyam*' I 114, 1. *c*. Thus they can pass judgement on the hymn. *d* stz 2 d.

(8) *Tr.* As well-informed ones you must carve for us out of the (priestly) works all humn enjoyments, brilliant highest reward, which gives mightly energy. You must carve for us treasure and young age.

Notes—8—9 the real request. *a—dhiṣaṇābhyaḥ pari*— Sāyaṇa—"*Stutibhyo nimittabhūtebhyaḥ*"—*dhiṣaṇāḥ* Cf IX 59, 20, Pischel—Ved. St. II 84—'From the three earths.'

(9) *Tr*. Grant us progeny here and treasure there. Carve for us the renown, which is associated with heroes, through which we must eclipse others. O Ṛbhus, you have bestowed on us this shining reward.

Notes a—almost identical with X 183, 1 C. *d*—I 48, 11. The perfect '*dadā*' anticipates the request as already fulfilled. Sāyaṇa—"*asmabhyaṁ datta*" So also Ludwig. Cf V 57, 7 b.

IV 37

Metre 1—4 Triṣṭubh; 5—8 Anuṣṭubh

(1) *Tr*. You gods, Vājas and Ṛbhuṣans, come here to our sacrificial performance by the ways traversed by gods, as you, bringing delight, have received the sacrifice of Manu in these clans on auspicious days.

Notes—In the first part, stz 1—4, this hymn many times reminds us of the foregone hymns, especially IV 34. The second part, stz 5—8, refers to an intended horse-sacrifice. *a* IV 34, 5 a. *b* VII 38, 8 d. *cd*—IV 34, 3; IV 37, 3—'*yathā yajñaṁ manuṣaḥ*' like '*yaṁ* (*yajñam*) *manuṣvat*' IV 34, 3. '*vikṣu*' of the present clans, is explained through 3 c.

(2) *Tr*. These sacrifices should be according to your heart and mind. Clothed in ghee they should come to you today, being agreeable. The Soma-draughts fully presented should arouse (?) your longings. When drunk they should give you delight in all possible ways.

Notes—Sāyaṇa gives two derivations for '*harayanta*,' from *hṛ* and from *hary*.

(3) *Tr*. O Vājas, O Ṛbhukṣans, as the......sacrifice has been ordained by the gods to you, and the hymn of praise was granted to you, therefore as Manu did, I (now) among the later-born clans, offer you Soma in company of the heavenly ones.

Notes—trudāyam is obscure. *tri* is well-connected to number three of the Ṛbhus or to the third Savana together. Cf. *tripṛṣṭha* of Soma. Sāyaṇa—"The food called Soma, which is linked with the courses of the three Savanas i.e. which belongs to the Third Savana." *b* IV 34, 4 cd C IV 34 3 b; IV 1 c.

(4) *Tr.* O richly-rewarded ones, you have sturdy horses, a shining chariot, iron-jaws, beautiful gold-ornament. Now O Son of Indra, O Sons of strength, the flower (of Soma) was awarded to you for your intoxication.

Notes—The eldest Ṛbhukṣan is addressed as 'Son of Indra.' Indra himself is often called Ṛbhukṣan.

(5) *Tr.* O Ṛbhukṣans, we call for the treasure (fabricated by) Ṛbhu, which is the most victorious ally in battle, which is accompanied by Indra, which is constantly winning, which consists of horses.

Notes a—Here *'rayim'* has the epithet *'Ṛbhum'* like *'Ṛbhukṣanam Ṛbhum'* in VIII 93, 34. For *'Ṛbhu'* here is scarcely any particular meaning ('handy' 'efficacicus'—Grassmann) to be thought of as the desired treasure—is to be heeded. Yet *'Ṛbhum'* can be short form of *'Ṛbhutaṣṭam'* (Cf *Vibhvataṣṭam* IV 36, 5). See particularly IV 36, 5. Then *'rayi'* is that sacrificial horse itself as in stz 8. With this all adjectives in stz 5 are suitable. (f.n.—As 'Agni' denotes treasure (rayi II 1, 12) or reward (*Vāja* II 1, 12; III 12; III 2, 4) or is compared with treasure, (I, 127, 9; I 128, 1). Sāyaṇa remarks—"As the Ṛbhus are the cause of the treasure, they are designated with this word.")

(6) *Tr.* O Ṛbhus, the mortal whom you and Indra favour, with his thought he must be the winner in the winning of mastery, the winner with his race-horse.

Notes—cf IV 36, 5 and 6. *cd*—VIII 40, 2 d; VI 45, 12; VIII 71, 12 cd; I 27, 9. C VIII 19, 9 C. Cf VII 94, 6.

(7) *Tr.* O Vājas, O Ṛbhukṣans, find out for us the ways for performing sacrifice. O liberal lords, after you have been praised (find out paths) for us so that we shall victoriously cross through all the quarters of the heaven.

Notes d—āśāḥ are to be compared to the quarters of the heaven, to whose divine protectors (*āśāpālāḥ*) the sacrificial horse is later recommended. (Śa. Br. XIII 4, 2, 16). Of course in this sentence lies the idea of '*digvijaya*' (VIII 53, 11).

(8) *Tr.* O Vājas, Ṛbhukṣans, Indra, Nāsatyas (bring back to us) from all lands this treasure (i.e.) the horse. Slaughter it for richer present.

Notes—cd śasta known through I 162, 18 d can only be 'slaughter' the roots *śams* or *śas* are quite impossible on account of the form. To '*sam*' is to be added a verb applicable to *ab* also. Now the horse, returning from its travel is handed over to the butcher for offering. Or is *sasta* to be understood as '*sunudhvam*' (IV 35, 4) ? Perhaps with this *Dadhikrāvan* is to be thought of and the end of IV 37 would then form the transition to the following *Dadhikrāvan-hymns*. (f.n. *pṛthvīm paryaṭantaṁ hi turagaṁ kāmacāriṇam* MB XIV 72, 13)

VII 48

Metre Triṣṭubh

(1) *Tr.* O Ṛbhukṣans, O Vājas, you liberal lords, delight yourselves in our Soma-juice. O Vibhus, my mind, like the spirits of the travellers, should guide yourselves and your manly chariot hitherwards.

Note a—Because each of the Ṛbhus includes others the individual names stand in plural. Cf IV 34, 3 C. *c* One has to think of *kratvaḥ* twice—'*yātām kratavaḥ*' the spirits of the travellers are the chariot-drivers. cf X 12, 5 d.

(2) *Tr.* As Ṛbhu with the Rbhus, as Vibhu with Vibhush, we must be superior to (other) mights through your might. Vāja should stand by us in the battle for the prize of victory. With Indra in alliance we would vanquish Vṛtra (the enemy).

(3) *Tr.* Since they surpass many (authoritative orders) through their authoritative order, they, the high lords overcome the whole world in (the battle for) superiority. Indra,

Vibhvan, Ṛbhukṣan, Vāja must break the strength of the rival, of the enemy in the contest (?)

Notes b—cf the decree wellknown from the Avesta. *Vanaitimea uparatātm* and '*vanvanta uparān abhisyuḥ*'—RV II 4, 9; I 151, 5; VIII 65, 9.

(4) *Tr.* Now O gods, provide free path for us. Be all of you unitedly to our help. The Vasus should give us enjoyment of food. Protect us ever with your blessings.

XI

Chitrav Siddheshvarshastri

I 20

Note

THE GROUP OF THE DEITIES, CALLED THE ṚBHUS :

In this hymn the group of semi-human divinities has been invoked. There are 10 more hymns addressed to these divinities. (I 110, 111, 161; III 60; IV 33-37; VII 48). They have been referred to casually in 100 more stanzas. According to the Bṛhaddevatā Ṛbhu and his brothers Vāja and Vibhvan were sons of the sage Aṅgiras. They were artisans of gods and pupils of Tvaṣṭṛ. With the favour of Tvaṣṭṛ they performed many skilful deeds (Br. Dev. III 83-88).

Their exploits :

Five exploits of the Ṛbhus, indicative of their skill are well-known. In this hymn two out of these have been referred to (1) They rejuvenated their parents (2 They fashioned four cups out of one wooden bowl, prepared by Tvaṣṭṛ. Elsewhere in the Ṛgveda there are allusions to the Ṛbhus (i) as having constructed a three-wheeled chariot for the Aśvins, a chariot that moves throughout the firmament. (I III, I; IV 33, 8; IV 36, 1) (i) as having fashioned two stallions for Indra (IV 33, 10) (iii) so also as having created for Bṛhaspati a cow yielding nectar (IV 33, 8; III 34, 9). In addition to these exploits other acts of the Ṛbhus like composing hymns (X 87, 7), fashioning the sacrifice and the two worlds (III 54, 12: IV 34, 9) supporting the heaven (X 66, 10) have also been referred to in the Ṛgveda.

Attainment of immortality :

Because of this efficacy of the Ṛbhus they became immortal and were entitled to drink Soma along with other gods. This incident has been referred to in the 8th stz. of this hymn.

Explanation of the deities – the Ṛbhus :

According to Macdonell the Ṛbhus in Ṛgveda represent the three seasons remaining steady during the period of the 12 days of the winter solstice. That they rejuvenated their parents means, that they newly fixed the days of the beginning of Northern and Southern Solstices.

According to the opinion of Macdonell the bowl in the legend of the Ṛbhus is the moon. The legend that they divided the bowl into four means that they conclusively fixed the four different stages viz. the Full-moon night, No-moon night and the two 8th days. The Aryans on the Artic pole knew only two seasons, the summer and the winter. The Ṛbhus added to this two more seasons, the spring and the rainy season and thus fixed the time of the descent and the solstices.

(1) *Tr.* On the occasion of the attainment of godhead by the Ṛbhus, the learned seers composed this gemlike brilliant hymn.

(2) *Tr.* We praise in this sacrifice the Ṛbhus, expert in their work, who, by the power of the mind, fashioned the two horses (of Indra), yoking themselves merely on word.

(3) *Tr.* The Ṛbhus constructed the comfortable chariot of Aśvins, moving around its axle. They created a cow yielding milk.

(4) *Tr.* The straight forward Ṛbhus, speakers of truth,

rejuvenated their decrepit parents with their special efficacy.

(5) Such as you are, O Ṛbhus, you attained the honour of drinking intoxicating Soma along with the Martus, Indra and the brilliant Ādityas.

(6) O, Ṛbhus, they fashioned (with your capability) four cups out of the one bowl prepared by god Tvaṣṭṛ.

(7) *Tr.* O Ṛbhus, while pressing the sacrificed Soma we have composed for you 21 songs. Give us 21 gems in exchange of these.

(8) The Ṛbhus became immortal and were entiled to the sacrificial oblation along with the gods.

I 110

Note

RESURRECTION OF A DEAD COW

In the 8th stz. of this hymn there is a reference to the Ṛbhus as having resurrected a dead cow. According to Skandasvāmin a cow, useful for *Agnihotra*, belonging to a sage was dead and lowing of the calf in her belly was heard by the sage. At the request of the Brahmin the Ṛbhus revived the cow. (See I 20 Exploits of the Ṛbhus).

(1) *Tr.* O Ṛbhus, O gods, this singer, who has already performed many sacrifices duly, is offering you a sacrifice anew, as also a sweet song.

(2) O Ṛbhus, you, who are like my ancient relatives, who are desirous of oblations from the worshippers, in ancient times, you reached the house of the liberal Savitṛ on the strength of your achievements.

(3) *Tr.* The all-seeing liberal Savitṛ gave you nectar. In order to drink it you divided into four each the nectarlike bowls prepared by the strong Tvaṣṭṛ.

(4) *Tr.* The Ṛbhus, the sons of Sudhanvan, though mortal became lustrous like the sun and became immortal.

Within the period of a year only they became recepients of songs in the capacity of gods.

(5) *Tr.* The Ṛbhus, desirous of the heavenly Soma and of oblations, divided into four the gaping bowl with their sharp implement, just as a surveyor divides an agricultural piece of land into equal parts.

(6) *Tr.* Let us offer to the Ṛbhus, the heroes of the firmament, who, by dint of their craftsmaniship have attained the capacity of the World-father and have gone to the divine world, this song like a ladle, offering ghee.

(7) *Tr.* By their capability and by their wealth the Ṛbhus became rich and beautiful gods, match for Indra. O Ṛbhus, give us might capable of facing and conquering the armies of the impious ones.

(8) *Tr.* O Sons of Sudhanvan, O heroes, by your Craftsmanship you united the cows with their calves. With your skill you rejuvenated your aged parents. You obtained the merit of many cow-sacrifices (You severed many cows from their hides).

(9) *Tr.* O Indra, along with the Ṛbhus come to your battlefield, with the help of your horses. Protect us and give us ample wealth. May Mitra, Varuṇa, Aditi, the Ocean and the Earth grant this desire of ours.

I 111

(1) *Tr.* The Ṛbhus, the skilful artisans fashioned for Indra, a good chariot and two sturdy stallions, rejuvenated their parents and gave a new mother to the orphaned calves.

(2) *Tr.* O Ṛbhus, make us young like you for the accomplishment of sacrifices. Give us nourishment for victory and strength. Make our army possessed of capability and enable us to stay at home carefree along with our sons and grandsons and along with the retinue.

(3) *Tr.* O Ṛbhus, obtain booty and bring it to us. Create in our chariots and in our horses the strength, necessary for

winning booty. Give us might to defeat enemies, our own or strangers.

(4) *Tr.* I invoke for our protection and for a draught of Soma the Ṛbhus and Indra, Vibhvan, Vāja, Maruts, Mitra and Varuṇa and the Aśvins, these deities superior even to the Ṛbhus. May they give us wealth, intellect and victory.

(5) *Tr.* May Ṛbhu and Vāja grant us wealth and protection, necessary for the battle. May Mitra, Varuṇa, Aditi, the Ocean and the Earth grant this desire of ours.

I 161

(A Dialogue hymn with the Ṛbhus, Agni and Dīrghatamas)

In this hymn the description of the exploits of the Ṛbhus is given in the form of a conversation among the Ṛbhus, Agni and Dīrghatamas (Other Ṛbhu-hymns I 20; III 60, 1-4; IV 33-37; VII 48, 1—3; X 53, 11 and X 176, 1). When the seer Ṛbhu was drinking Soma along with his brothers named Vibhvan and Vāja, Agni came and sat amongst them, assuming a form similar to theirs. The present Dialogue-hymn has been composed on the background of this legend. In stz 1 the Ṛbhus are expressing a doubt as to which one amongst the four is Agni. In stz. 2 Agni, revealing himself, is describing the exploits of the Ṛbhus. Stz 3-14 contain the praise of the Ṛbhus by the Seer Dīrghatamas. Out of these stzs in stz 11 – 14 the Ṛbhus have been described as the rays of the sun (Āditya) Nirukta XI 16.

Exploits of the Ṛbhus :

In addition to the wellknown exploits of the Ṛbhus, described in I 20 present hymn refers to the Ṛbhus as having created the animals, the carriers for the conveyances of Indra, Aśvins and Bṛhaspati and as having discovered the primary element in the universe. Stz. 10 describes some minor deeds of the Ṛbhus. Stz. 3 refers to the Ṛbhus as creating a horse, a chariot and a cow and stz. 6 refers to those being given to Indra, Aśvins and Bṛhaspati respectively. Stz. 6 refers also to the cow Viśvarūpā, assuming all forms, as used by Bṛhaspati for his conveyance.

The discovery of primary elements in the universe

Stz. 9 refers to the Ṛbhus as having discovered the primary elements in the universe, viz., fire and earth (For comparison Sec—*Apo eva sasarjādau*—Manu 18: *Adbhyāḥ pṛthvī* (Tai Up II 1, 1).

Miscellaneous exploits

Stz. 10 allegorically describes the Ṛbhus as making the streams flow, as classifying the flesh-element in the bodies of the living beings and as teaching the art of throwing away excretion from the body.

The Ṛbhus in the form of the rays of the Sun

In Stz. 11—14 the Ṛbhus are praised being considered as rays of the Sun. According to Lokamanya B.G. Tilak the Ṛbhus stopped their work during the Inter-calary month occuring once in 3 years and that time they rested at leasure at the house of the sun. The dog mentioned here is the 'dog—star' near the constellation Mṛga. When the Sun approached it and the seasons of spring began the Ṛbhus awoke and once again started their work (Vedakāla—nirṇaya—B.G. Tilak pp 80-81).

(1) *Tr.* (The Ṛbhus) "Is our eldest or youngest brother present among the host of gods drinking Soma ? Or is the divine messenger Agni present here (assuming the form of our brother) ? O brotherlike Agni, we are not blaming the bowl of great origin. We are describing its attainment."

(2) *Tr.* (Agni) 'O Ṛbhus, O Sons of Sudhanvan, I have come to inform you about the order of gods that you should divide one bowl into four equal parts. If you do that you will be entitled to accept sacrificial oblations like the gods.'

(3) *Tr.* (Dīrghatamasa) O brotherlike Ṛbhus, you told the messenger Agni that you were engaged in fashioning

a horse, a chariot and a cow and in endowing new youth to your parents. You assured him that you would come to the place of the sacrifice after all this was over.

(4) *Tr.* O Ṛbhus, when you searched for the messenger Agni after having performed these exploits, you found him keeping himself concealed among the group of women near the bowl prepared by Tvaṣṭṛ.

(5) *Tr.* Tvaṣṭṛ spoke about his desire to kill the Ṛbhus, who had begiled the bowl dear to the gods. Since then the people do not utter the names of the Ṛbhus while drinking Soma. Even the mother of the Ṛbhus loves them with other names.

(6) Indra accepted the bay horses, Bṛhaspati the cow Viśvarūpā. The Aśvins accepted the chariot of the Ṛbhus. They endowed godhead on Ṛbhu, Vibhvan and Vāja, the three brothers expert in sacrifice. Since then they obtained sacrificial oblation.

(7) *Tr.* O Ṛbhus, O Sons of Sudhanvan, with the power of your intellect you drew out a cow from the hide of a dead cow. You rejuvenated your parents. From one horse you created another. You yoked it to your chariot and reached the gods.

(8) *Tr.* O Ṛbhus, O Sons of Sudhanvan, drink this water purified with Muñja grass. If you do not want that be delighted in the third libation of the sacrifice.

(9) *Tr.* O truth-speaking Ṛbhus, two of your brothers expressed the opinions about the water being the best and the fire being the best. On the contrary, the third one spoke about the earth being the best. Thus you divided the bowl into four.

(10) *Tr.* (O Ṛbhus), Two of your brothers drew out a lame cow from the waters and divided her flesh for the prupose of sacrifice. The third one took out the cowdung from her bowls and cleaned her. What more service can the son in the form of the priest do to the parents in the form of the sacrificer ?

(The praise of the Ṛbhus in the form of the rays of the Sun).

(11) *Tr.* O Ṛbhus, skilled in the art of leading (in the form of the rays of the sun), you were sleeping in the house of the inapprehensible sun in the ancient times. You created grass on high lands on the earth through your skill and created water in low lands.

(12) *Tr.* O Ṛbhus, (in the form of the rays of the sun) you pervade all the worshippers and encircle around them. You cursed them who opposed you at the time of this exploit and conferred boons on your glorifiers. Where were your parents in the form of the sun and the moon at that time ?

(13) *Tr.* O Ṛbhus, (in the form of the rays of the sun) when you were sleeping in the house of Savitṛ, whom none can hide, he told you that the dog in the form of the wind was inspiring you in your work. Accordingly you created a new universe after the rainy season.

(14) O Ṛbhus, (in the form of the sun), O sons of Strength, out of your love the Maruts move through the heaven and Agni through the earth. The wind goes through the firmament and Varuṇa through expansive waters.

III 60

(1) *Tr.* O Ṛbhus, O valiant Sons of Sudhanvan, extirpating the enemies, with your knowledge and skill you performed various exploits in this world.

(2) *Tr.* O Ṛbhus, possessed of physical, intellectual and mental capability, you performed great exploits of dividing the bowl, creating a cow and fashioning the horses for Indra. You attained godhead because of your exploits.

(3) *Tr.* The Ṛbhus, the Sons of Sudhanvan, human by birth, performers of good actions, skilful and of good character, obtained the friendship of Indra and immortality.

(4) *Tr.* O Sons of Sudhanvan, O Ṛbhus, O ideal worshippers coming with Indra in his chariot for drinking Soma, you

enjoying whatever you desire, your exploits and your good deeds are indescribable.

(5) *Tr.* O mighty and manly Indra, you praised by the worshippers, bountiful one, come to our sacrifice along with Ṛbhu and Vāja and drink with both the hands our Soma, giving delight.

(6) *Tr.* O Indra, you controller of gods and human beings and of the cycle of days, O much praised one, be delighted in our sacrifice along with the brothers Ṛbhu and Vāja.

(7) *Tr.* O Indra, having thousand eyes, accept our sacrificial song along with the brothers Ṛbhu and Vāja, with the help of your hundred speedy horses.

IV 33

The twelve days of Āditya

The 7th Stz. of this hymn refers to the Ṛbhus as spending 12 days in the hospitality of Āditya (Agohya). According to Sāyaṇācārya this is intended to refer to the 12 constellations Ārdrā and others in rainy season. In Stz. 11 we find the maxim 'A toiling person alone attains friendship of the gods.'

(1) *Tr.* I am sending my songs to the Ṛbhus as messenger for obtaining a milch-cow, for mixing Soma with milk, to the Ṛbhus, pervading the firmament, speedy as the wind and possessed of efficacy—

(2) *Tr.* the Ṛbhus, who served their parents with skilful acts obtained the friendship of gods and broguht prosperity to their own mind.

(3) *Tr.* May Ṛbhu, Vāja and Vibhvan, who gave new youth to their own parents, that were rendered useless like dilapidated pillar, who are drinkers of Soma, come to the place of our sacrifice.

(4) *Tr.* The Ṛbhus, the performers of marvellous tasks, who guarded for one year each the cow, the flesh of the cow and the lustre of the cow, were endowed with the boon of immortality.

(5) *Tr.* O Ṛbhus, the eldest of you proposed to make the bowl into two. The middle one proposed to make it into three. At last you fashioned four bowls on the suggestion of the youngest one. Tvaṣṭṛ, the divine artisan, was pleased with this work.

(6) *Tr.* Tvaṣṭṛ was pleased on seeing the four bowls, dazzling like the day-light. It is because of this that the Ṛbhus were entitled to sacrificial oblation.

(7) *Tr.* The Ṛbhus, who stayed as guests for 12 days at the house of the brilliant Āditya made the fields on the earth fertile. They made the rivers flow. They planted herbs in desert-land and made waters flow in low-lands.

(8) T*r.* May the Ṛbhus, performers of good deeds, glorious and skilful, who fashioned a speedy chariot for the man and the all-impeiling cow Viśvarūpā for Bṛhaspati, may they create for us wealth in all quarters.

(9) *Tr.* The Ṛbhus, who attained godhead by their efficacy and by the brilliant capacity of their mind, became dear friends of Indra, Varuṇa and other gods respectively.

(10). *Tr.* O Ṛbhus, praised in songs, working for the welfare of the worshippers, who by the skill of the intellect, fashioned the horses Harī for Indra you give us wealth, prospecrity and treasures.

(11) *Tr.* O Ṛbhus, it is true that there can be no friendship with the gods without toiling. You obtained the right to the draught of Soma in the particular part of the day on account of your skill. Drink Soma in the third libation and give us wealth.

IV 34

(1) *Tr.* O Ṛbhus, come to us along with the two brothers Vibhvan and Vāja and along with Indra in order to drink the intoxicating Soma offered by the Deity of Speech and give us ample wealth.

(2) *Tr.* O Ṛbhus, who have attained godhead, who are rich in food, give to the worshippers offering you Soma, excellent progeny and wealth.

(3) *Tr.* O brilliant Ṛbhus, having excellent human form, accept our sacrifice and the Soma, captivating the mind and longing towards you.

(4) *Tr.* O Ṛbhus, O Vāja, expert in the art of leading, make gift of ample wealth to the worshippers, apt in service, offering intoxicating Soma and oblation in the third libation.

(5) *Tr.* O Ṛbhus, O Vājas, having ample wealth, expert in the art of leading, come to us. The Soma in the third libation is running towards you like a recently delivered cow, running towards the house.

(6) O generous and knowledgeful Ṛbhus, O Sons of Strength, you, invoked with a song, come to the place of our sacrifice and drink Soma along with your dear friend Indra.

(7) *Tr.* O Indra, with gratified mind, drink Soma along with Maruts and Varuṇa, along with the gods desirous of drinking Soma and along with your wife.

(8) *Tr.* O Ṛbhus, drink Soma in company of Ādityas, in company of the mountains, so also in company of the rivers, bestowing wealth and in company of god Savitṛ and be delighted.

(9) & (10) *Tr.* O Ṛbhus, you who bestow a new existence upon your parents, upon the Aśvins, upon the cow and upon the horse, who separate the heaven and the earth, who perform good deeds, who are rich in cows, horses, progeny, wealth, food etc. who have precedence in drinking Soma, give us wealth.

(11) *Tr.* O blameless Ṛbhus, do not go back from our sacrifice, without satiating thirst. Find delight in the place of our sacrifice along with Indra and Maruts and give us wealth.

IV 35

(1) O Ṛbhus, O Sons of Strength, O Sons of Sudhanvan, donors of sacrificial wealth, do not refuse. Come to us. Drink intoxicating Soma immediately after Indra.

(2) *Tr.* O Ṛbhus, O Vājas, who divided the bowl, possessed of skill, efficient ones, drink the pressed Soma and make us gifts of ample treasures.

(3) *Tr.* O Ṛbhus, O Vājas, expert in the work, because of your capability in dividing the bowl you reached among the host of gods by the heavenly ways.

(4) *Tr.* O skilful Ṛbhus, of what material was the bowl made, which you divided ? Drink the intoxicating Soma, pressed by the priests.

(5) *Tr.* O skilful Ṛbhus, rich in wealth, you rejuvenated your old parents. You fashioned the bowls for the gods and speedy horses for Indra.

(6) *Tr.* O valiant Ṛbhus and Vājas, give army and wealth to your worshippers, pressing Soma for you in the evening–libation.

(7) *Tr.* O Indra, having bay horses, friend of the Ṛbhus, drink Soma in the morning and at mid-day along with the Ṛbhus, possessed of skill and donors of wealth.

(8) *Tr.* O Ṛbhus, O Sons of Strength, O Sons of Sudhanvan, you who have attained godhead because of good deeds, who are staying in heaven, give us ample wealth and be immortal.

(9) *Tr.* O skilful Ṛbhus, you who bestow ample wealth in the third libation, performers of good deeds, drink our intoxicating Soma along with Indra.

IV 36

(1) *Tr.* O Ṛbhus, who raise the heaven and the earth to prosperity, because of your skilful act of stationing in

the firmament the three-wheeled chariot without horse and without reins, you attained godhead.

(2) *Tr.* O Ṛbhus, O Vājas, possessed of knowledge, having mental strength, you who fashion a speedy chariot, not deviating, we invoke you for a draught of Soma.

(3) *Tr.* O Ṛbhus, O Vājas, O Vibhvan, your act that you rejuvenated your aged parents, was praised among host of gods.

(4) *Tr.* O Ṛbhus, O Vājas, you became immortal among the group of gods because of your praiseworthy acts that you divided the bowl and created a living cow out of the hide of a dead cow.

(5) *Tr.* O Ṛbhus, O Vājas, protectors of the worshippers, give us your wellknown, praiseworthy wealth so also the indescribable war-chariot, fashioned by Vibhavan.

(6) *Tr.* A worshipper, protected by Ṛbhu, Vāja and Vibhvan, becomes a mighty warrior, skilled archer and invincible hero. He attains prosperity in wealth and progency. He becomes a seer through his poetic ability.

(7) *Tr.* O Ṛbhus, O Vājas, you who are in high up place, charming, possessed of knowledge and connoisseurs, accept our songs, of ours who are proclaiming your name.

(8) *Tr.* O Ṛbhus, possessed of knowledge, create for us glorious wealth beyond imagination, beneficial to the people. Create power, wealth and strength and give these to us.

(9) *Tr.* O Ṛbhus, loving worshippers, give us wonderful prosperity, rendering all other people powerless. So also give us progeny wealth, sons and grandsons and glory.

IV 37

(1) *Tr.* O Charming Rbhus, O Vājas, come by divine ways to

our human place for sacrifice on an auspicious moment and accept our sacrifice.

(2) *Tr.* O Ṛbhus, may the brilliant Soma in the vat delight you and may it inspire you to fresh exploits.

(3) *Tr.* O Ṛbhus, O Vājas, I am offering you along with a song, this brilliant, beneficial, god-given Soma in the third libation of the human world.

(4) *Tr.* O mightly Ṛbhus, O Sons of Strength, O Sons of Indra, you have iron-helmets, a shining chariot and sturdy horses. Be gratified with the Soma in the third libation and give wealth.

(5) *Tr.* O brilliant, victorious, mighty Ṛbhus, staying together, accompanied by Indra, we invoke you.

(6) *Tr.* O Ṛbhus, accompanied by Indra, may the worshipper, whom you protect, obtain sacrificial horse and excellent capability.

(7) *Tr.* O Ṛbhus, O Vājas, praised by the worshippers, possessed of knowledge, direct us the ways so that we can cross through all quarters safely.

(8) *Tr.* O Indra, O Ṛbhus, O Vājas, confer upon us boons for wealth and for acquisition of glory.

VII 48

(1) *Tr.* O Ṛbhus, who posses a chariot beneficial to the world, who stay in the firmament, who are possessed of wealth, who are expert in the art of leading, Soma has been offered to you. Turn the horses of your chariot, deligent in work and capable, in our direction.

(2) *Tr.* O Ṛbhus, vanquishers of enemies, who render the worshippers great and capable, may the brother named Vāja amongst you give us help in battle and enable us to kill the demon like Vṛtra.

(3) *Tr.* May the overpowering brothers Ṛbhu, Vibhavan and Vāja, who have become conquerers of enemies and slayers of enemies through the help of Indra, extirpate the might of the enemies.

(4) *Tr.* O praiseworthy, Ṛbhus, glorified by the worshippers, protect us and give us wealth and nourishment. O gods, you bless us and protect us.

XII

S.A. Upadhyay

I 20

(1) *Tr.* This hymn, the bestower of gifts, is composed for the godly family by the eloquent priests with (their) mouth.

Notes—In this modest effort of presenting the annotated translation, I have derived much help from all the existing material on Ṛgvedic studies—in particular from the works of Sāyaṇācārya, Oldenberg, Geldner, Renou and Velankar to whom I owe a debt of gratitude. The details of the different deeds of the Ṛbhus are not discussed in the notes as it is proposed to include them in an andependent article. *devāya janmane* refers to the group of the three Ṛbhus. At IX. 108.8b, the expression refers to the gods in general. For *āsayā* cf. *bhāramyaṅguśam āsyena* at I.61.3b; *vacāṁsyāsā.... takṣam* at VI. 32.1 d etc. For *stoma* in the context of the Ṛbhus cf. *stomaḥ dade* at IV. 37.3B; also IV. 36.7ab. The hymn is *ratnadhātama* only through the favour of the Ṛbhus, who are described as *ratnadhā* at IV. 44.6D; IV. 35.7c. cf. also *ṛbhuḥ vasur dadiḥ at* I. 110.7; *maho naro draviṇasaḥ* at IV. 34.5b; *ṛbhavo vājaratnāḥ* at IV. 35.5; *Vājaśrutāsaḥ naraḥ at* iv. 36 5b. On account of their liberal gift, Ṛbhus h ve been addressed as *sūrayaḥ* at IV. 37.7c; also *maghavānaḥ* at VII. 48.1b. For *ratnadhātama* stoma cf. *vasuvidaḥ dhiyaḥ* at VIII. 60.12d; *kṛdhi dhiyaṁ jaritre vājaratnām* at X.42.7d etc.

(2) *Tr.* They, who, for Indra, fashioned with (their) mind the two bay horses that are yoked by (mere) word, attained sacrifice through (their) works.

Notes—(a) – *vacoyuj* is exclusively used for Indra's horses. This adjective explains the significance of *suyuj* at IV. 33.10b. The *harī* of Indra are also called *brahmayuj* at III. 35.4a; VIII. 2.27a. (b)—*tatakṣur manasā*—cf. *harī manasā niratakṣata* at III. 60.2c; also *harī medhayā...cakruḥ* at IV. 33.10ab; *śacyā harī ataṣṭa* at IV. 35.5c. For *takṣ* in context of *harī* and the Ṛbhus cf. I. 111.1b. c)—The Ṛbhus, though mortals, were deemed as meriting a sacrifice on account of their artistic skill and deftness; cf. I. 20.8bc; I. 161.6d; III. 60.1 cd etc. The word *śamī* ('a pious work') is generally used in the context of a human worshipper who employs *śamī* as a supplement to his hymn; cf. II. 31.6d; IX. 74.7c etc. In case of the Ṛbhus, their *śamī* has helped them to attain godly status and to acquire a share in the sacrifice; cf. *saudhanvanāso amṛtatvam erire...śamībhiḥ* at III. 60.3cd; *śamībhir amṛtatvam āśuḥ* at IV 33.4d.

(3) *Tr.* They fashioned a light-rolling and all-round moving chariot for Nāsatyas. They fashioned the cow Sabardughā.

Notes—(a)—Read *nāsatī ā bhi am* for metre; at IV. 37.8b read nāsatī (a. c)—The cow *Sabardughā* (also known as Viśvarūpā) is fashioned for Bṛhaspati; cf. I. 161.6b; IV. 33.8b etc. The Ṛbhus fashioned a *suvṛt* (I. 111.1a; IV. 33.8a; IV. 36.2a) *tricakra* (IV. 36.1b), *parijman*, *avihvarat* (IV. 36.2b) and *sukha* chariot for the Aśvins, the ever-willing helpers, to enable them to go quickly anywhere. The Chariot, thus, is rightly described as *ukthya* (IV. 36.1a) and *vidathesu pravācya* (IV. 36.5c). The different epithets suggest the mechanic deftness of the Ṛbhus. The adjectives *suvṛt* (exeept at X. 70.3c; X. 85.20B; X. 107.11B) and *tricakra* (except at VIII. 58.3a) where Uṣas may have been intended) are exclusively used of the chariot of the Aśvins.

(4) *Tr.* The honest Ṛbhus, whose chants are unfailing, through (their) work, made (their) parents young, once again.

Notes—For the rejuvenation of the elders cf. I. 110.8d; I. 111.1c; I. 161.3c, 7b; IV. 33.2ab; IV. 34.9a; IV. 35.5a; IV. 36.3cd. (b)—The Ṛbhus are called *satyamantrāḥ* as the chants employed by them for achieving their purpose are always effective at VII. 76.4d the *pitṛs* i.e. the Aṅgirases are called *satyamantra ṛjuyavaḥ ṛjuyu-ṛjuyu ṛjuṛbhavaḥ* : cf. *ṛjukratuḥ* (*indraḥ*) at I. 81.7b. (c)—Read *viṣṭī akrata* for metre. Viṣṭī (inst. sing. of viṣṭi the root viś) 'by skilful work;' cf. *arcanti nārir* apaso na *viṣṭibhiḥ* at I. 92.3a.

(5) *Tr.* Your intoxicating Soma-juices have united themselves with Indra associated with the Maruts and with the Ādityas, the kings.

Notes—The reference is to the third *savana* which is common to Ṛbhus, Indra, Ādityas, etc; cf. III. 64.4a, 5ab; IV. 35.1d etc.

(6) *Tr.* And you, again made fourfold that cup, the new work of the God Tvaṣṭṛ.

Notes—camasam caturaḥ akarta—cf. I. 110.3CD; 5ab; I. 161.2a, 4c; III. 60.2a; IV. 33.6cd; IV. 35.2d, 3a, 4ab, 5b; IV. 36.4a.

(7) *Tr.* Such as you are, bring jewels to us; thrice sevenfold (jewels) to the presser of Soma. (Bring) each and every (jewel) on account of (our) good praises.

Notes—ratnāni dhattana—The Ṛbhus are called *ratnadhā* (IV. 34.6d; IV. 35.7c) *Vājaratna* (IV. 34.2b; IV. 35.4d) and *mahaḥ draviṇasaḥ nṛ* (IV. 34.5b)—*trirā saptāni*, according to sāyaṇa, refers to their 'three-fold jewels and seven-fold sacrifices' or to 'thrice seven sacrifices'. The expression suggests abundance of jewels; cf. *tribhiḥ saptebhir avatām* at VIII. 59.5d.

(8) *Tr.* The priets upheld (their life); through good work, they obtained a share in the sacrifice among the gods.

Notes—(a)—Supply *prāṇān* i.e. they, though mortals, made themselves immortal. This is clarified in bc. Oldenberg (Noten

I, p. 17) understands *bhāgam* as the object of *adhārayanta* in view of VIII. 36.1d; VIII, 100.1c. *vahnayaḥ* are the Ṛbhus who are called vāghataḥ at I. 110.4a, III. 60.4c. bc)—cf. *svapaso yajñiyam bhāgam aitana* at I. 161.6d; *Saudhanvanāso amṛtatvam erire viṣṭvī śamībhiḥ sukṛtaḥ sukṛtyayā* at IV. 35.8a; also 2a above; III. 60.1d, 2abc. 4d; IV. 36.4c etc.

I 110

(1) *Tr.* My work was extended (earlier); once again, it is indeed extended; the most sweet prayer is recited for the praise (of the Ṛbhus). This ocean (of Soma) is here for all gods; be, indeed, well pleased, O Ṛbhus (with Soma) which is offered with the svāhā call.

Notes—(a)—*apaḥ*, in view of b refers to the pious activity of composing a hymn. The root *tan* is often associated with a hymn; cf. *dhiyam atnata* at I. 180.16a; *viśvā matir ā tatāne* at VII. 29.3c; *dhiyā ā tanudhvam* at X. 10.2a; also V. 47.6a; X. 106.1b; II. 28.5c etc. *apaḥ*, according to sāyaṇa refers to sacrifice; cf. *yajñaḥ...tataḥ* at X. 130.1a; *yajñasya tantuḥ ātataḥ* at X. 57.2ab etc.; also cf. VI. 9.2a, 3a; VIII. 13.14c, 18b; VIII. 59.6d; VIII. 92.21b; IX. 102.7c; X. 90.15c. At VII. 10.2b *tanvānāḥ* is the common property for both *yajña* and *manman*.

(b)—For *svādiṣṭhā dhitiḥ* cf. *svādiṣṭhayā girā at* III. 53.2d; *vacaḥ svādoḥ svādīyaḥ* at I. 114.6ab. Indra is requested to bestow *svadmanam vacaḥ* at II. 21.6d. (c)—refers to the third *savana* which belongs to all gods. (d)—Supply *andhasaḥ*. This is an irregular *Jagatī Pāda* with 13 letters.

(2) *Tr.* When you as some wise and forward-moving relaions of mine had set out (on your way), seeking nourishment, you, O Sons of Sudhanvan, reached the home of the worshipful Savitṛ after much of wandering.

Notes—(a)—*ābhogaya* (*ā*+*bhoga*+*ya*) occurs only at this passage; ābhoga at VII. 94.12c refers to a person who is given to undue and over enjoyment (and not a serpent as Grassmann explains in his Wörterbuch zum Rig-Veda); also cf. ābhog at I. 113.5b. (b)—*āpayaḥ*—Both Sudhanvan the father of the Ṛbhus and Kutsa, the Ṛṣi of the hymn, were the descendants of

Aṅgiras. *a-pāka*—'not simple' i.e. 'wise.' Agni is called *su-apāka* at VI. 11.4z; VI. 12.2a. *prāñca* (*pra-ac*) i.e. 'moving forward.' Geldner understands *apāka* and *prāñca* as meaning 'westward' and 'eastward' respectively. (c)—*bhūmanā* (inst.) is from *bhūman* (m. bhu) meaning 'abundance, fullness.' The other instrumental form viz. *bhūna* (note the shift of the accent) which occurs at X. 82.4b and X. 149.3b, has probably, the adverbial sense, though at X. 82.4b Sāyaṇa interprets *bhūmnā* as *stotrena*. Is it that *bhūmnā* is employed for preserving the *Triṣṭubh* cadence ? Howerver at X. 82.4b, the line, though having 12 syllables, has the cadence of *Triṣṭubh* which is the metre of the whole hymn. Also note *bhūman* (neu.) means 'the earth.' (d)—dāśuṣaḥ—(from *dāsvas*, perfect participle from *dāś*) *savituḥ*—cf. *dāśvān indraḥ at* X. 104.6d; *varuṇāya dāśuṣe* at X. 65.5a; *viśve devāsaḥ. dāśvāṁsaḥ* at 3.7bc.

(3) *Tr.* When you came invoking Agohya, then Savitṛ assigned immortality to you. You, certainly, made that cup, the drinking vessel of Asura, fourfold (though) it was one (only).

Notes—(b)—*agohya* (one who cannot be concealed) refers to Savitṛ; cf. I. 161.11C, 13B; IV. 33.7A. Indra (VIII. 98.4b) and Agni (X. 64.3a) are also called *agohya.* (c)—*Asura* is Tvaṣṭṛ. Elsewhere the cup is described as *devapāna* (I. 161.5b; IV. 35.5b). For the root *bhakṣ* in the sense of 'to drink' cf. *kalaśāḥ abhakṣayam* at X. 167.3d; also X. 167.4a. (cd)—See notes on I. 20.6.

(4) *Tr.* The priests having worked with pious activity and strength reached immortality though being mortals. The Ṛbhus, the sons of Sudhanvan, shining line the Sun, became united (with their goal) in a year, on account of (their) thoughts.

Notes—(a)—*viṣṭvī* is absolitive of the root viś 'to work.' For '*śamī*' see notes on I. 20.2c. For taraṇitva of the Ṛbhus cf. *taraṇibhiḥ*...pari *dyām*...babhuvuḥ, at IV. 33.1 cd; also v. 6 below. vāghataḥ—cf. III. 60.4c; *vahnayaḥ* at I. 20.8a. (c)—*sūracakṣas* in the context of the Ṛbhus occurs only here; elsewhere it qualifies the *harī* of Indra I. 16.1c). *viśve devāḥ* (I. 89.7c) and the ordinary gods (VII. 66.10a), Geldner translates as 'die sonnenaugigen' (the sun-eyed ones) which according to Gonda (Epithets in the Rig-Veda, Hague 1959, p. 122) is a quality which characterises the Ṛbhus as divine. (d)—*dhītibhiḥ* i.e. 'on account of their intelligence.' Or, construe *dhītibhiḥ* sam *apṛcyanta* i.e. 'became united with (their thoughts-goal).'

(5) *Tr.* Being praised, the Ṛbhus with the sharp instrument measured out the one yawning vessel, like a plot of land, imploring the highest (reward) and desiring fame among the immortals.

Notes—(a)—*tejana*—(the root tij) occurs only here in the Ṛgveda. It refers to some sharp (tij) instrument with which the Ṛbhus measured (as it were) the cup before making it fourfold; also cf. Atharvaveda I. 2.4; VI. 49.1. (b)—*jehamānam*—(the root jih to throw out) 'yawning' i.e. 'having a broad opening or mouth;' cf. *vijehamānaḥ...jihvām* (of Agni) at VI. 3.4c. Sāyaṇa explains it as 'striving (for the sacrificial rites).' (c)—*upamam nādhdmānaḥ* is clarified by d. (cd)—cf. *indreṇa yātha sarathaṁ sute sacāḥ/atho vaśānāṁ bhavatha saha śriyā* at III. 60.4ab.

(6) *Tr.* With knowledge, we will offer a hymn to the heroes of the mid-region as ghee with a ladle. The Ṛbhus, who with their strength clung to the strength of this father, have climbed up the reward of the hevenly region.

Notes—(a)—possibly is a *Triṣṭubh* pāda in view of its cadence. (cb)—*manīṣām juhavāma*—cf. *giraḥ...juhomi* at II. 27.1ab; *manma—juhvati* at II. 41.18cd. (c)—*taraṇitvā*, according to Geldner, refers to 'the punctuality.' It is to be constructed as both accusative and instrumental—*asya pituḥ* refers to *camsasya pituḥ* i.e. Tvaṣṭṛ (Geldner) or to *Sūrya* (*Sāyaṇa*). *asya* is not accented as it is unemphatic. (d)—*vājam*—'prize' i.e. the heaven—immortality—cf. *taraṇbhiḥ...pari dyām...babhūvuḥ* at IV. 33.1cd. Sāyaṇa understands it as referring to 'soma-offerings'. *vājam aruhan*—cf. IX. 83.5c; IX. 86.40c.

(7) *Tr.* Ṛbhu, on account of (his) strength, is new Indra to us; Ṛbhu with Vājas and Vasus is a good giver. O gods, with

your help, let us, on a favourable day, overpower the attacks of those who do not press soma.

Notes—(a)—like v. 6a, possibly is a *Triṣṭubh Pāda*; or read *navya* an to make up the *Jagatī* cadence. Grassmanns reading, *navyasā* makes up the *Jagātī* cadence, yet it is unpreferrable as it is against the traditional text and the idea in *navyasā* śavasā is less emphatic than *navīyān indraḥ*. Aśvins (IV. 43.3 ab). Savitṛ (VII. 34.4b), Soma (IX. 88.4a), Manu (X. 84.5a) etc. are compared to Indra; also read I. 131.2; IV. 39.5a; IV. 42.8. cd; X. 139.3d; X. 166.2ab etc. (b)—See notes on I. 20.1c. Perhaps a pun on *Vājebhiḥ* (with Vājas; with rewards) and *asubhiḥ* (with Vasus; with wealth) is intended. (c)—*priye ahani* refers to the day of sacrifice; cf. VII. 56.2 ab. (d)—*pṛtsuti* (*pṛt+suti su*) 'march for battle' i.e. 'an attack; cf. I. 169.2c; V. 4. 1d; X. 38.1a.

(8) *Tr.* O Ṛbhus, you formed a cow out of the hide and (thus) once again, united the mother with the calf. O Sons of Sudhanvan, with (your) good skill, you, O heroes, made the old parents young.

Notes—(a)—*Niścarmaṇaḥ* refers either to the hide of a dead cow or to the cow who had lost her blood and flesh and thus having only hide, as it were, over her skeleton; cf. I. 161.7a, III, 60.2b; IV. 36.4b. *apiṁśata*—the root *piṁś* is often associated with this feat of enlivening the cow; cf. I. 161.10b; IV. 33.4b. (b)—cf. *takṣan vatsāya mātaram* at I. 111.1d. (cd)—cf. I. 20.4; I.111.1c; I. 161.7b; IV. 33.3ab; IV. 34.9a; IV. 35.5a; IV. 36.3cd.

(9) *Tr.* With Vājas, help us in the winning of rewards; O Indra, in the company of Ṛbhu, give us the lovely wealth. May Mitra, Varuṇa, Aditi, sindhu, Pṛthivī and Dyauḥ grant that to us.

Notes—(a)—A pun on the word *vājebhiḥ* is intended. 'With Vājas' (i.e. the three Ṛbhus), help us in a battle with rewards (*vājebhiḥ*). For Vāja standing for three Ṛbhus cf IV. 35.6b.

I 111

(1) *Tr.* (The Ṛbhus), who are active with (their) wisdom, fashioned a good-rolling chariot; they fashioned the two bay-horses that carry Indra and possess mighty wealth. The Ṛbhus fashioned the young age for (their) elders, they fashioned an accompanying mother for the calf.

Notes—(a)—*ratham* is for the Aśvins; see notes on I. 20.3. Note that every Pāda begins with the unaugmented form *takṣan*. The poet uses the root *takṣ* in the first three stanzas of this hymn. *apasaḥ*—cf. I. 161.6d; IV. 33.1d, 8d. (b)—*vṛṣaṇvasū* (Bv. compound) 'mightily wealthy;' the *harī* of Indra are so called as they lead to the acquisition of mighty wealth, cf. Indra is called *vasupati* at I. 9.9a; I. 170.5a. etc. *Vasudā* at VIII. 99.4a. (also note that a cow is called *Vasupatnī* a at I. 164.27a). The epithet *vṛṣaṇvasū* is generally used of the Aśvins. (c)—See note on I. 20.4. (d)—See notes on I. 110.8b.

(2) *Tr.* Fasion out for us, the skilful strength for the sacrifice: (fashion out) the food accompained by good progeny for wisdom and skill. Give to our clan that good Indra-like strength so that we may dwell with (our) people consisting of all heroes.

Notes—(a)—has 13 syllables and a defective cadence. (b)—cf. IX. 36.3c. *kratve dakṣāya* is an oft-recurring phrase; cf. IV. 37.2d; V. 43.5b; IX. 100.5a; IX. 109.2b; X. 57.4b. Supply *takṣata* to complete the sentence.

(3) *Tr.* Fashion out, for us, on all sides, O Ṛbhus, the acquisition (of wealth), the acquisition for (our) chariot, the acquisition for (our) race-horse, O heroes. May you, everyday, grant us the victorious acquisition, overcoming a relation as well as stranger in battles.

Notes—The repetition of *Sātim* is for emphasis. (a)—has defective cadence. (c)—*jaitrīṁ sātiṁ meheta*—cf. *jaitraṁ kratum...vṛṇmahe* at X. 36.10cd. *sam maheta*, occuring only here, is either 2nd person plu. in view of *takṣata* in a or 3rd person sing, as sāyaṇa construes. (d)—*jāmi*, here, is a relative who is inimical; cf. *jāmim ajāmim pra mṛṇihi śatrūn* at IV. 4.5d;

also VI. 19.8d; VI. 25.3a etc. *sakṣaṇim* used with accusative; cf. IX. 110.1b; or as Geldner, supply *vīram.*

(4) *Tr.* I invoke Ṛbhukṣan Indra for help, (I invoke) the Ṛbhus, the Vājas, the Maruts, both Mitra and Varuṇa and indeed, the Aśvins for a drink of Soma; may they impel us on to the acquisition, wisdom and victory.

Notes—(a)—For restoring *Jagatī* cadence, read, as Oldbenberg suggests, *Indaram a hva ūtaye. ṛbhukṣan*—'great'—Sāyaṇa. Indra is often called *Ṛbhukṣan* (ṛbhu+the root kṣi) 'the ruler of Ṛbhus' i.e. 'powerful.' (d)—*hinvantu dhiye*—I. 27.11c; or construe *dhiye* to a hymn which is a result of acquisition and victory.

(5) *Tr.* May Ṛbhu well sharpen (us) for the acquisition of loot; may Vāja the victorious one in battles, help us. May Mitra, Varuṇa, Aditi, Sindhu, Pṛthvī and Dyauḥ grant that (wealth) to us.

Notes—(b)—*samaryajit* occurs only here. samarya '(a battle)' is from sam+the root *ar* (to go); according to Sāyana, from *sa-marya.* (cd)—See I.110.9cd.

I 161

(1) *Tr.* Why, indeed, the best one, the youngest one has come to us ? With what message, he comes ? What was that which we spoke ? We have not blamed the cup which is of great origin. O brother Agni, we have spoken only about the origin of the wood.'

Notes—According to Sāyaṇa, Agni, on seeing the three Ṛbhus exactly resembling each other while performing a sacrifice and about to drink Soma, assumed the similar form. The three Ṛbhus, being confused at seeing the fourth one, inquire. 'Is the eldest one or is the youngest one come to us ?' In b, it appears that the Ṛbhus recognise the fourth one to be a messenger of gods. However, it is not necessary to presume that Agni had assumed a form resembling to that of the three Ṛbhus. *śreṣṭhaḥ* and *yaviṣṭhaḥ*, thus refer to Agni. (c) *camasam*—Wilson's rendering 'ladle' is not very satisfactory. (cd)—indicates the Ṛbhus' apprehension at the arrival of Agni. They fear that the gods might have sent instructions prohibiting them from speaking heedlessly about the cup of Tvaṣṭṛ. The next stanza, however, makes it clear that Agni has come with a favourable and encouraging mission. The speech of the Ṛbhus about the cup must have been quite heedless, cf. c and verse 5.

(2) *Tr.* (Agni speaks) "Make (this) one cup into four (cups); that the gods have told you; for that I have come to you. O Sons of Sudhanvan, if you do this, you will become worthy of a sacrifice alongwith the gods."

Notes—(b)—*tat* refers to the work of fashioning four cups out of the single cup of Tvaṣṭṛ. Sāyaṇa understands also the other works like fashioning a chariot, horses etc. as implied by the word *tat*.

(3) *Tr.* What you replied to Agni, the messenger, (is this): "A horse is to be fashioned and a chariot is to be prepared here. A cow is to be fasioned and the two are to be made young. O brother when we have done these (deeds) we follow you."

Notes—(b)—*aśvaḥ*—see notes on v. 7 cd. (c)—Read *yuvaśā kartva a dvā* for preserving the *Jagatī* cadence. The stanza helps us to determine the order of different deeds performed by the Ṛbhus.

(4) *Tr.* Ṛbhus, having done that, you asked: "Where has he, the messenger, who had come to us, gone ?" When Tvaṣṭṛ observed the four cups that were fashioned, immediately then, he hid himself among the goddesses.

Notes—a and c have irregular cadence; the eighth letter is short in both these pādas. Tvaṣṭṛ's relations are worth observing: here he feels ashamed; in the next verse he is angry; at IV. 33.5, 6 he admires the skill of the Ṛbhus. (d)—*gnāsv antar ny ānaja*—"He annointed himself amongst the goddesses i.e. he, feeling ashamed, considered himself a woman." (Sāyaṇa).

(5) *Tr.* When Tvaṣṭṛ spoke, "We shall strike them who blamed the cup, the drinking vessel of the gods." they

assumed other names at the time of Soma—(sacrifice); the maiden protected them with other names.

Notes—(a)—see notes on v. 10. (b)—*camasam devapānam*- cf. IV. 35.5b a and b have irregular cadence. (c)—*anyā nāmāni*—Sāyaṇa finds herein the origin of the names of the priests viz. *Hotṛ*, *Adhvaryu* and *Udgātṛ* (d)—*kanyā*, according to Sāyaṇa, refers to the self-engendering mother of the Ṛbhus (and not only 'mother' as Geldner represents). Possibly, *kanyā* is the daughter of Tvaṣṭṛ.

(6) *Tr.* Indra yoked the (two) bay horses; the Aśvins (yoked) the chariot. Bṛhaspati drove out (the cow called) Viśvarūpā. When you—Ṛbhu, Vibhvan and Vāja went to the gods, you, the skilful ones, secured the sacrificial share.

Notes—the things fashioned by the Ṛbhus are accepted and put to use by the gods. (c)—cf. v. 7d. (c)—cf. *śamībhir yajñam āśata* at I. 20.2c; *ābhajanta sukṛtyayā / bhāgam deveṣu yajñiyam* at I. 20.8bc; also III. 60.1cd.

(7) *Tr.* You with (your) thoughts, made the cow to come out from the hide; you made those aging (parents) young. O sons of Sudhanvan, you fashioned a horse; you having yoked the chariot, went to the gods.

Notes - (a)—IV. 36.4b; read notes on I. 110.8a, For *dhītibhiḥ* cf. *yayā dhiyā gām ariṇita carmaṇaḥ* at III. 60.2b. (b)—Read notes on I. 110.8cd. (c)—aśvam for Indra or for themselves, in view of d. In case of Indra generally the dual form *harī* is used; also cf. *aśvaḥ* kartvaḥ in v. 3b.

(8) *Tr.* You spoke : "Drink this water or drink, indeed this (Soma) which is filtered through Muñja-grass." (The gods then said) : "O sons of sudhanvan, if you do not delight in that, you may, indeed, rejoice yourself in the third libation."

Notes—(ab)—constitutes the speech of the Ṛbhus uttered sarcastically to the gods expressing their discontentment at the first two libations only. c is the speech of the gods. According to Sāyaṇa the whole stanza constitutes the speech of the gods. a has 13 letters. (b) *muñjavejanam* refers to the Soma-juice filtered through the sieve of Muñja-grass; cf. Śatapatha Brāhmaṇa IV. 3.3.16. The word *muñja* is not used in the Ṛgveda elsewhere, The hiding reptiles in the *Muñja* grass are refered to as *muñjāḥ* at I. 191.3c.

(9) *Tr.* One spoke : "The water is the best one." The other one said : "Agni is the best." Another one declared the thundering weather (to be best) from amongst many (seasons). Speaking the unfailing (words), your carved out the cups.

Notes—a, b and c have irregular cadence. The word *abravīt* is repeated at the end of the first three pādas : a, b and c are the speeches of the three Ṛbhus. Each one gives the root-credit of helping the act of making the Tvaṣṭṛ's cups fourfold to different, objects. (c)—*vadharyantīm* (participle from *vadhary*)—'(the rainy season) which throws a weapon' i.e. the lightning; also read Wackernagel, Altindische Grammatik, Band II, 2, 111 *vadha* (mas.) *vadhana* (mas.) mean 'a weapon.'

10. *Tr.* One drives the lame cow to the water; the other one minces the flesh which is brought in a basket; one carried away the dung up to the sun-set. Have the parents helpes the sons ?

Notes—*śroṇām gām*—Nowhere else the cow enlivened by the Ṛbhus is referred to as *sṛoṇa* or crippled. *śroṇām*, therefore, is to be interpreted in the broad sense : 'lame' i.e. 'unable to walk on account of extreme weakness'; cf. notes on I. 110.8a. (b)—*yat saṁvatsam Ṛbhavo mā apiṁṣan* at IV. 33.4b. *sūnā* the (*siv*) is a wickerbasket in which the flesh is purchased. (c)—nimṛuc (*ni*+the root *mṛuc* 'to go down)' refers to the evening time; cf. a *nimṛuca uṣasaḥ* at I. 151.5d; *sūryasya nimṛci* at X. 151.5c. *śakṛdeko apābharat*—The *śatṛt* of the cow is referred to only here. The accumulated *śakṛt* (mala) in the cows body not only obstructed her nourishment but made her extremely weak—almost dead. The clever Ṛbhus removed the *śakṛt* and thus enlivened the cow.

(11) *Tr.* For him; you laid out the grass on the heights and water in the depths, with good skill, O heroes. That (act viz. that) you slept at the house of Agohya that (act)—you, to-day, now do not follow, O Ṛbhus.

Notes—(a)—*asmai* i.e. for the people. (ab)—cf. *dhanvā tiṣṭhannoṣadhir nimnam āpaḥ* at IV. 33.7 d. (c)—cf. v. 13 below and IV. 33.7 ab.

(12) *Tr.* Having enveloped the creatures, when you moved about, where were your dear parents ? You cursed him who seized you by the arm; he who spoke, to him, you retorted.

Notes—(a)—Geldner construes : *sammīlya, bhuvanā parya sarpata* i.e. 'when, with closed eyes, you encompassed the creatures.' (b)—*pitarā* i.e. the sun and the moon (Sāyaṇa), probably the heaven and the earth are meant. (c)—*karasna* (*kara+sna san*) is formed with the addition of—*sna* which is graded form of suffix—*san*; cf. *vadhasna*. (Sāyaṇa alternatively explains. 'He who speaks harshly (pra) to you, you censure him.' The prefix pra is used twice to indicate that the Ṛbhus replied in the same tone.

(13). *Tr.* Ṛbhus, you who had slept, asked : "O Agohya, who, now, has awakened us ?" The ram spoke of the dog as the awakener. You have, to-day, shown yourself after a year.

Notes—(c) *basta* is used only here.

(14) *Tr.* The Maruts go to the heaven; Agni on the eath, this wind goes to the atmosphere; Varuṇa goes to the waters and oceans—seeking you, O Children of strength.

III 60

(1) *Tr.* Here and there, through (their) mind, relationship and knowledge have the Uśijs known these (deeds) of yours by which supernatural skills, you, the sons of Sudhanvan, assuming another form according to impluse, attained the share in the sacrifice, O heroes.

Notes—(a)—*badhutā* refers to the human nature of the Ṛbhus; cf. *saudhanvanāḥ* in d. (b)—*Uśijaḥ* are the ancestors of the poet who had learnt about the skill of the Ṛbhus (c)—*pratijūtivarpasaḥ* '(assuming a form according to (their) impulses)' occurs only here. This refers to the different forms assumed by the Ṛbhus when Tvaṣṭṛ sought to kill them for blaming the *devapāna camasa*; cf. I. 161.5d. *varpas* is a form assumed through craft (*māyā*); cf., *varpanti* of Indras as opposed to his *śardhanti* at III. 34.3ab. (d)—see notes on I. 20.8bc.

(2) *Tr.* O Ṛbhus, you have well-attained the godhead by that, by which arts you divided the cups, by which thought you carved out the cow from the hide, by which mind, you fashioned the two bay-horse.

Notes—(a)—*śacīhiḥ apiṁśata*—cf. *śacyākarta camasam devapānam* at IV. 35.5b; also see notes on I. 20.6. (b)—see notes on I. 20.3c; I. 110.1a and I. 161.7a. (c)—see notes on I. 20.2b.

(3) *Tr.* The Ṛbhus well-obtained the friendship of Indra; the sons of Manu have betaken themselves as artists. The sons of Sudhanvan, the skilful ones, have attained immortality having worked with pious activity and through artistic deeds.

Notes—(a)—The poet has used the verb as in the first three stanzas. (b)—*manor napātaḥ* indicates the human nature of the Ṛbhus. *apasaḥ*—cf. IV. 33.1d. Ṛbhus are often called *svapasaḥ* I. 161. 6d; IV. 33.8d and *suhastāḥ* at IV. 33.8d, 9b; VII. 35.12a: X. 66.10 a on account of their skill. (d)—Ṛbhus' activity is often referred to as śamī; cf. I. 20.2c; I. 110.4a; IV. 33.4d.

(4) *Tr.* With Indra, in the same chariot, you go to the pressed out Soma-juice; now be you in association with the glory of (your) wishes. O bards, O Sons of Sudhanvan, nothing is there to measure out your skilful deeds, heroic acts, O Ṛbhus.

Notes—(cd)—The deeds and the achievement of the Ṛbhus are praiseworthy; cf. *tad vo Vājā Ṛbhavaḥ supravācanam*/

deveṣv abhavan mahitvanam at IV. 36.3ab; also IV. 36.4cd. The inimitable acts of the Ṛbhus justify their attainment of immortality.

(5) *Tr.* O Indra, with the Ṛbhus and the Vājas, drink in both the hands, the soma which is wellswollen (with water) and pressed'out. O liberal one, being incited by (our) hymn, rejoice at the home of the worshipper, together with the sons of Sudhanvan, the heroes.

Notes—(a)—has 13 letters. (b)—*gabhastyoḥ*—Locative in the sense of instrumental *gabhastyoḥ* may be constructed with sutam; cf. *gabhastipūtam....Somam* at II. 14.8c; also *dadhanvire gabhastyoḥ at* VII. 13.7c; *mṛjyamāno gabhastyoḥ* IX. 20.6b; IX. 36.4; IX. 65.6b etc.

(6) *Tr.* O Indra, rejoice strongly, here, together with Ṛbhu and Vāja, in this our libation, O much-praised one. These meadows (of Soma) have spread out for you in accordance with the ordinances of gods and laws of men.

Notes—(b)—*śacyā* is adverbially used; cf. *śacyā dhamantam* at VIII. 96.13c or construe it as instrumental: 'on account of (your) strength' or 'with sacī, (Sāyaṇa). (c)—svasara is a region where one moves in order to find one's food; cf. viśve devāso apturaḥ/sutamāganta *tūrṇayaḥ*/usrā iva svasarāṇi at I. 3.8. Sāyaṇa understands svasarāṇi as 'days.' Here *svasarā* refers to the profuse quantity of *Soma*: Cf. VI. 58.10d; VIII. 99.1d etc. Renou compares Avestic vastra 'pasture' (Yasht 35.7) and explains svasara as su-vasara (the root vas-to graze; cf. the Indo-European root wes—to graze) which is reduced to svasara; read: Renou, Vedic *Svasara* in Vishveshvaranand Indological Journal, vol I, No. 1, March, 1963, pp. 37-9.

(7) *Tr.* O Indra, come here, striving for the worshipful hymn of the singer, together with the Ṛbhus and the Vājas; knowing a thousand ways, (come to the call of the sacrifice) with hundred ardent desires for the son of Āyu.

Notes—(a)—has 13 letters. (b)—*Stomam...yajñiyam*—cf. *dhiyam yajñiyam* at X. 101.9a.

IV 33

(1) *Tr.* To Ṛbhus, I send forth (my) hymn like a messenger; I pray the śvaitarī cow to spread out itself—(to the Ṛbhus) who, the skilful artists, impelled by the wind (as it were), in a moment, surrounded the heaven with (their) quick zeal.

Notes—(b)—*śvaitarīm* (*vṛddhi* formation from *śvetara*), dhenum—'a white cow' i.e. white milk of the cow, which is to be spread out like a carpet for the Soma-juice; milk is referred to as *śukram upastiram* for *Soma* at IX. 62.28c. The idea in ab is that both the hymn (vācam) and the Soma—offering mixed with milk (*śvaitarīm dhenum*) are offered to the Ṛbhus. (c)—*vātajūtāḥ* i.e. 'swift as the wind.' This epithet which is generally used in the context of Agni and his horses, is employed here to emphasis the sense of *'sadyaḥ'* in d. *taraṇibhiḥ evaiḥ*—Sāyaṇa explains the expression as 'with swift horses.' (d)—*apasaḥ*—see notes on III. 60.3c.

(2) *Tr.* When the Ṛbhus have served (their) parents with service, work and skill, immediately then, they attained the friendship of the gods. The wise ones have brought prosperity to the prayer.

Notes—(ab)—see notes on I. 20.4. (b)—*pariviṣṭi* (*pari*+the root *viś*) is personal service; *veṣaṇā* (viś) is work in general and *daṁsanā* is the artistic skill. (c)—*dhīrāsaḥ* at IV. 36.2a.

(3) *Tr.* May they—Vāja, Vibhvan and Ṛbhu—who relish the sweet food, who are associated with Indra and who made (their) old aging parents, who were lying low like sacrificial posts, young, once again, favour our sacrifice.

Notes—(ab)—The simile is very apt; cf. IV. 36.3cd; also see notes on I. 20.4. (d)—*psaras* (*psa—psar*) is 'food', 'enjoyment.' Soma is called *mahī psaras* at IX. 2.2a; IX. 74. 3a and *devapsaras* (with irregular accent) at IX. 104.5b; IX. 105.5b. Vāyu is described as *supsarastama* at VIII. 26.24. a; even a hymn is referred to as *mahī—psaras* '(a great enjoyment)' of Varuṇa at I. 41.7c.

(4) *Tr.* When the Ṛbhus protected the cow for a year, when the Ṛbhus minced the flesh for a year (and) when they brought her life (to her) for a year—(then) with those holy acts, they obtained immortality.

Notes—(a) – *saṁvatsam—saṁvatsaram.* It appears that the Ṛbhus worked for one year to enliven the cow; see notes on I. 20.3c; I. 810.8a; I. 161.10. (b) *bhāsā*—the root bhās) is 'light;' in the present context 'life.'

(5) *Tr.* The eldest one said : "Let me make two cups."; the younger one said : "Let us make three." The youngest one spoke : "Let me make four." Tvaṣṭṛ admired that your speech, O Ṛbhus.

Notes—(d)—has 12 syllables; read quickly *sta* and *r* (i.e. *tnaṣṭarbhava*) so as to form one syllable to restore the Triṣṭubh measure. For Tvaṭṣṛ's reaction see notes on I. 161.4.

(6) *Tr.* The heroes spoke the unfailing (word); they did thus only; the Ṛbhus followed this their own will (in this case). Tvaṣṭṛ on seeing loved the four cups which were shining like (bright) days.

(7) *Tr.* When the Ṛbhus were sleeping (in the home) of Agohya for twelve days, enjoying in (his) hospitality, they made the fields fertile and carried forward the rivers. The plants stood up (i.e. grew) on the desert; the waters (followed down) the low (places).

Notes—(ab)—For Ṛbhu's sleeping at the abode of *Agohya* read I. 161.11 cd, 13ab. (cd)—See notes on I. 161.11ab.

(8) *Tr.* May those Ṛbhus, the good helpers, the good artists, the defthanded ones, who made the easy–rolling chariot which waits upon a hero and who (carved out) the all-impelling Visvarūpā cow, fashion out wealth for us.

Notes—(a)—*suvṛtam*—see notes on I. 20.3, *nareṣṭhām* occurs only here. At VII. 78.1d, the chariot of the Ṛbhus is called *naryam.* (b)—*viśvajuvām* occurs only here. (c)—a *takṣantu rayim*—cf. *atakṣata sātim* at I. 111.3a *rayim*...a *takṣata* at IV. 35.6cd; a...*rayim*...*takṣata vayah* at IV. 36.8d. the root takṣ is often used in the context of the Ṛbhus. (d)—*svapasaḥ suhastāḥ*—See notes on III. 60.3b. Note the alliteration in this *Pāda*.

(9) *Tr.* For the gods liked their work while pondering (over it) with (their) intelligence and attention. Vāja became the artist of the gods, Ṛbhukṣan of Indra and Vibhvan of Varuṇa.

Notes—(a)—The unparalalled acts of the Ṛbhus were duly appreciated by the gods; also read : *na vaḥ pratimai sukṛtāni vāghtaḥ/saudhanvānā Ṛbhavo vīryāṅi* ca at III 60.4cd. Not only the gods intelligently (abhikratvā manasā dīdhyānāḥ) approved the work of the Ṛbhus but also accepted them as their artists. (d)—has 12 letters; pronounce *indrasyarbhukṣā* to restore the Triṣṭubh measure.

(10). *Tr.* O Ṛbhus, you who delighting in (our) hymns, fashioned with (your own) intelligence, the two easily-yoked bay-coloured horses for Indra, bestow on us treasures and abundance of wealth like home-loving ones, the friendship.

Notes—(ab)—see notes on I. 20.2ab (d)—has 12 letters. For the simile and the use of *dhā* cf. II. 4.3b; VI. 15.2a etc.

(11) *Tr.* This time of the day (the gods) have appointed for your drink and enjoyment; the gods do not (accept) for friendship (any one) except one who toils (for them). Such as you are, O Ṛbhus, grant us riches at this third libation.

Notes—(a)—referes to the third *savana*; cf. (cb)—This is the moral lesson taught through the example of the Ṛbhus.

IV 34

(1) *Tr.* Ṛbhus, Vibhvan, Vāja and Indra—go towards this our sacrifice for bestowing rich gifts; for the goddess Dhiṣaṇā has fixed this time of the day for your drink. Your delights have gone together.

Notes—In this hymn, the Ṛbhus are invited to drink Soma at the third *Savana* and to grant liberal gifts. Except in v. 9, the deeds of the Ṛbhus are not referred to in this hymn.

(2) *Tr.* Knowing (your) births, O Possessors of valuable gifts, delight (yourself) according to the proper times, O Ṛbhus. Your delights and Purandhi have gone together. Send to us wealth comprising of good heroes.

Notes—(a)—construe *janmanaḥ* as genitive in the sense of accusative in view of *vid*; cf. VII. 99.1d; IX. 81.2cd; also read Oldenberg—Noten I. *Vājaratnāḥ*—Elsewhere the Ṛbhus are called *maho naro draviṇasaḥ* at v. 5b; *ratnadhāḥ.* at v. 6d; see notes on I. 20.1c.

(3) *Tr.* O Ṛbhus, this sacrifice, which you have received from ancient days like Manu, is prepared for you. The delighting (Soma drinks) have gone to you; and you, O Vājas, have become foremost of all.

(4) *Tr.* Now has come the time for rewarding rich gifts to your worshipper, O heroes. O Vājas, O Ṛbhus, drink; for you is given the great third libation for (your) delight.

(5) *Tr.* O Vājas, O Ṛbhuksan, O lords of great wealth, come near us, being praised. At the close of the day these drinks go to you as (the cows) who have delivered recently, to (their) home.

Notes—(d)—The simile suggests the eagerness and affection with which the drinks are offered to the Ṛbhus.

(6) *Tr.* O Sons of Strength, being invoked with homage, eome near to this sacrifice. O patrons, you who are givers of rich gifts and associated with Indra, together with (other gods) drink of this sweet (Soma) whose (lords) you are.

Notes (a) *napātaā śavasaḥ*—cf. I. 161.14d; IV. 35.la; 8c; IV. 37.4c. (c)—*sūrayaḥ*—cf. IV. 37.c. (d)—*ratnadhā*—see notes on I. 20.1c.

(7) *Tr.* O Indra, together with Varuṇa drink the Soma; O lover of hymns, drink in the company of the Maruts, in company of the first drinkers who drink in accordance

with the proper time and in association with the goddessesss, wives who are granters of riches.

Notes—*pādas* a and b begin with the word *sajoṣāḥ*—c and d end with the same word. (c)—*agrepābhiḥ* refers to the Ṛbhus; cf. *agrepā Ṛbhavaḥ* at v. 10c below. *ṛtupābhiḥ*—cf. *ṛtubhiḥ... mādayadhvam* at v. 2b above. (d)—*ratnadhābhiḥ*, the characteristic epithet to the Ṛbhus, here, belongs to *gnāspatnībhiḥ* and in v. 8 to *sindhubhiḥ*.

(8) *Tr.* O Ṛbhus, delight yourself in the company of Ādityas together with the Parvatas, in association with divine Savitṛ, and in the company of reward-bringing rivers.

Notes—All the four *Pādas* begin with the word *sajoṣāḥ*. (d)—The poet has used the word *ratnadhā* in 1b, 4b, 6d, 7d, 11d of this hymn.

(9) *Tr.* Those Ṛbhus, who with (their) help, (pleased) the Aśvins and the parents and who fashioned the cow and the two horses, the armours and the two worlds separately; those, the Vibhvans, the heroes who made good progeny.

Notes—The stanza is to be construed with the principal sentence *asme dhatta* in the next stanza. (c)—*aṁsatra*—The fashioning of armours by the Ṛbhus (for the gods as Sāyaṇa suggests) is referred to only here in the Ṛgveda.

(10) *Tr.* You, who hold treasure abounding in cows, booty, good horses, riches and ample food—may they—O Ṛbhus—the first drinkers, being delighted, give to us (that) and to those who praise (your) gifts.

Notes—The construction of verses 9 and 10 is anakoluthic; 10 ab is directly addressed to the Ṛbhus; 10 cd has *ṛbhavaḥ* as vocative though the verb *dhatta* is in the third person. (d)—refers to both the singers and the patrons.

(11) *Tr.* O Ṛbhus, do not be far away; we have never kept you thirsty; (be you) not blamed at this sacrifice. O gods, delight yourself with Indra, with Maruts and with kings for awarding gifts.

Notes—(ab)—Construe b as an independent sentence and *aniḥśastāḥ* as predicative adjective; or construe—*na vo titṛṣāma... asmin*-as one sentence and *aniḥśastāḥ* as vocative.

IV 35

(1) *Tr.* O Sons of strength, O Sons of Sudhanvan, O Ṛbhus, come here; do not be far away. For, in this libation is your reward; your delights have gone after Indra.

Notes—(b)—cf. IV. 34.11a. (c)—*ratnadheyam*—cf. v. 2a and 9a.

(2) *Tr.* Here has come the reward of the Ṛbhus; the drink of the well-pressed out Soma was (here); for, you made the one cup fourfold by (your) good work and skill.

Notes—(d)—cf. v. 3a; see notes on I. 20.6.

(3) *Tr.* You made the cup fourfold; you said, "O friend, distribute (these cups)." Then, O Vājas, O Ṛbhus, O deft-handed ones, you went to the path of immortality, the group of gods.

Notes—(b)—is addressed to Agni. vi *sikṣa* (desiderative of *śak* 'to distribute)' cf. *śikṣo śikṣasi dāśuṣe* VIII. 52.8b; *tvaṁ viśikṣuḥ* (*agne*) at 2a, 10d; Geldner's translation 'probiere' (test or rehearse) has a challenging note which, probably, is incompatible with the nature of the Ṛbhus and with the address *sakhe*. (cd)–cf. I. 161.2 (d)—*suhastāḥ*—see notes on III. 60.3b.

(4) *Tr.* Of what (material) was this cup which you made four-fold with (your) wisdom ? Now press out the libation for delight; O Ṛbhus, drink of this sweet Soma.

Notes—(a)—The cup was made of wood; cf. I. 161.1 cd. (b)—Ṛbhus are presented as the pressers of their own Soma, probably for consecrating the four cups.

(5) *Tr.* With strength you made the parents young; with strength you made the cup, the drinking-vessel of the gods. O Ṛbhus, O possessors of rich gifts, with strength,

you fashioned the two quick-running bay-horses that carry Indra.

Notes—Note the emphasis on the word *śacyā* which is used at the beginning of the first three *pādas*. (a)—See Notes on I. 20.4. (b)—See notes on I. 20.6; *camasam devapānam*—cf. I. 161.5b. (c)—See notes on I. 20.2b (d)—*vājaratnāḥ*—See notes on I. 20.1c.

(6) *Tr.* To him, who, at the end of the day, presses the strong libation for you, O Vājas, for (your) delight, fashion out O Ṛbhus, O strong ones, being delighted, a treasure consisting of all heroes.

Notes—(a)—has defective cadence. (cd)—*rayim...atakṣata*—see notes on IV. 33.8c.

(7) *Tr.* O lord of the bay-horses, you drank the pressed-out (Soma) in the morning, the midday libation belongs to you alone; O Indra, drink together with the reward-granting Ṛbhus whom you have made friends on account of (their) good deeds.

Notes—(c)—*Ṛbhubhiḥ....ratnadhebhiḥ*—see notes on I. 20.1c. (d)—cf. *indrasya sakhyam Ṛbhavaḥ sam ānaśuḥ* at III. 60.3a.

(8) *Tr.* O Sons of strength, you, who became gods with good work and who sat down in the heaven like eagles, give treasure (to us). O Sons of Sudhanvan, you became immotals.

Notes—(a)—cf. *saudhanvanāso amṛtatvam erire*|...*sukṛyayā* at III. 60.3cd.

(9) *Tr.* O deft-handed ones, the third libation, (your) reward, which you earned with (your) good work, is presented to you, O Ṛbhus. Drink this with delight like that of Indra.

Notes—(a)—cf. v. 1c, 2a. (b)—*suhastāḥ*—See notes on III. 60.3b.

IV 36

(1) *Tr.* The praiseworthy, three-wheeled chariot, created without horses, without reins, surrounds the space. That is your great declaration of godly (nature) that you, O Ṛbhus, nourish heaven and earth.

Notes—(a)—see notes on I. 20.3a *anaśvaḥ rathaḥ* cf. I. 112.12b; I. 120.10ab; the chariot of Maruts is similarly described at VI. 66.7; read : *aneno vo Maruto yamo astv anaśvaś cid yam ajatyarathiḥ/anavaso anabhiśū rajastūrvi rodasi pathyā yāti sādhan.* At I. 152.5a the Sun is described as *anaśvo jāto anabhiśur arvā.* Sometimes the chariot of the Aśvins is described as *jirāśva* as at I. 157.3b *ukthyaḥ*—cf. X. 41.1a. (b)—*tricakrḥ* is exclusively used for the chariot of the Aśvins; cf. I. 118.2b; I. 157.3a; I. 183.1b; VIII. 58.3a; X. 41.1b; X. 85.14b.

(2) *Tr.* O Vājas, O Ṛbhus, we invite you to the drink of this libation—they (i.e. the Ṛbhus), the wise ones, who prepared the easyrolling, unfaltering chariot by (mere) thought of the mind.

Notes—(a)—See notes on I. 20.3.

(3) *Tr.* O Vājas, O Ṛbhus, O Vibhvans, that your greatness has been well—proclaimed among the gods (viz.) that you made (your) elders, once again, young though old and always aging, in order that they may walk.

Notes—(ab)—See notes on III. 60.4cd, (cd)—See notes on I. 20.4.

(4) *Tr.* You have made the one cup four-fold; you have carved out the cow from the skin with (your) thoughts. Then you attained immortality among the gods. O Vājas, O Ṛbhus, that (attainment) of yours deserves to be praised gloriously.

Notes—(a)—See notes on I. 20.6; b)—I. 161.7a.

(5) *Tr.* The wealth from the Ṛbhus, which the lords who have become famous through rewards, have created, is the first most renowned; (the chariot) fashioned by Vibhvan is

worthy of praise in the assemblies. He whom the gods favour, is the wise one.

Notes—(b)—refers to the Ṛbhus; see notes on I. 20.1c. (c)—*vidatheṣu pravācyaḥ*—cf. ukthyaḥ in v. 1a.

(6) *Tr.* He is the strong race horse; with eloquence he is the sage; he is the brave defender, invincible in battles; he holds for himself the abundance of wealth and good heroic strength he, whom Vāja, Vibhvan, Ṛbhus have favoured.

(7) *Tr.* The best and the attractive ornaments are placed on you; a hymn (is offered to you) O Vājas, O Ṛbhus; enjoy it, For, you are the wise, eloquent poets; we invite you with this prayer.

Notes—(a)—refers to the *stoma* mentioned in b. (c)—*kavayo vipaścitāḥ* is the rare adjective of the Ṛbhus. This, probably, explains why the poet employs *brahman* for inviting the Ṛbhus.

(8) *Tr.* You, knowing (everything), (give) us from Dhiṣanā, all enjoyments of heroes, the illustrious booty and the best powerful strength. O Ṛbhus fashion out for us the treasure and the strength.

Notes—(a) *Vidvāṁsaḥ*—cf. *sucetasaḥ* in v. 2. (b)—*naryāṇi* bhojanā—cf. *naryam vasu* at VI. 53.2a. (d)—Ṛbhus are often solicited to fashion out (take) riches etc. for the worshippers; cf. v. 9b; I. 111.3a; IV. 35.6cd.

(9) *Tr.* Bestowing (on us), here, the progeny and the treasure, fashion out for us, here, the fame associated with heroes, with which we may surpass others; O Ṛbhus give us that wonderful wealth.

Notes—(ab)—*iha* is repeated thrice for emphasis. (b)—*śravo vīravat* cf. *vīravad yaśaḥ* at IV. 32.12c; V. 79.6a etc. (c)—cf. II. 2.10b.

IV 37

(1) *Tr.* O Vājas, O Ṛbhukṣans, O Gods, by the godtrodden paths come near to our sacrifice as you, o delightful ones, hold for yourself a sacrifice among these people of Manu on the auspicious days.

Notes—It may be noted that the deeds of the Ṛbhus are not referred to in this hymn. (b)—*pathibhir devayānaiḥ*—This phrase in all its places of occurrence occupies this position viz. comprising break and cadence of the *Triṣṭubh pāda*; cf. I. 183.6c; V. 43.6d; VII. 38.8d; read Velankar H.D. Ṛgveda Maṇḍala VII., Bhāratiya Vidyā Bhavan, Bombay, 1963, p. 102 (notes on VII. 38.8).

(2) *Tr.* Let these sacrifices be to (the joy of) your heart and mind; let the delighting and the ghee-clad (Soma-juices) go (to you) today. The completely pressed out (Soma-juices) activate you : being drunk, they delight you for (performing) a powerful and skilful (act).

Notes—(b)—*ghṛtanirṇijāḥ*—Supply *sutāsaḥ*. *ghṛtavantaḥ sutāsaḥ* at X. 29.6c etc. (c)—*hṛde manase*—An appeal both to the mind and heart of the deity; cf. I. 73.10b; VII. 98.2c.

(3) *Tr.* As the thrice going is laid down by the gods for you, and a hymn is given to you, O Vājas, O Ṛbhukṣans, I offer, like Manu, Soma to you in the company (of other gods) in the great heaven, among the late-born people.

Notes—(b)—For *stoma* in context of the Ṛbhus cf. I. 20.1b. (d)—supply *deveṣu.*

(4) *Tr.* O Strong ones, you have the strong horse, the shining chariots, the iron-jaws and good gold-ornaments. O Son of Indra, O Children of strength, the foremost (drink) is known to you for delight.

Notes—(b)—*ayaḥśipraḥ*—At VIII. 102.3c the messenger of Mitrāvaruṇa is described a *ayaḥśīrṣan suniṣkan*. The Maruts are thus described at VII. 56.11a. (c)—At IV. 35.7d the Ṛbhus are referred to as the friends of Indra; also cf. *indrasvantam* in the next verse.

(5) *Tr.* O Ṛbhukṣans, in a battle, we invoke Ṛbhu, the treasure, the strong one, the companion, associated with Indra, always winning and accompanied by the horses.

Notes—(a)—Ṛbhu is concieved as a treasure. Geldner in view of VIII. 93.34b understands ṛbhum *rayim* as *Ṛbhutaṣṭam rayim*. In view of the verb *havāmahe* it is preferrable to construe Ṛbhum as the object.

(6) *Tr.* Let that mortal, indeed, whom you, O Ṛbhus, and Indra favour be with (his) prayers and a horse, a winner in the winning of holy food.

Notes—*arvatā* probably refers to the horse referred to in v. 8 below.

(7) *Tr.* O Ṛbhukṣans, O Vājas, being praised, find out for us the ways to the sacrifice—for us in order to cross all the quarters, O liberal ones.

Notes—(d)—V 10, 6d 10, 6d.

(8) *Tr.* O Vājas, O Ṛbhukṣans, O Indra, O Nāsatyas, from all people (bring back) to us that treasure, the horse; slaughter it well for ample gifts.

Notes—(b)—See notes on I. 20.3a. (c)—*carṣaṇibhyaḥ* a—cf. I. 84.20d; VI. 48.15a; a; a following an ablative has the sense of from, away from; cf. *hṛdā* a at I. 60.3a; *asmad* at I. [63.5c; VIII. 18.11a. However at I. 92.16a : V. 56.3b, a, though following an ablative, has the sense of 'towards, around' etc.

VII 48

(1) *Tr.* O Ṛbhukṣans, O Vājas, O liberal heroes, enjoy (this) pressed—out (Soma-juice) amongst us. May (your)

powerful (horses) like the wisdom of travellers, bring you who are inclined towards us and (your) chariot, which favours men, (amongst us), O Vibhvans.

Notes—Read Velankar H.D., Ṛgveda Maṇḍala VII, pub. Bhāratīya Vidyā Bhavan Bombay, 1963. The different deeds of the Ṛbhus are not referred to in this humn. (a)—has ten letters. (b)—*maghavānaḥ*—See notes on I. 20.1c. (d)—*rathaṁ naryam*—cf. *vajram naryam* at X. 74.5d; *śuṣmam naryam* at VI. 72.5c; *apāṁsi naryāṇi* at VII. 21.4b; *naryeṣu bahuṣu* at I. 166.10a Supply *aśvāḥ*; cf. *pivoaśvāḥ* at IV. 37.4a. *Vibhvaḥ* (Nom. plu. and voc.) illustates the poet's economy of words. Geldner supplies *kratavaḥ* (from the simile) as the subject.

(2) *Tr.* May we, as skilful ones with the Ṛbhus and powerful ones with the Vibhvans, overpower the mights (of the enemies) with your might, O Vibhvans. May Vāja favour us in acquisition of loot; may we conquer the enemy with Indra as (our) companion.

Notes—Note the deliberate attempt at alliteration and pun in a, b and c.

(3) *Tr.* Indeed, they have overpowered the many (wiles) by (their) power, have conquered all (their) enemies for (acquiring) perfect superiority; may the noble Indra, Vibhvan, Ṛbhukṣan and Vāja destroy the might of the enemy with (their) crushing strength.

Notes—(a)—Ṛbhuḥ (sing for plu.) and Vibhvaḥ qualify *vayam* to be supplied. (a)—Supply *māyāḥ*; cf. III. 20.3cd. sāsā (śās) f. as Grassmann explains in his Wōrterbuch zu, Rig-Veda. (b)—*uparatāti*—Loc. of *upara-tāt*. The suffix *tāt* is added to indicate completeness or perfectness; cf. *devatāti* at I. 95.8d; I. 128.2c; *sarvatāti*—at III. 54.11d; *saytyatāti* at IV. 4.14c; *jyeṣṭhatāti*—at V. 44.1b etc. (also cf. Avestan haurvatat); read Wackernagel, Altindische Grammatik, Band II, 2, 463, 464.

(4) *Tr.* O Gods, now make us blissful; be you all in harmony; be for our protection. May the gods grant us vitality; may you, (O gods) protect us with (your) blessings, for ever.

Notes—(a)—For *varivas kṛ* (used with Dative of the person) cf. I. 59.5d; X. 52.5b etc.

XIII

H.D. Velankar

III 60

(1) *Tr*. The (ancient) eager priests have known those (miracles) of yours O heroes, just here, through contemplation, through relationship and through (transmitted) knowledge, (performed) with the help of the mysterious powers, through which, assuming many different forms according to the needs of the occasion, you enjoyed the sacrificial share, O Sons of Sudhanvan.

Notes—bandhutā is relationship with the divine beings. This is claimed with Agni at IV. 4.11; with Indra at X. 144.5; with Aśvinā at V. 73.4 and VIII. 20.22; X. 64. 13; see above on 54.16 and on VII. 72.2. tāni : supply *sukṛtāni* (cf. v. 4) after *tāni* in b and tāśca (i.e. māyāḥ) in c. These are understood (*abhi-jagmuḥ*) by *manas* 'thinking.' *bandhutā* 'relationship.' i.e. divine favour and *vedas* 'acquired or traditional knowledge.' At VIII. 87.2d it is the knowledge of the deity, the Aśvinā who are known as *viśvavedasā* at I. 47.4. *pratijūtivarpasaḥ*—for *varpas* see on 58.9 above; for *jūti* see I. 116.2, also Upadhyaya, Bhāratīya Vidyā, vol. 22, p. 70.

(2) *Tr*. You attained god-head, O Ṛbhus, through (mental) powers with which you designed the (four) cups (out of one), through that wisdom with which you released a cow

from a mere cowhide and through that contemplation with which you fashioned Indra's bay steeds.

Note—devatvam ānaśa; cf. IV. 33.4d; also I. 110.4.

(3) *Tr*. The Ṛbhus enjoyed the friendship of Indra; the sons of Manu, who were skilful, ran successfully. Having worked hard by means of pious labours and with good action, the pious sons of Sudhanvan enjoyed immortality.

Notes—dadhanvire : *dhanv* secondarily means 'to be active' cf. VIII. 31.5b *manor napātaḥ*; cf. *martāsaḥ santo* at I. 110.4. *viṣṭvi*—cf. I. 110.4a; X. 94.2c. *sukṛtyayā* : cf. IV. 35.2c.

(4) *Tr*. Together with Indra in the same chariot you go (to the sacrifices), when the juice is pressed (and kept ready); and then you become associated with the glory of your (attained) desire. O Skilful singers, neither your well-fashioned works nor your heroic deeds can be imitated O Rbhus, O Sons of Sudhanvan,

Notes—vaśā is a desire; cf. VI. 24.5; X. 142.7; X. 171.4. *vaśānām śriyā saha-bhavatha* i.e. *śriyam sacatha*; cf. I. 116.17d; aiso I. 43.7ab. *pratimai* (dative infinitive of *prati mā*) : cf. *anu etave* at VII. 33.8d.

(5) *Tr*. Together with the Ṛbhus including Vāja, O Indra, pour well (in your belly) the pressed out Soma-juice well mingled (with water) Maghavan, rejoice at the house of your worshipper, together with the heroic sons of Sudhanvan.

Notes—samukṣitam : i.e. with water; cf. VIII. 4. 12c; IX, 99.5a; also apsu māmṛje at IX. 2.5 etc. Supply jaṭhare in b; cf. I. 104.9; X. 96.13. *gabhastyoḥ somaḥ* at II. 14.8 and IX. 86.34; *mṛjyamānāḥ gabhastyoḥ* at IX. 20.6; IX. 36.4.

(6) *Tr*. Along with the Ṛbhus including Vāja, rejoice here at this our libation, owing to your power, O Indra praised by many. These are the laws of the gods, together with the fixtures of men.

Notes—svasrāṇi : The *Savanas* are offered to you as your own homes; you may rest at these at will as at your own home.

vratā devānām—really hangs loose; we get these same words above at 7.7d; 55.1c; and 56.1b; of these the poet has probably the first in view (*devā devānām anu hi vratā guḥ*); accordingly *vratā devānām* must be taken as an independent parenthetical clause 'these or such are the laws of the gods' or *anu* be supplied corresponding to the instrumental *dharmabhiḥ*. Really speaking d is an anakoluthic combination (as indicated by ca) of two sentences viz. *vratair devānām ca dharmabhiḥ* and *vratā ca dhrmā*. The latter was actually contemplated, but *later given up in view of the metre i.e. Jagatī* cadence, and *dharmā* turned into *dharmabhiḥ*.

(7) *Tr.* Together with the Ṛbhus including Vāja, do come here to the hymn of the singer, which is brought at the sacrifice, thus strengthening it O Indra, along with a hundred stimulating intentions (helpful) to man and being possessed of a thousand resources as you are, when the sacrificial offering is poured into the fire.

Notes—*vājibhiḥ*—*vājavadbhiḥ* (v. 5). *yajñiyam* 'fit for or offered at the sacrifice.' vājayan is a causal form as the accent shows. keta 'an intention, will' cf. *praketaiḥ* at VII. 33.9. *sahasranīthaḥ*; cf. *sahasracetaḥ*, *śatarithaḥ* at I. 100.12b. *nītha* is 'guidence,' same as *praṇīti*; cf. IX. 85.4; *sahasranīthāḥ kavayaḥ* at X. 154.5, (where however, as in word like *nīthavid*, the word has the secondarily sense of 'a vehicle in the form of hymn' and is comparable with the word *vahas*); cf. also *sahasranīti* used of Soma at IX. 71.7; as well as *sunītha* (8.8 above) and *sunīti* (VI. 47.7) both used in the same sense. *homani* (from hu to offer) 'pouring' dropping of the oblation in the fire; cf. I. 84.18c.

IV 33

(1) *Tr.* I send my hymn like a messenger to the Ṛbhus.—I pray to the śvaitarī cow for spreading itself out (like a carpet)—the skillful artists, impelled by the wind (as it were), who have reached the heaven by their own active natures.

Notes—*dūtam iva*—For the same simile see V. 43.8ab; VI. 63.1ab; *śvaitarī dhenuḥ* i.e. (*śveta-rā*) a white cow, consequently cow's white milk, *upastire* is infinitive *upat* the root *stṛ* spread out' as a seat or carpet; milk is called *śukram upastiram* at IX. 62.28 (a white spread out carpet) and at IX. 69.5 water is said to be Soma's *upastaraṇam* ('a spread out seat or carpet'). *vātajūtāḥ—vātāḥ na jūtāḥ*, see IV. 17.12d; IX. 97.52c. *apasaḥ* is significant; they are said to have become divine by means of their *apas* or skilful work at IV. 35.8ab; also I. 110.6cd; I. 161.7d.

(2) *Tr.* When the Ṛbhus served their parents with personal attendance, active service and skilful labour, just then they obtained the friendship of the gods. The wise ones have brought prosperity to our prayer.

Notes—pariviṣṭī and *veṣaṇā*, both instru. sing. in form are from the root viś 'to work;' also Upadhyaya S.A., Hymns to the Ṛbhus in the Ṛgveda, in Bhāratīya Vidyā XXII, 1962. vv. 2 and 3 refer to the miraculous rejuventation of their parents by the Ṛbhus, *puṣṭim avahan* 'brought prosperity' by their rich gifts; see v. 10c, IV. 41.10ab. Or as Geldner suggests *puṣṭi* in the sense of 'glory' as at VI. 63.6—'They brought glory, beauty to our hymn' by being mentioned in it. *mana* (man) 'a prayer, a hymn', here; but at II. 33.5 it means 'thought.'

(3) *Tr.* May Vāja, Vibhvan and Ṛbhu, the followers of Indra and the enjoyers of the sweet food, who made their old worn out parents, lying low like (the newly cut) sacrificial posts, young once more, favour our sacrifice.

Notes—sanā-jarāṇā are both adjectives of only *pitarā*, śayānā is the common property and *yūpā* are the freshly cut trees, laid low on the ground for drying before they are raised and fixed as sacrificial posts; see ıII. 8.7ab. *psaras* is food; Soma is called *mahi psaras* at IX. 2.2 and IX. 74.3. At I. 41.7, a hymn is metaphorically called *mahi psaraḥ*.

(4) *Tr.* The Ṛbhus attained immortality by these holy works when for an year they guarded the cow, when for an year they painted flesh over her, and when for an year they brought to her the light (of life).

Notes—maḥ apiṁśan—The means of decoration, painting etc., is sometimes put in the accusative as here; see also *māṁsam ekaḥ piṁśati* I. 161. 10, where the same legend is recorded. *bhāsas* (n. from bhās to shine) here signifies brightness of life, life-breath; at I. 161.10c in the same context *śakṛt* seems to signify just the opposite, the unessential parts, which were removed (*apa abharat*).

(5) *Tr.* The eldest said, Let me make two cups (out of the one); the younger said, Let me make three; the youngest said, Let me make four. Tvaṣṭṛ admired that speech of yours, O Ṛbhus.

Notes—According to I. 161.1—5 the gods promised through Agni, that the Ṛbhus would be admitted to a share at the sacrifice, if they could perform the miracle described here, namely, making of four cups out of a single one (this probably) refers to the moon and her four phases). Tvaṣṭṛ was not very sure about their capacity to do this, in the beginning; but he admired their work, when he actually saw it. kareti-kara-karai iti (against *Pada Pāṭha*).

(6) *Tr.* The heroes (i.e. the Ṛbhus) spoke what was bound to come off. Thus indeed they performed (the miracle). (In that) the Ṛbhus followed their own will. Tvaṣṭṛ loved it when he saw the four cups, shining like the days.

Notes—satyamūcuḥ is explained by *evā hi cakruḥ*; they said only what they could execute. *anu svadhām jagmur etām*—'they followed their own inclination'; *anu* is to be construed with *jagmuḥ*—see '*Indra svadhām anu hi no babhūtha*' O Indra, you have followed our will, inclination' I. 165.5d. For this sense of *svadhā* cf. II. 35.7.

(7) *Tr.* When the Ṛbhus slumbered for twelve days at the house of Agohya enjoying his hospitality, they made his lands fertile; they led the rivers (through them). The plants grew on the dry land; waters flowed over the low ground.

Notes—For the story of *Agohya*, see also I. 110.2.3; I. 161.11-13 and Macdonell VM p. 133 cd—They brought fertility to the land by leading canals of water into it.

(8) *Tr.* May those helpful, skilful, deft-handed Ṛbhus who created the easy-rolling chariot that waits upon the heroes, who produced the all-inspiring and all-beautiful cow, bring us wealth.

Notes—nare-ṣṭhām—nara here refers to the Aśvinā, for whom the chariot was fashioned according to I. 20.3. The cow was for Bṛhaspati; see—I. 161.1ab.

(9) *Tr.* For the gods liked their work when they carefully considered it with wisdom and attention. Vāja became the skilful artist for the gods, Ṛbhukṣan for Indra and Vibhvan for Varuṇa.

Notes—kratvā manasā dīdhyānāḥ—'taking stock of it with the help of their wisdom and intelligence'; the expression *hṛdā manasā* is slightly different, *hṛd* refering to the heart, i.e. feeling or sentiment, in addition to *manas*, i.e. pure reason.

(10) *Tr.* Being delighted with our hymns, bestow on us O Ṛbhus, abundance of riches and treasures as persons longing for a lasting home bestow their friendship (upon the neighbours),—you, who fashioned with your natural intelligence the easily—yoked bay horses for Indra.

Notes—mitram dhā 'to bestow friendship'; cf. X. 108.3; the word *mitram* is used in the sense of both 'a friend' (cf. III. 59.1) and 'friendship'. *kṣemayantaḥ* 'longing for a lasting home'; see *kṣeti kṣemebhiḥ sādhubhiḥ* at VIII. 84.9 and *dhruvakṣemāsaḥ parvatāsaḥ* at III. 54.20. For the same simile, see *agnim devāso mānuṣīṣu vikṣu priyam dhuḥ kṣemayanto na mitram* at II. 4.3. *rāyas poṣam dhatta* is to be construed with *ukthā madantah* in a; the root *mad* is used with an accusative as at VII. 49.4.

(11) *Tr.* They (i.e. the gods) have appointed your drink and enjoyment at this time of the day. Gods do not stand for the friendship of any one except him who toils hard for them. Such as you are, bestow riches on us, O Ṛbhus, at this third libation.

Notes–ida ahnaḥ—see—*idānīm ahnaḥ* at IV. 54.1b. *dhuḥ*—The subject is *devāh. ṛte* governs the ablative; so supply *sakhyāt* after *śrāntasya* and *anyasya* before *sakhyāya. śrānta*—the root *śram* is generally used in the sense of a 'a fruitless labour'; though at IV 12.1a and VIII. 67.6 ab, it conveys the sense of 'a pious labour'; at I. 179.3a, which passage contains the same idea as ours, the word *mṛṣā* is added to make it more emphatic *na mṛṣā śrāntam yad avanti devāḥ* 'since the gods do not favour a person who has laboured in the wrong direction i.e. who does not offer a sacrifice to the gods.'

VII 48

(1) *Tr.* O Ṛbhukṣans, O Vājas, O bounteous heroes, do rejoice with us in our pressed out juice. May your mighty (horses), like the wise counsels of the travellers, bring you, who have turned towards us, O Vibhus, and your man-favouring chariot here.

Notes—(b)—Construe *asme* (loc.) *sutasya mādyadhvam*. *arvācaḥ* is accu. plu. as at I. 168.1cd. In d I supply *aśvāḥ* after *vibhvaḥ* (nom. pl. of *vibhu* as in v. 2) and compare VII. 1.3ab below and *vibhavo hi aśvāḥ* at III. 6.9. As a matter of fact vibhaḥ stands for both the vocative and the nom. pl. See trans, and note on 66.12 below. In the simile the horses of the Ṛbhus are compared with the wills or wisdoms (*kratu*) of the travellers, the point of similarity being 'capacity to lead aright'. Geldner takes *vibhvaḥ* as vocative (along with the other two names) and supplies *kratavaḥ* (from the simile) in the chief clause : May my wisdom like that of the travellers, lead you and your chariot hereword, O Vibhus.' This is not quite satisfactory.

(2) *Tr.* May we, as Ṛbhus in the company of the Ṛbhus and (Vibhus) in the eompany of the Vibhus, O Vibhus, overpower the mights (of the enemies) by your power. May Vāja favour us in the battle; may we conquer an enemy with Indra as our companion.

Notes—*ṛbhu* (sing. for Pl.) and *vibhvaḥ* are intended to qualify *vayam* supplied, (cf. *abhi syāma*) a pun on the two words being intended; the third word is left out as Vāja cannot be construed as an adjective; yet the word *vājasātau* is used for a pun. For a similar pun see 52.1a below. Construe *vaḥ* with *śavasā*; or better with *vayam* supplied; see on 30.4a above and

52.2; 56.24; 88.6 below. It is not an object of *abhi syāma* at either place.

(3) *Tr*. For, even they have over-thrown the many (wiles) by their ruling power and have conquered all their enemies for winning eminence. May the noble Indra, Vibhavan, Ṛbhukṣan and Vāja completely put to rout the might of the enemy with a crushing attack.

Notes—Supply *māyāḥ* after *pūrvīḥ* cf. I. 10b above. *śāsā* (instru. sing. of śās); cf. X. 20.2b; and *kṣiyema* at 46.2 above. *viśvan aryaḥ* (accu. pl.) cf. VIII. 65.9ab; *uparatāti* (loc)—*upara tāti* is complete superiority, *upara* being 'superior' as at VI. 21;11d. *tāt* to *tāti* is a suffix showing completeness or fulness; see on 39.1 above. In c *aryḥ* is either nom. pl. of *ari* or nom. sing. of *arya*, going individually with Indra and others. *mithati* is a noun from the root *mith* 'to oppose' (cf. X. 34.2a); cf. 93.5 below where the two opposing armies are called *mahī mithatī*.

(4) *Tr*. Now O gods, give us bliss; with a concordant mind, be all of you for our protection. May the gods bestow on us nourishment together. Do you protect us (O gods), with your blessings for ever.

Notes—*varivaḥ kartana*—see on *varivo dhā* at 47.4 above.

XIV

Louis Renou

I 20

(Hillebrant p. 92)

(1) *Tr*. Here is a collection of praise addressed to the divine race, (which) has just been prepared by inspired orators, with (their) mouth, (praise) which confers treasures better (than any thing else).

Notes—deva—adj.; the use is not established (and this in restricted limits only) in nt. EVP XII p. 71.

(2) *Tr*. (The Ṛbhus) who, with (an applied) mind, have fashioned for Indra the two bay-horses, yoked by word, have attained thanks to their efforts (the right to) sacrifice.

Notes—'*vacoyuj*' instant epithet of the horses of Indra. The play between *vacas* and *manas* (the third term karman being present under *śamībhiḥ* c and cf *viṣṭī* here *in* stz 3, *sukṛtyayā* stz 8) *samī* is in dependance of *viś* III. 60.3 below. Thus the shade is not the same as in the formula *dhiyā śamī* II. 31.6. 'by the poetic act and the (manual) effort (in the rite)'.

(3) *Tr*. They fashioned for the two Nāsatyas the chariot easy (to drive), which moves all around (the world). They

fashioned the milch-cow, which allows herself to be milked eternally.

Notes—takṣan succeeding *tatakṣuḥ* in stz 2; the perfect introduces the narrative sequence; unmarked verbal forms follow (here, unaugmented preterative). *Sabardughā* is necessarily appelative (epithet) in III. 6.4 and elsewhere.

(4) *Tr.* The Ṛbhus, whose sacred formulae become reality, (these gods), with the just thoughts, have managed by their work, (in a manner) that the two parents (become) young again.

Notes—satyamantra cf. *mantrebhiḥ satyaiḥ* I. 67.5—Lüders p. 545 "They have rejuvenated their parents with true *mantras*" *viṣṭī* here (and in I. 92.3), cf EVP III p. 35 on 3a in relation with *śamībhiḥ* stz 2 cf. viṣṭvī III. 60.3 cited earlier.

(5) *Tr.* Your exhilarating draughts (of Soma) have united with (those of) Indra, aceompanied by the Maruts and with (those of the Adityas), the kings.

(6) *Tr.* And the celebrated cup of god Tvaṣṭṛ, new(ly) prepared by him, you have made it again (so that there are) four.

Notes—niskṛta is verbal adjective in relation to substantive *niṣkṛta*, Note that the instrumental complement is evident by a genitive dependent (theoretically) of *camasa*; *akarta*—above Atmane *akrata* in 4 to designate an act less 'external.'

(7) *Tr.* (Being) such, confer on us treasures thrice the group of seven (treasures) for the Soma-presser, one by one (as prize) for good recitations.

Notes—sāpta with *triḥ* as one has *tribhiḥ saptebhiḥ* VIII. 59.5. 'three groups of seven.' Lüders p. 682—('friendship' for *Sāpta* VIII. 55.5 Geldner is very much doubtful). On II. 19.7 and on of the use, see the notes of Geldner and of Oldenberg. (Oldenberg thinks of a double sense, based upon *sapta* and on *sapti* 'a team') cf also EVP VII p. 29. *suśastibhiḥ* Instrumental of the thing desired as a prize.

(8) *Tr.* Conductors (of the rite) they secured for themselves and from the performance of their good activity they obtained as their part, a sacrificial portion among the gods.

Notes—dhāray Atmane is 'to remain (firm)' with *kṣatram, indriyam ṛtam* etc., yet with no marked shade in each act to the active : Here one will admit a value somewhat distinct from *bhāgam adhārayan* VIII. 56.1 or *dīdharo bhāgam* VIII. 100.1. 'to fix (as) a part' may be 'to secure' or perhaps 'to revendicate.' The line develops the idea contained in stz 2 c.

I 110

(1) *Tr.* My (poetic) work (had been) interwoven (previously). This (same work) is (now) woven anew. The sweetest poetic intuition is recited (at this moment) for (taking the form of) a hymn. Here is the occean (of Soma, which is) prepared for all the gods. Drink together to your heart's content O Ṛbhus, the Soma in which (the ritual cry) 'Svāhā' is uttered.

Notes—samudra—borrowed from Book IX, '*tṛp*' is said of the beverage (but the object is *annasya* after the RV.—'to taste' ŚB X. 3.5.13; in fact of Soma).

(2) *Tr.* As you, going forward, advanced, searching your recompense, (thinking) "I have friends, whatever their (worth), (may be) towards the East, (may be) towards the West" (finally) O Sons of Sudhanvan, after a long time you arrived towards the house of Savitṛ, the donor of offerings.

Notes—ābhogaya (Sieg. ZII V p. 212, and on the entire verse) derivative of a rare type probably formed on the Dative *ābhagāya* of the neighbouring hymn 113.5; where the word is parallel with *rāye-caritasya* bhūmanā cf. though somewhat different '*bhūyo vi cakrame*' X. 117.8, '*bhūriṁ carantam*' I. 185.2 *dāśvān* is rare as applied to a divinity—some examples in Books I and X (So also for the personal forms of *dāś* in addition to II. 19.4 by contamination).

(3) *Tr.* Then Savitṛ stirred up as a gift for you immortality when you came to Agohya, making yourselves heard (by a cry of appeal). you have made fourfold, the celebrated cup, the means of drinking of Asura (Tvaṣṭṛ), (the cup) which was one.

Notes—Savitṛ link with stz 2 d. *amṛtatva*—followed from the right to sacrifice and from the *yajñiya bhāga.* I. 20.2 and 8. *bhakṣay* (and *bhakṣ*) refers exclusively 'to drink' in the RV and the ancient Vedic literature. In this regard—ŚB III. 6.1.23 is typical and cf—*Dvandva 'bhojanabhakṣaṇe'* of Śr. *sūtras.* In the domestic sūtras the change takes place, an intermediary situation being that of '*prāṇabhakṣam*' 'eating or drinking by the breath (only, being equal to the odour of the dish or the beverage inhaled').

(4) *Tr.* After having laboured with efforts (and) success (these) officiating ones, though being mortal, attained immortality. The Ṛbhus, the Sons of Sudhanvan, who see the sun, were gratified with the (divine) intuition in one year.

Notes—taraṇitvā—cf. *taraṇibhirevaiḥ* IV. 33.1 below, the dominating idea is that of an act which allows overcoming the obstacles and thus leading to decisive success, '*sūracakṣas*' a doublet rarer of '*svardṛs*' EVP XII p. 81; also *svarcakṣas* Hapax d Gonda—'Vision' p. 191.

(5) *Tr.* As (one measures) a field, the Ṛbhus have measured with a reed the unique cup, which opened wide, (these gods) invoked with praise, imploring for the supreme (favour), seeking renown (which is the lot) of the immortals.

Notes—Or *nādhamānāḥ* passive 'implored' like *upastutāḥ, upamam* then directly connected with śravas ? But the use would be isolated. It is true that elsewhere '*nādh*' never has an objective case.

(6) *Tr.* We will just offer in oblation an inspired poem to the lords of the mid-region, as (one offers) the melted butter

with the sacrificial ladle. The Ṛbhus, who by (their) efficient action have followed (the example) of the Father here, have ascended to the space of the heaven (as) their prize of victory.

Notes—*manīṣām hu*—is not a real zeugma; the verb being at its place with *ghṛtam*. Moreover one has *giraḥ juhomi* II. 27.1; *manma juhvati* II. 11.18 and some such other places. It is difficult to make the Genitive *pituḥ* depend upon 'śāc.' One is thus led to understand '*taraṇitvā ye*,' '*taraṇitvam pituḥ*' *taraṇitvā* is inst. sg. rather than Acc. pl. cf stz 4 and general usage in these derivatives. cf also *svapasyayā* stz 8—*vidmanā* I. 111.1; *sukṛuyayā* I. 20.8; For the sense cf stz 4. *d*—zeugma 'to climb to the space and to attain the prize.' cf. nevertheless *vājam āruh* IX. 83.5; X. 86.40.

(7) *Tr.* The Ṛbhu (is) for us a newer Indra as regards the vigour. Ṛbhu, with the Vājas (and) the Vasus (is himself) a Vasu (as) donor. With your assistance, O gods, may we, on the beloved day, overcome the agressions of those who do not press (Soma).

Notes—The verbal play (Geldner) which is repeated in stz 9 a is extended to *vasuḥ* also which is both sg. of *vasubhiḥ* that precedes and also at the same time the adjective 'good,' though this meaning may be doubtful. EVP XII p. 76. By the side of '*dadi*' one would expect 'rich' a forged acception, which has to be extracted (from) vasu nt. 'riches.'

(8) *Tr.* (Starting with) the hide (as the premier material) O Ṛbhus, you have artistically fasioned the cow. You have made the mother join with the calf. O Sons of Sudhanvan O Lords, due to your skill in work, you have acted (in such a manner that) the two decrepit parents could become young again.

Notes—The allusion to the cow is apparently to be put together with I. 161.10 and IV. 33.4 below. cf. also Old—b The allusion clearer in I. 111.1 below. (in *sṛj* subsists readily the idea of creation.—*jīvrī*—cf. IV. 36.3 below (*pitur na jīvreḥ*) I. 70.9.

(9) *Tr.* Help us with the Vājas for gaining the prize of victory O Indra, whom the Ṛbhus accompany, make a marvellous favour burst forth. cd=94, 16.

Notes—aviḍḍhi Narten Aorist p. 87—*Ṛbhumant*, both 'accompanied by the Ṛbhus' and 'joined (as it happened) to the Ṛbhus'. *ā darṣi*—image of a hidden treasure, which one obtains as by burglary. cf. V. 39.3. On tne imperative type in *si* and its immediate connection with the subjunctive in—*sat*. Cardona Language 41, P. 1.

I 111

(Fragments of inserted dialogue)

(cf. ti V. 8.9—Caland-Henry p. 355)

(1) *Tr.* They fashioned the chariot, which rools smoothly, they who work with knowledge. They fashioned the two bay—horses, which Indra drives, the two rich in manly force. (These) Ṛbhus fashioned for the two parents, a young age. For the calf they fashioned a mother, keeping (it) company.

Notes—The verb *takṣ* is taken again in 1—3 forming a zeugma, being a typical verb of the activity of the Ṛbhus. Here the Preterite inserts itself following I. 20.2 above. On the ambiguous morphological base *takṣ* see Narten Aorist P. 124. *vṛṣaṇvasū* is usually epithet of the Aśvins, introduced here because of latent allusion to the Aśvins in *pāda a*. *yuvan* has no Nt, hence the invention of a Nt stem *yuvat* based on the fem. *yuvatī*. (Fem in—*i* like *Jānī* and on the other hand maghava (n) t. (Wackernagel III p. 265) where a base in—*an* and one in—a(n)t. alternate. *sacābhū* is formed on the analytical formula *bhavā sacā* I. 40.1. (*sacābhavā san* I. 71.4) or *abhavat sacā* VI. 57.4 and analogous; hence the duplication '*abhavaḥ sacābhūḥ*' X. 70.9.

(2) *Tr.* Fashion for us (similarly) for the sacrifice the vital force proper to the Ṛbhus. For (our) spiritual-power (and our) active—thought (fashion) an enjoyment, consisting of progency. Be pleased to confer on our troop the force-

of-Indra, so that we reside with (our) tribe having its full force of useful men.

Notes—Therefore *ā takṣ* with the figurative regime (also stz 3) responds to *takṣ*, with the regime in its proper sense (line 1). *Ṛbhumat*, like *Indriya* in *d* a word implying comparison. '*vayas*' is here taken in its usual sense and *not in the rarer sense which it has in stz 1 c* (mixed VII. 97.1 youthful strength Geldner). *sarvavīra* or 'having ones men sound and safe' (On this sense of *sarva* EVP III p. 53, IV 107)--Less probable—Thus Geldner's translation of I. 51.15 and I. 106.19 to be rectified. *Śardha*—'(troop EVP X p. 59) figures near Indra in IX. 39.6 and so on. The term implies the idea of 'force;' hence '*indriya*' here, is the force peculiar to Indra.' EVP ibid p. 66, from where 'an attribute comparable to that of Indra.'

(3) *Tr.* O Ṛbhus, carve out for us the gain, gain for the chariot, gain for the steed, O Lords. Please give us generously the gain that befits a victor; (and this) for all the time to come (give us a hero) capable of dominating in battles (the enemy) of the same race (and the) alike as well.

Notes—jaitrī from *jetṛ*—Debrunner—Suffix—708 on this rare type of derivative. *sam—maheta* seems to have been formed on *saṁ mahema* I. 94.1 (which moreover has a some what different meaning 'to execute magnificiently.' cf EVP XII 96) '*mahema*' is 'to magnify' VII. 2.3 jāmi i.e., *śatṛ* following IV. 4.5 and elsewhere; hence secondarily the sense unfavourable to to the formula '*jāmimajāmim*' (and ajāmi alone Geldner VII. 83.6).

(4) *Tr.* I call for help Indra, the Ṛbhukṣan, (as well as) the Ṛbhus, the Vājas, the Maruts in order to drink the Soma, (and also) both (of these two gods) Varuṇa and Mitra (and finally) the two Aśvins, at present. May these (gods) stimulate us to victory, to the poetic vision, in short, to be victors.

Notes—dhiye has double appearance cf *dhiyaḥ san and so on.—jiṣe* is infinitive of the type *śluṣe*, but more specialised. Also I. 112.12.

(5) *Tr.* May the Ṛbhu sharpen (for us) the gain so that (we) win (the stake). May Vāja, who is victorious in the competition, help us. May Mitra, Varuṇa, Aditi, Sindhu, the Earth and Heavn grant that to us.

Notes—bhara—EVP XII p. 104. *saṁ* śā apart from its proper sense 'to sharpen' also means' to stimulate' with 'poetic faculty' or analogous regime. Here there occurs a semantic deviation due to the pressure of the word '*sāti*' (masc.) of stz 4. *Vāja* (prize) in the Nomative with the use of the word as a proper noun. So II. 1.10 (Geldner). V. 15.5 (?); X. 12.5(?).

I 161

(Sieg ZII V p. 203 (Detailed interpretation)
Hillebrandt p. 93; Dumezil Tarpeia p. 215)

(1) *Tr.* (The Ṛbhus) "Why has the very beautiful, the very young (Agni) come to us ? For which message does he advance ? What (is-it) that we have said by way of reply ? We have not criticised the cup, which is of a good race. O Agni, O brother, it is the quality of the wood that we have spoken about."

Notes—Exchange *kim* : *kad* as X. 12.5 (also less directly. IV. 3.5 EVP XIII p. 93). *śreṣṭha, yaviṣṭha* usual qualifications of Agni. The two words are not exactly in opposition to each other. Difference between '*vac*' to say and '*vad*' 'to speak of.' In Veda *bhūtī* (also *bhūti*) is only prosperity, good state. cf. *bhūyiṣṭha* stz 9 and with an enlargement *bhūṣ*.

(2) *Tr.* (Agni) 'From one cup make four.' This is what the gods have said to you. That is (why) I have come to you. O Sons of Sudhanvan, if you are inclined to do so, you will become worthy of sacrifice, jointly with the (other) gods.

Notes—Only use of '*yadi*' with (double) future. cf. stz 8. *sākam*—ak infixed on '*sam*' or less probably, a base in *sañc* (as *apāka* on *apāñca*, a *bhike* on *abhyañc*) *āke* on *añc*.

(3) *Tr.* (The Reciter) What you replied to Agnı, the messenger. (here it is) "A horse (yet remains) to be fashioned, and a chariot (remains) to be prepared here. A milch-cow (remains) to be fashioned and (finally) two (beings are) to be rejuvenated. When we shall have done (all) these things, then O brother, we will go to you."

Notes—kartva said of a work, which is 'to be done' without any obligative shade, but in strict parallelism to *kartum.*

(4) *Tr.* O Ṛbhus, when you had done (all these things), then you asked, "where indeed has gone that famous (person), who had come to us (as) a messenger ?" After Tvaṣṭṛ had cast his glance on the four cups, prepared, then he intermeddled among the (divine) Women.

Notes—nyañja TB (cited by Geldner) is adherence (of the grains to the vessel in which they are cooked).—*añj* with preverbs has different (figurative) meanings—Sieg. 'to have a make-up' 'to anoint oneself' etc.

(5) *Tr.* When Tvaṣṭṛ had said, "we shall kill those, who have criticised the cup, serving towards the beverage of the gods, (the Ṛbhus) then, take other names for (the oblation of) pressed (Soma). It is with the other names that the young girl placed them under her protection.

Notes—devapāna the same type of derivation as *devayāna.* EVP XIV pp. 62 on 7 and p 79. The names cited in stz 6. (Geldner) or rather *nāman* identical with *rūpa* (I. 185.1; IX. 75.1; IX. 94.2; X. 123.7) *Kanyā* (Hoffmann Munch. Stud. VI p. 39. Does it refer to the daughter of Tvaṣṭṛ (X. 17.1) ?

(6) *Tr.* Indra had yoked the two bay-horses, the Aśvins the chariot. Bṛhaspati had led (the cow) Viśvarūpā. Ṛbhu, Vibhvan, Vāja, you, came to the gods; having worked well you obtained a sacrificial portion.

Notes—aitana—d—distinct from agacchata of c.

(7) *Tr.* With the help of your poetic intuitions you took out a cow from a hide (taken as the primary material). You

have rejuvenated the two (beings), that had grown old. O Sons of Sudhanvan, beginning with one horse, you have fashioned another) horse. Having yoked the chariot, you have approached the gods.

Notes—*rī* has abnormal values—EVP III p. 65; VIII p. 64; IX p. 81; X p. 89. Here with *nis*, 'ex-tract'. according to 110.8 above, where *niḥpiś* occurs; hence the use without preverb in the same sense in III. 60.2 below. cf *sam rī*. It seems that nothing remains of the primary sense of the verb ('to imagine,' to flow '[as in a mould]' would be risky) and *rī* has become a substitute of takṣ which occurs here in *c* (with the preverb to be replaced according to *a*) and in 111.1 *d* above. *c*—Sieg. prefers "you have fashioned a second horse, after a first one."

(8) *Tr.* You said, "Drink this water or drink that water purified by Muñja (grass)." Then the gods replied) 'O Sons of Sudhanvan, if you do not find pleasure in this, then (it is expected that) you will exhilarate yourselves (with Soma) at the Third pressing.'

Notes—Distinction between *udaka* (also stz 10) here with depreciatary intention ?—and *āp* (taken as the element), this latter in juxtaposition with *agni* and *bhūmi*.

(9) *Tr.* "It is water which is the most important," said one (of the Ṛbhus). "It is fire that is most important," said the other. The other (i.e. the third one) said that (the earth, which) desires the (celestial) arm (i.e. the lightning was) absolutely at the head (of the other elements). It is (thus) by telling (the things related to) elementary—Order that you have fashioned the cup artistically.

Notes—Lüders p. 544 (on the ṛta as even an instrument of the Ṛbhus); cf. Sieg (who places the verse in the mouth of the gods)—*bhūyiṣṭha*—the sense conforms with *bhūyas* IV. 24.9 (*apām bhūmānam* X. 98.12) *pra-brū* cf. stz. 12; but following Siege it is better to join '*bahubh-aḥ pra*' *ṛtāvad*—'to speak of that which concerns the cosmic oder.' In this sense note plural of *ṛtā* but—'holy word' Sieg.

(10) *Tr.* One leads to water the paralytic cow; one (i.e. the second) cuts the meat brought by means of a basket.

One (i.e. the third one) has carried away the dung before the sunset. Probably did the two parents lend help to their sons ?

Notes—piś is said of the meat. cf. IV. 33.4 below and *piśita* from the AV onwards. *nimṛcaḥ*—the complete expression figures in I. 151.5. (in the sense of 'upto the evening ?' which in any case possible here (and elsewhere).—*nimṛci*, (without any other determination), VIII. 27.19.

(11) *Tr.* In the high—lands you have created the grass for these (people) here. In the low-lands (you made) water (flow), because of your skill in work, O lords, ever since you have slept in the house of Agohya. O Ṛbhus, do not repeat such acts today.

Notes—*ab* slight zeugma.—The use of *ni* in *b* is suggested by IV. 33.7 below, passage where *nimnan āpaḥ* is in apposition to *dhanva*, and *oṣadhiḥ* as *tṛṇa* here.

(12) *Tr.* When you were still going around the (terrestial) beings, closing the eyes, probably your dear parents, were somewhere (on the spots) ? Have you cursed him, who has taken you by the arm ? Did you in return address words to him, who was addressing words to (you) ?

Notes—*a*—cf. MS cited in Geldner's note. *kva svid* as *kim svid* in stz. 10. *cd*—interrogative according to Sieg.—also in 13—but doubtful.

(13) *Tr.* O Ṛbhus, when you had awakened from sleep, did you (not) ask, "O Agohya, who is he that has awakened us thus ?" Has not the ram said that the dog (had been) the awakener ? Have you opened the eyes (just that very year) ?

Notes—*idam* in *d* conforms to *idam* in *b* and above all to *adyedam* in stz. 11 *b* (Sieg.). Note that this adverbial use of the word is relatively rare in the (ancient) RV—*vi—khyā* is generally to look around oneself' thus equally close to *budh* IV. 1.18, secondarily 'to shine' 'to render visible by shining'—analogous dispositions in *vi—cakṣ*.

(14) *Tr.* The Maruts go to the sky, Agni on the earth, this wind, here goes in the mind-region. In the waters, in the oceans goes Varuṇa, (all this) in search of you, O Sons of Vigour.

Notes—Instrumental of location common with *yā*, *śavaso napātaḥ*, specially typical of the Ṛbhus.

III 60

(stanzas 5—7 to Indra)

(1) *Tr.* Here (and) there, (may be) by (application of) thought (may be) by family-tie, (may be) by their (own) knowledge, O lords, (O Ṛbhus) the model priests have learnt these things from you (i.e.) the altering powers, due to which, O Sons of Sudhanvan, by (assuming) a changed form at every (new) instigation, you have obtained a sacrificial part.

Notes—vedas—here and in VIII. 87.1; elsewhere the words signifies (material) possession.; but *jāta-vedas* and probably *viśva-vedas* are based upon *vedas 'science.'*

(2) *Tr.* The powers by means of which you have antistically fashioned the cups, the poetic-intuition by means of which you have drawn (out) a cow (from) a hide, the thought by means of which you have fashioned the two bay-horses, thanks to (all) that, O Ṛbhus, you have fully obtained godhead.

Notes—ariṇīta cf. I. 161.7 above.

(3) *Tr.* The Ṛbhus have fully obtained friendship of Indra. (These) nephews of Manu, (good) workers, have come forward. The sons of Sudhanvan, clever in fabricating, with skill in fabricating, have obtained immortality after having worked with efforts.

Notes erire—EVP XII p. 100.

(4) *Tr.* With Indra you go on the same chariot towards the pressed (Soma). Thus are you (united) with the glory of your (fulfilments). O Ṛbhus, officiating priests, O Sons of

Sudhanvan, your skills in working would not be imitated and (your) heroic-acts (cannot be limited either).

Notes—sute sacā—stable formula (rare variant *sacā someṣu, sacā savaneṣu*) *b*—or '(masters) of wishes, with glory'? prati-mā is at first 'to create (a melody) in conformity with (a verse), hence the substantive *pratīmā* as a sacrificial term, (identical with post-Ṛgvedic *vikṛti* ?)

(5) *Tr.* O Indra, along with the Ṛbhus (that is) with the Vājas, let flow within you the Soma washed (with water, which has been) pressed in the hands. O Liberal one, moved by the poetic intuition, intoxicate yourself in the house of the worshipper with the sons of Sudhanvan, the lords (the Ṛbhus).

Notes—Vājavant or rather—'allias the Vājas' cf. stz. s 6 and 9. ā vṛṣ—EVP VIII p. 83.

(6) *Tr.* O Indra, (you who are) accompanied by the Ṛbhus, (i.e.) the Vājas, intoxicate youself here in this pressing of ours, with (all your) power, o (god) widely praised. These pastures here, have always offered themselves to you; the rules—of—alliance between the gods and the human beings (have been formed) according to the natural-dispositions.

Notes—svasara (cf. Vishveshvar Indological Journal I p. 37). As usual the word alludes to Soma. *d*—Oldenberg, so also Schmidt—vratā p. 91, who compares to it V. 63.7, where *vratā* occurs by side of *dharmaṇā* (as here by the side of *dharmabhiḥ*) in dependance of *rakṣethe*. A similar elipsis will be presumed here. The same juxtaposition is found in V. 72.2 (J. As. 1964 p. 160) The relation of the Genitives remains uncertain.

(7) *Tr.* O Indra, you, who along with the Ṛbhus (i.e.) the Vājas, give strength (to the mankind), come here towards the collection of the sacrificial praise of the singer, (come) with hundred long-lived intentioos, for Man, you who (know) thousand approaches, when the offering of the sacrifice is in question !

Notes—homan—the same meaning in VIII. 63.4. In spite of the Genitive complement it is probably a semi-infinitive.

IV 33

(Geldner Commentary p. 74)

(1) *Tr.* I send forward the speech, a messenger as it were to the Ṛbhus. I invoke the milch-cow Śvaitarī, (whose milk) is to be spread under (the site of the offerings). (I send the speech to the Ṛbhus), the (good) workers, who, moved by the wind, with their movements capable of surmounting (the obstacles), have always gone round the heaven in one day.

Notes—upastire after the *upastaraṇa* of the ritual; or figurative as in EVP IV p. 42. *taraṇibhir evaiḥ* cf. *taraṇitvā* I. 110.4 and 6 above.

(2) *Tr.* After these Ṛbhus had served the two parents with their attentive care, with their work, with their marvellous acts, it is then that they acquired the friendship of the gods. The Expert (workers), they brought an (element of) prosperity to the religious thought.

Notes—aram kṛ is either to 'serve (some one),' 'to satisfy by ones service,' or 'to arrange, to dispose'—double sense which is purely apparent, resulting from the difference of complement. *aramkṛt* is 'he who arranges' (used absolutely viz the sacrifice); but apparently 'he, who serves,' VIII. 1.10. *aramkṛti* is the service rendered (to a god, in fact, by the hymns)'—*aram bhū* 'to be at dis-position' *pariviṣṭi* distinguishes itself from *pariviṣṭa* in I. 116.20, (which is from *viś*) and even from X. 68.6 above. (which is, as here, from *viś* and is less restricted than post—Ṛgvedic '*pariviṣ*' to serve (at a table),' the meaning is however beginning to appear. X. 62.10. Here the use can be related to *viṣṭvī* I. 110.4 and *viṣṭī* I. 20.4 above.

(3) *Tr.* They, who made the two the parents young again (these) old (parents), who lay decrepit like (sacrificial) posts, they (i.e.) Vāja, Vibhvan, Ṛbhu (all) accompanying Indra, they who have the (beverage of) sweet (Soma) for their rejoicing, may they come to help our sacrifice.

Notes—maphupsaras after *devapsaras.*

(4) *Tr.* Because the Ṛbhus had watched over the cow the whole year, because the Ṛbhus had fashioned the fiesh the whole year, because they had carried away the dung of this (cow) for the whole year, due to (all) these efforts they obtained immortality.

Notes—saṁvatsam—hapax (identical with *saṁvastsaram* and *saṁvatsare* normal forms in the same context I. 110.1, I. 161.13).—cf. *trivatsā* (VS, etc) and the simple *vatsa* as noun for 'an animal of the year.' mās—Wackernagel III p. 250; also RV V. 29.8—bhāsas—Sieg ZII V p. 210.

(5) *Tr.* The eldest said, "I will make two cups." The younger said, "we will make three," The youngest said, "I will make four." O Ṛbhus, Tvaṣṭṛ propogated this speech of yours.

Notes—Note the variation karā : *kṛṇavāma.* Pāṇini-Sieg ZII V p. 204.

(6) *Tr.* The lords had spoken truth, for they did as (they had said); the Ṛbhus conformed to this disposition (which was) theirs. Tvaṣṭṛ wideopened his eyes when he saw the four cups shining like day-light.

Notes—anu-svadhām (also, *anu-ṣvadhām*)' according to this (their) own nature, analogous with I. 165.5 (a passage referred to by Geldner, which should be rendered as "you have been always faithful to your own nature" (Otherwise EVP X pp. 55, 115). On the root *'ven'* in this passage—Gonda Vision p. 360), (vague EVP IV p. 118). The idea is that of a look coloured with emotion.

(7) *Tr.* Ever since the Ṛbhus had enjoyed the hospitality of Agohya, sleeping (in his house) they saw (to it that) twelve days (every year) the tillable lands (were) beautiful. They directed the course of the rivers (for irrigation). Plants were in the dry soil, waters in the low place.

Notes—sukṣetrā kṛ, the type described above VII. 97.8—The root *nī* in Atmane means to direct beneficiently, as (figuratively) in I. 141.7. *dhanvan* often opposed to *kṣetra* (elsewhere ajra) and to āp (and sindhu). Sieg ZII V. p. 213.

(8) *Tr.* They, who have prepared the smoothly-going chariot remaining (at the disposition) of the warrior, they, who (have fashioned) the milch-cow *Viśvarupā*, that animates all, may these (gods), the Ṛbhus, fashion for us wealth, they, who are helping well, working well, skilled as far as the hands are concerned.

Notes—nareṣṭhā—the other compounds, in *sṭhā* have a locative final—e and the Dative is generally not used in the first member of a Vedic compound. It is nevertheless probable here at least as a substitute for *nari* (cf. dive for *divi*) and as a counter-part to ratheṣṭha. The warrior being rathesthā, the charict-will be naresthā ā—takṣ—I. 111.2 above.

(9) *Tr.* Because the gods had appreciated their work considering (it) with their spiritual power (and their) (well-pondered) thought, Vāja became the good worker of the gods, Ṛbhukṣan (that) of Indra, Vibhvan (that) of Varuṇa.

Notes—'kratvā manasā'—hendiadyn—Relation between Ṛbhukṣan and Indra I. 63.3 and so on.

(10) *Tr.* They, who (reciting) the hymns (and) intoxicating themselves (with Soma) fashioned for Indra, by means of their inventive wisdom, the two bay-horses, easy to be yoked, (being) like that. O Ṛbhus, (confer) upon us prosperity of wealth, of material goods. Contract (with us) a pact as (people), who desire peace.

Notes—'ukthā mad'—an expression pregnant with meaning. cf. IV. 49.1. dhatta-slight zeugma—*mitram dhā* almost a formula (mitra-dhita, *mitra-dhitī* and is specified by *kṣemaya* which is more precise here than in III. 7.2 or V. 47.4.

(11) *Tr.* At this (instant) of the day (the gods) have conferred upon you beverage and intoxication. The gods who (are) not (inclined) to friendship with (the human being), who gets tired during the rite. This (being) so, O Ṛbhus, confer upon us now gifts for this third pressing.

Notes—*idā* generally occurs with the Genitive *ahnaḥ*; *b*—we follow Lüders p. 427 who, rightly, separates *ṛte* (without) which has here as elsewhere Ablative. The difficulty is that śram ordinarily is said of a person, who labours (with a happy result). Neverless in a negative phrase one has for instance VIII. 4.7. "May we not tire in your friendship." (*sakhye*, as here *sukhyāya*). *dadhāta*: *dhatta* 10.

VI 34

(1) *Tr.* Ṛbhu, Vibhvan, Vāja, Indra, come towards this sacrifice of ours, for the gift of the treasures. For at this (instant) of the days the deity Dhiṣaṇā has conferred upon you the (right of) the beverage. Your intoxications have united themselves.

Notes—*Dhiṣaṇā* here as 'a Teacher' 'she who confers.'

(2) *Tr.* O Ṛbhus, you who know (your) origin, who have booty for treasures, intoxicate yourselves according to the ritual-times. Your intoxications have united themselves, Puraṁdhi is united. Set in motion for us the riches made up of select-men.

Notes—*vidānā* with Genitive as in X. 77.6, which is in favour of vid 'to know.' *vājaranta* identical with *vajavant* (epithet of the Ṛbhus) ratna is attracted by the stanzas 1, 4, 7, 8 and 11. *Puraṁdhi*—semi-personification EVP IX p. 83.

(3) *Tr.* O Ṛbhus, this sacrifice here has been prepared for you, (sacrifice) which you have received (as your lot), as Manu (has received it) from times immemorial. The appreciated (intoxications) have presented themselves here for you, and all of you, O Vājas, you have been the beneficiaries of the first share.

Notes—or does *jujuṣāṇaḥ* '(satisfied)' refer to the Ṛbhus, with *vaḥ* as expletive ?—*agriyā* could be an adverbial Instrumental. Other explanations—Geldner (Oldenberg).

(4) *Tr.* O lords, now here, at this (instant) (has come) the gift of treasures for the mortal worshipper, for him, who serves

you. Drink O Vājas, O Ṛbhus. The great third libation has been given to you for intoxication.

Notes—*dade* without preverb is passive, here and in IV. 37.3 (otherwise ā *dade* is non-passive).

(5) *Tr.* O Vājas, O Ṛbhukṣan, O lords (masters) of the great material good, being chanted (by us), come to us. At the fall of nights these beverages come to you just as (the cows) that have delivered newly come to the house.

Notes—*naro draviṇasaḥ* extension of *naro divaḥ* or supply *draviṇodaḥ* as in I. 15.7; I. 96.8. *abhipitve ahnām* cf. *prapitve ahnām* IV. 16.12. 'in the morning of the day.'

(6) *Tr.* O Sons of Vigour, being called by oral-homage, come towards this sacrifice—here. O Masters, being of one accord, you who confer treasures, accompained by Indra, drink of the sweet (Soma), (of this Soma), whose (masters) you are.

Notes—*yātana*—*yāta* stz. 5. One should presume a haplology *sūrayaḥ sūrayaḥ yasya* ca 'can be the mark of this strong' ellipsis.

(7) *Tr.* O Indra, of one mind with Varuṇa, drink the Soma, (Drink) of one mind with the Maruts, you who have pleasure in chants. (Drink) of one mind with (the Ṛbhus), who drink first, who drink at the ritual-times. (Drink) of one accord with (the divine) Wives, conferring the treasures.

Notes—*sajoṣasaḥ*—(plural as in stz. 6) or *sajoṣāḥ* (Sg) is almost always with the Instrumental, thus leading to the idea of 'in concert with' similarly '*sajuṣ gnāspatnī*—hapax formed on *gnāspati*— cf. Oldenberg.

(8) *Tr.* O Ṛbhus, intoxicate youselves, being of one accord with the Ādityas, being of one accord with the Mountains, of one accord with the divine Savitṛ, of one accord with the Rivers, that confer the treasures.

(9) *Tr.* The Ṛbhus, who (have helped) the Aśvins, who (have rejuvenated) the two parents, who by means of their helpful-act, have fashioned the milch-cow, the two horses, the two armours, the two Worlds separately, they, the lords—Vibhus who worked (so that men) have a good progeny.

Notes—abc., distinct verbs to be supplied, while admitting that *takṣ* can suffice for all in the cycle of the Ṛbhus. cf. Oldenberg. This is the only allusion in this hymn to the exploits of the Ṛbhus. *ṛdhaks* EVP IV. p. 82; here one could presume a double sense 'separately' and 'with success.' But the proper meaning is the image of the Worlds created in such a manner that the Heaven 'be seperated' from the Earth. *Vibhu* (*Vibhū*—here) a variant of *Vibhvan* in the plural; influenced the final of Vibhu. svapatyāni kṛ—style pregnant with meaning, cg. VII. 97.8 above.

(10) *Tr.* You, who confer riches in the form of the cows, in the form of booty, in the form of select—men, in the form of material—goods 'in the form of numerous cattle, O Ṛbhus (being like that, you)—who drink first, who intoxicate yourselves, confer (this wealth) on us and (on the patrons) who sing of (your) good deeds.

Notes—mandasānā—comparatively clear participle value; sometimes, as here, absolutely, sometimes with Instrumental or Locative regime. (The Instrumental confirms this value—VI. 17.5 and VI. 26.6). In this regard the words stand little apart in the series in (a)—sāna.

(11) *Tr.* O Ṛbhus, you have not remained aside. We have not left you thirsty, in this sacrifice (as people) excluded from the praise. Intoxicate yourselves with Indra, with the Maruts, with the kings, for the gift of the treasures, O Gods.

Notes—apa—bhū precised by IV. 35.1; which joins the next hymn with the present stanza—beginning. *aniḥśasta* : but niḥśasā is without the intention of doing evil' (TB *niśasā*

III. 7. 12. 4. 'refusal'—Dumont) modelled on *āśasā, abhiśasā*. ibid.

IV 35

stz. 7 to Indra

Caland—Henry p. 345

(1) *Tr.* O Sons of Vigour, O Sons of Sudhanvan, O Ṛbhus come hither, not stand aside. For in this libation has been placed the gift of treasures (emanating) from you. May your intoxications go towards Indra.

Notes—apa—bhūta—connected with 34, 11.

(2) *Tr.* See here has come the gift of treasures (emanating) from the Ṛbhus, the drinking of well-pressed Soma has taken place. Since with your skill in working, with your capacity to work, you acted (in such a manner) that the unique cup (was) di (vided) in four.

Notes—vi kṛ in this precise sense seems to occur only in this cycle.

(3) *Tr.* You acted (so that) the single cup be divided in four. You said, "O friend (Agni), get to work now" O Vājas, O defthanded (gods) Ṛbhus, then you went on the path of immortality, towards the group of gods.

Notes—akṛṇota—cakre 2 *d. vi* added to *śikṣ* seems to be due to *vy* (*akṛṇota*), which precedes, but there occurs a hapax *viśikṣu*, said of Agni in II. 1.10 near the mention of Ṛbhu) 'he who distributes.'?

(4) *Tr.* Out of what, indeed, (was) this cup made, which you have formed into four by (dividing it) by the effect of your poetic power ? Then press for yourselves the (Soma, destined) for the pressing in view of the intoxication. Drink O Ṛbhus, of the Somic sweet beverage.

Notes—kāvyena—value analogous with *śacyā* in stz. 5, viṣṭī in similar context, *sunudhvam* the middle voice of *su*—which is normally passive : *savanam* internal Accusative value—meaning pregnant, identical with '*sundudhvaṁ somaṁ sutam.*'

(5) *Tr.* O Ṛbhus, O (gods), you, who have booty for treasure, with your power you have rejuvenated the two parents. With your power you have fashioned the cup, which serves for the drink of the gods. With your power you have fashioned the two bay-horses, (these) coursers, mounted upon by Indra.

Notes—dhanutarau is not a comparative (cf. Oldenberg). The term attests a form *dhanoti* (*confirmed by dhanvati*) cf. *sanutṛ* (*sanutara*) *sanoti* and *tarutṛ* (cf. *tarute*). The morphological gap (suffix *tara*) is in relation with the aberrant character of the verbal base.

(6) *Tr.* O Vājas, he who, at the fall of night, presses for you, in order to intoxicate you, the strong (Soma of) the libation, O Ṛbhus, O male (gods), having intoxicated yourselves (with Soma), fashion for that (man) the wealth made up of select-men in total-number.

Notes—savanam su stz. 4. *sarvavīra* cf. IV. 50.10 above.

(7) *Tr.* O (Indra), you whose horses are bay-coloured, in the morning you have drunk the pressed (Soma) The libation of the midday belongs to you alone. Drink with the Ṛbhus, conferring the treasures, whom O Indra, you have made your friends, on account of their skill in work.

Notes—apibaḥ—saṁ pibasva the middle voice is limited to some examples with *sam.* Separately with *pra*—X. 114.7 and with *vi*—III. 53.10 (shade of reciprocity).

(8) *Tr.* You, who have become gods due to your skill in work, who have alighted in the heaven like eagles (in their nests), such as you are, O Sons of Strength, O Sons of Sudhanvan, confer the treasure. You have become immortal.

(9) *Tr.* The third (Soma of) the pressing, which you have made a gift of treasure for yourselves by means of your

skill in work, this (Soma), O (gods) with deft hands, O Ṛbhus, this Soma (has been) poured for you. Drink it together with the intoxications of Indra.

Notes—pariṣikta confirms that *savana* is identical with *Soma* (stz. 4) *indriya* means *indrasya* or *indreṇa*.

IV 36

(1) *Tr.* Born without a horse, without reins, the chariot with three wheels, worthy of the hymn, rolls around the space. Such is the great proclamation of your divine-character, O Rbhus, that you make the heaven and the earth prosper.

Notes—ab—cf. VI. 66.7 *cd—tad-yad* in correlation as in stz. 3.

(2) *Tr.* They, the prudent ones, who have fashioned the smoothly rolling chariot, which does not overturn (and that) by an intuition (proceeding from) the spirit, these (Ṛbhus), we (invite) them to drink this (Soma of) the libation. O Vājas, O Ṛbhus, we send (this invitation) to you.

Notes—dhiyā—hapax, similar in meaning to *dhīti* stz. 4; *pari*—intermediary between the usual shade 'starting with' and the abstract shade which one has in *dharmaṇaḥ pari.* ā *vedaya* slight zeugma between *c* and *d*. cf. stz. 7.

(3) *Tr.* O Vājas, O Ṛbhus, this grandeur of yours, happy to be proclaimed has (manifested) itself among the gods, O Vibhus, (consisting in this) that you make the two parents, although quite decrepit and worn out by age, young again (and capable of) walking.

Notes—ab perhaps better as "This has been the grandeur... (which distinguishes you), among the gods, (viz.) that you. In any case *supravācanam—mahitvanam* forms a variant of 1. C.

(4) *Tr.* The cup that was one you managed so that it be divided in four. From the hide (as the primary material) you have drawn out the cow by means of your intuitions.

Thus by your obliging nature you have obtained immortality among the gods. O Vājas, O Ṛbhus this (achievement) of yours (is) worthy of being praised.

(5) *Tr*. From the Ṛbhus, springs forth the wealth of foremost renown, that which the lords, known (under the name) of Vājas, have created, (wealth) fashioned by Vibhvan, worthy of being proclaimed in the repartitive ceremonies. O gods, he, whom you favour, he sur (passes) the masses.

Notes—d—vi carṣaṇi or 'he crosses over (the obstacles), goes beyond them.' In correlating *carṣaṇi* with *car*. see EVP IV p. 38.

(6) *Tr*. The man, whom Vāja, Vibhvan, the Ṛbhus have helped (is) a prize-winning horse. He (is) a prophet by eloquence. He (is) a heroic archer unsurmountable in battles. He receives a prosperity (made up of) riches. He (receives) abundance of select men.

(7) *Tr*. The most beautiful chiselled ornament (viz.) an admirable collection of praise has been placed upon you. O Vājas, O Ṛbhus, appreciate it. For you are expert poets, who are connoisseurs of inspired-speeches. It is with this Formula-of-energy that we send (this invitation to you, who are) like that.

Notes—piś eventually has *vācam* as its object VII. 103.6. *vedayāmasi*—cf. stz. 2 *d*—where the formula is more explicit. *veday* is 'to announce' in the Veda (and 'to know, to recognise' in the Classical skt the meaning 'to perceive, to experience' must be from the root *vid*, like *vedana* 'perception' specially 'a sorrowful perception).'

(8) *Tr*. You, who are the knowledgeable ones, (fashion) for us, (starting from) the primitive-structures, all enjoyments suitable to human beings, a dazzling booty, conferring a male vigour, the highest (prize) that (there can be). O Ṛbhus, fashion for us wealth and vital-force.

Notes—dhiṣaṇā in plural. cf. the rare passages quoted in EVP VII p. 50, Geldner V. 69.2. Here, are they the archetypes of the creation ? or simply 'at the beginning of the world?' as in 37.8—hereafter, by the pluralisation of the dual *dhiṣaṇe* ?

(9) *Tr.* By giving progeny here, wealth there, fashion for us a renown consisting of select-men, thanks to which we can distinguish our (selves) further than others. O Ṛbhus, this outstanding prize-of-victory, you have already given to us.

Notes—citay—more concrete in II.2.10 'to distinguish oneself, to be in the lime-light' is the usual meaning; (as a result EVP XII p. 42 *ad* II 2.5 to be modified); occasionally 'to signal, to describe' (EVP III p. 72), apart VII. 60.6. (where *citay* is apparently a denominative); in the participle he 'who distinguishes himself (eventually by applying his mind to something)' would suffice. (The only transitive use in I. 131.2)' 'that, which distinguishes (the god); 'being identical with.' He who deigns him a distinction (by means of sacrifices).' *dada*—perfect by way of prospective Aorist or rather a slip for *datta*.

IV 37

Generalisation in stz. 8 i.e. the final stanza

(1) *Tr.* O Vājas, O Rbhukśan, O Gods, come towards us by the paths which serve for the gods to move on, since you have always received the sacrifice from man in these tribes, in the happy moments of the days, O givers-of-joy.

Notes—Ṛbhukṣāh in plural as in stz 3 and so on in this hymn (so also 34.5 above), but under the more usual form in—*aṇaḥ* ? The singular is not at all impossible cf. 4 c below and avoids a morphological anamoly. *devayāna* EVP XIV p. 62. *dadhidhve* as in 34.3 above (a passage compared to by Geldner). *sudina* EVP III p. 65, generally occurs with a noun (in apposition or in objective case) for 'day.' The semantic dwindling is confirmed by the figurative use *viśvā sudinā*. cf. *sudināha* gramm-lex.

(2) *Tr.* May these sacrifices be to your heart (and convenient) to (your) thought. May they, covered in clarified butter, quite agreeable, come today. May the pressed (Somas), filled (in the cups), push you forward. May they, (once) drunk, excite you to spiritual-power (and) active thought.

Notes—harayanta—doubtful; modelled *on harṣayanta* which follows, *ahārṣam* : *harṣate* ? *harsayanta* with Dative as *harsasva dātave* VIII. 19. 29.

(3) *Tr.* Since (the pressing) at three times (has been) fixed by the gods for you and (since) the collection-of-praise has been destined for you O Vājas, O Rbhukṣans, I (thus) offer the Soma, in the nearby tribes, as Manu did long ago. (I offer it) for you (in company of the gods dwelling) at the height of the heaven.

Notes—upara opposed to the idea of distant past included in the suffix—*vat* (cf *manuṣvat*)—*bṛhaddiva* is epithet of *amṛta* II. 2.9; hence the absolute use here, as well as in IX. 79.1; eventually also in I. 167.2.

(4) *Tr.* For you have sturdy horses, brilliant chariots, visors of iron, beautlful ornaments (of gold), O (gods) you, O Sons of Indra, you, Sons of Vigour, the first fruits (of Soma) (prepared) for your intoxication have been assigned to you.

Notes—anu ceti meaning analogous with *anu—jñā*.

(5) *Tr.* O Rbhukṣans, Ṛbhu (who is) the wealth, (this god), the richest in booty for obtaining the prize, (this god), associated (with the other Ṛbhus), accompanied by Indra, we invoke him, he who always wins better (than any one else), he, who is rich in horses.

Notes—ṛbhum—abridged from '*Ṛbhutaḥ* (*rayiḥ*)' in 36.5 above ? In fact the word is at the confines of the appalative without ever entering in this category really. Suppose one excludes the appalative (adjective) one would be obliged to admit harsh juxtapositions as here. (Geldner felt it for X. 144.2 and X. 176.1) Look at once at 'We call Ṛbhu' and 'We call the (mighty) wealth.' *indrasvant*—hapax by the side of *indravant*, after the doublet *manuṣvat* (here stz. 3) and *Manuvat*.

(6) *Tr.* O Ṛbhus, the mortal whom you support, likewise whom Indra supports, may he be always winning specially in wisdom due to his poetic-intuitions, he, with his steed.

Notes—redundant *sed...sa. medhasāti* and *arvatā* are near each other VIII 40,2 passage, compared by Geldner. cf. also *arvatā—brahmaṇā* II. 2.10.—The two fundamental and often indiscernable competitions—the race of the horses and the oratory jousting.

(7) *Tr.* O Vājas, O Ṛbhukṣans, O Patrons, (once that you will have been) praised, find out for us the paths for the sacrifice, so (that we can) traverse all the regions (of the space).

Notes—vi ci 'to make a way by removing (the fallow—land)' EVP IV p. 21 *yaṣṭave asmabhyam*, same meaning as 'in order that we can sacrifice'—Not the syntax analogous with *yajadhyai d*—cf. Oldenberg.

(8) *Tr.* O Vājas, O Ṛbhukṣans, O Indra, O Nāsatyas, this wealth, (collect it) together for us from (all the human) establishments, (Lead) the horse, (which incarnates its essence). Give it generously in (the form of) conferring of gifts.

Notes—ā śasta is it 'immolate' (Geldner) ? cf. *āśāsana* and the arguments given by Geldner. In spite of the morphological difficulties and uncertainty of sense, we prefer to resort to ā—saṁs the sense 'to assign' (in fact there is semantic indecision between *saṁs* and *saś*).

VII 48

Velankar p. 115

(1) *Tr.* O Ṛbhukṣans, O Vājas, O liberal lords, let yourselves be intoxicated at our place in (the beverage) of the pressed (Soma). O Vibhus, may (our active–thoughts) like the active–thoughts of the travellers, turn your powerful chariot in this direction.

Notes–māday with Genitive like *mad* and so on, like (the partitive Genitive) with *pā* 'to drink'. *cd* or 'you and (your) chariot,' which seems preferable because of the Accusative *arvācaḥ*; however the beginning of the *pāda* has possibly been inspired from ā vo' rvācaḥ I. 168.1. The subject of *ā-vartayantu* in I. 71.3 is the horses. a subject, which could be restored here (*vaḥ*, then being an expletive).

(2) *Tr.* (Being just like the Ṛbhu with the Ṛbhus, like Vibhu with the Vibhus, may we prevail upon (the enemies), thanks to your force. May Vāja help us in order to win the booty. With Indra as the ally may we dominate the enemy.

Notes–ab–another translation–Geldner IV p. 260, who avoids the anomaly of the Nominative *vibhvaḥ*. Better perhaps to admit an anacoluthon. 'May Ṛbhu (help us) with the Ṛbhus—May we prevail–etc' Kuiper Lingua XI p. 225 proposes to analyse *vibhva—u—Hillebrandt*—Mythology II 2 p. 122.

(3) *Tr.* Indeed ! These (gods) prevail upon the multiple commands (of the enemies). They vanquish all the enemies when (the question of) superiority (is at stake). May Indra, Vibhvan, Ṛbhukṣan, Vāja, destroy, by the combat, the virile-force of the stranger, of the enemy.

Notes--a–so if one reads (*śāsāḥ*). Otherwise *pūrvīḥ* remains in the air becoming a type of feminine plural epithet, with some substantive dropped. Velankar adds '*māyāḥ.*' *ari*

(Thieme—Fremdling 'stranger' p. 53) must have necessarily the same sense in *b* and *c*. *uparatāti* (here and in I. 151.5) identical with *abhike* ? This meaning would maintain contact with *upara*, moreover EVP IV p. 80. *mithati*—same shade as the (feminine) participle *mithatī* VII. 93.5; cf VI 25.2 and 9.

(4) *Tr.* Well, make for us a large space. O gods, be all of you of one accord in order to help us. May the Vasus together be deigned to give us the ritual-enjoyment. As for you, protect us ever with your blessings.

प्रथमं मण्डलम्।

[द्वितीयोऽध्यायः ।।२।। व० १.३८] (२०)

८ मेधातिथिः काण्वः। ऋभवः। गायत्री।

अयं देवाय जन्मने स्तोमो विप्रेभिरासया। अकारि रत्नधातमः १
य इन्द्राय वचोयुजा ततक्षुर्मनसा हरी। शमीभिर्यज्ञमाशत २
तक्षन् नासत्याभ्यां परिज्मानं सुखं रथम्। तक्षन् धेनुं सबर्दुघाम् ३
युवाना पितरा पुनः सत्यमन्त्रा ऋजूयवः। ऋभवो विष्ट्यक्रत ४
सं वो मदासो अग्मतेन्द्रेण च मरुत्वता। आदित्येभिश्च राजभिः ५
उत त्यं चमसं नवं त्वष्टुर्देवस्य निष्कृतम्। अकर्त चतुरः पुनः ६
ते नो रत्नानि धत्तन त्रिरा साप्तानि सुन्वते। एकमेकं सुशस्तिभिः ७
अधारयन्त वह्नयो ऽभजन्त सुकृत्यया। भागं देवेषु यज्ञियम् ८

(११०)

६ कुत्स आङ्गिरसः। ऋभवः। जगती; ८, ६ त्रिष्टुप्।

ततं मे अपस्तदु तायते पुनः स्वादिष्ठा धीतिरुचथाय शस्यते।
अयं समुद्र इह विश्वदेव्यः स्वाहाकृतस्य समु तृप्णुत ऋभवः १
आभोगयं प्र यदिच्छन्त ऐतनापाकाः प्राञ्चो मम के चिदापयः।
सौधन्वनासश्चरितस्य भूमनागच्छत सवितुर्दाशुषो गृहम्। २
तत् सविता वोऽमृतत्वमासुवदगोह्यं यच्छ्रवयन्त ऐतन।
त्यं चिच्चमसमसुरस्य भक्षणमेकं सन्तमकृणुता चतुर्वयम् ३
विष्ट्वी शमी तरणित्वेन वाघतो मर्तासः सन्तो अमृतत्वमानशुः।
सौधन्वना ऋभवः सूरचक्षसः संवत्सरे समपृच्यन्त धीतिभिः ४
क्षेत्रमिव वि ममुस्तेजनेनँ एकं पात्रमृभवो जेहमानम्।
उपस्तुता उपमं नाधमाना अमर्त्येषु श्रव इच्छमानाः ५

आ मनीषामन्तरिक्षस्य नृभ्यः स्रुचेवं घृतं जुहवाम विद्मना।
तरणित्वा ये पितुरस्य सश्चिर ऋभवो वाजमरुहन् दिवो रजः ६
ऋभुर्न इन्द्रः शवसा नवीयानृभुर्वाजेभिर्वसुर्ददिः।
युष्माकं देवा अवसाहनि प्रियेऽभि तिष्ठेम पृत्सुतीरसुन्वताम् ७
निश्चर्मण ऋभवो गामपिंशत सं वत्सेनासृजता मातरं पुनः।
सौधन्वनासः स्वपस्यया नरो जिव्री युवाना पितराकृणोतन ८
वाजेभिर्नो वाजसातावविड्ढ्यृभुमाँ इन्द्र चित्रमा दर्षि राधः।
तन्नो मित्रो वरुणो मामहन्तामदितिः सिन्धुः पृथिवी उत द्यौः ९

(१११)

५ कुत्स आङ्गिरसः। ऋभवः। जगती, ५६ त्रिष्टुप्।

तक्षन् रथं सुवृतं विद्मनापसस्तक्षन् हरी इन्द्रवाहा वृषण्वसू।
तक्षन् पितृभ्यामृभवो युवद् वयस्तक्षन वत्साय मातरं सचाभुवम् १
आ नो यज्ञाय तक्षत ऋभुमद्वयः क्रत्वे दक्षाय सुप्रजावतीमिषम्।
यथा क्षयाम सर्ववीरया विशा तन्नः शर्धाय धासथा स्विन्द्रियम् २
आ तक्षत सातिमस्मभ्यमृभवः सातिं रथाय सातिमर्वते नरः।
सातिं नो जैत्रीं सं महेत विश्वहा जामिमजामिं पृतनासु सक्षणिम् ३
ऋभुक्षणमिन्द्रमा हुव ऊतय ऋभून् वाजान् मरुतः सोमपीतये।
उभा मित्रावरुणा नूनमश्विना ते नो हिन्वन्तु सातये धिये जिषे ४
ऋभुर्भराय सं शिशातु सातिं समर्यजिद्वाजो अस्माँ अविष्टु।
तन्नो मित्रो वरुणो मामहन्तामदितिः सिन्धुः पृथिवी उत द्यौः ५

१४ दीर्घतमा औचथ्यः। ऋभवः। जगती, १४ त्रिष्टुप्।

(१६१)

किमु श्रेष्ठः किं यविष्ठो न आजगन् किमीयते दूत्यं१ कद् यदूचिम।
न निन्दिम चमसं यो महाकुलोऽग्ने भ्रातर्द्रुण इद् भूतिमूदिम १

एकं चमसं चतुरः कृणोतन तद् वो देवा अब्रुवन् तद् व आगमम्।
सौधन्वना यद्येवा करिष्यथ साकं देवैर्यज्ञियांसो भविष्यथ २

अग्निं दूतं प्रति यदब्रवीतनाश्वः कर्त्वो रथ उतेह कर्त्वः।
धेनुः कर्त्वा युवशा कर्त्वा द्वा तानि भ्रातरनु वः कृत्व्येमसि ३

चकृवांस ऋभवस्तदपृच्छत क्वेदभूद् यः स्य दूतो न आजगन्।
यदावाख्यच्चमसाञ्चतुरः कृतानादित् त्वष्टा ग्नास्वन्तर्न्यानजे ४

हनामैनाँ इति त्वष्टा यदब्रवीच्चमसं ये देवपानमनिन्दिषुः।
अन्या नामानि कृण्वते सुते सचाँ अन्यैरेनान् कन्या३ नामभिः स्परत्। ५

इन्द्रो हरी युयुजे अश्विना रथं बृहस्पतिर्विश्वरूपामुपाजत।
ऋभुर्विभ्वा वाजो देवाँ अगच्छत स्वपसो यज्ञियं भागमैतन ६

निश्चर्मणो गामरिणीत धीतिभिर्या जरन्ता युवशा ताकृणोतन।
सौधन्वना अश्वादश्वमतक्षत युक्त्वा रथमुप देवाँ अयातन ७

इदमुदकं पिबतेत्यब्रवीतनेदं वा घा पिबता मुञ्जनेजनम्।
सौधन्वना यदि तन्नेव हर्यथ तृतीये घा सवने मादयाध्वै ८

आपो भूयिष्ठा इत्येको अब्रवीदग्निर्भूयिष्ठ इत्यन्यो अब्रवीत्।
वधर्यन्तीं बहुभ्यः प्रैको अब्रवीदृता वदन्तश्चमसाँ अपिंशत ९

श्रोणामेक उदकं गामवाजति मांसमेकः पिंशति सूनयाभृतम्।
आ निम्रुचः शकृदेको अपाभरत् किं स्वित् पुत्रेभ्यः पितरा उपावतुः १०

उद्वत्स्वस्मा अकृणोतना तृणं निवत्स्वपः स्वपस्ययो नरः।
अगोह्यस्य यदसस्तना गृहे तदद्येदमृभवो नानु गच्छथ ११

संमील्य यद् भुवना पर्यसर्पत क्व स्वित् तात्या पितरो व आसतुः।
अशपत यः करस्नं व आददे यः प्राब्रवीत् प्रो तस्मा अब्रवीतन १२

सुषुप्वांस ऋभवस्तदपृच्छतागोह्य क इदं नो अबूबुधत्।
स्श्वानं बस्तो बोधयितारमब्रवीत् संवत्सर इदमद्या व्यख्यत १३

दिवा यान्ति मरुतो भूम्याऽग्निरयं वातो अन्तरिक्षेण याति।
अद्भिर्याति वरुणः समुद्रैर्युष्माँ इच्छन्तः शवसो नपातः १४

तृतीयं मण्डलम्।

(६०)

७ गाथिनो विश्वामित्रः। ऋभवः, ५-७ इन्द्र ऋभवश्च। जगती

इहेह वो मनसा बन्धुता नर उशिजो जग्मुरभि तानि वेदसा।
याभिर्मायाभिः प्रतिजूतिवर्पसः सौधन्वना यज्ञियं भागमानश १
याभिः शचीभिश्चमसाँ अपिंशत यया धिया गामरिणीत चर्मणः।
येन हरी मनसा निरतक्षत तेन देवत्वमृभवः समानश २
इन्द्रस्य सख्यमृभवः समानशुर्मनोर्नपातो अपसो दधन्विरे।
सौधन्वनासो अमृतत्वमेरिरे विष्ट्वी शमीभिः सुकृतः सुकृत्यया ३
इन्द्रेण याथ सरथं सुते सचाँ अथो वशानां भवथा सह श्रिया।
न वः प्रतिमै सुकृतानि वाघतः सौधन्वना ऋभवो वीर्याणि च ४
इन्द्र ऋभुभिर्वाजवद्भिः समुक्षितं सुतं सोममा वृषस्वा गभस्त्योः।
धियेषितो मघवन् दाशुषो गृहे सौधन्वनेभिः सह मत्स्वा नृभिः ५

इन्द्र ऋभुमान् वाजवान् मत्स्वेह नो ऽस्मिन् त्सवने शच्या पुरुष्टुत।
इमानि तुभ्यं स्वसराणि येमिरे व्रता देवानां मनुषश्च धर्मभिः ६
इन्द्र ऋभुभिर्वाजिभिर्वाजयन्निह स्तोमं जरितुरुप याहि यज्ञियम्।
शतं केतेभिरिषिरेभिरायवे सहस्रणीथो अध्वरस्य होमनि ७

चतुर्थं मण्डलम्।

(३३)

११ वामदेवो गौतमः। ऋभवः। त्रिष्टुप्।

प्र ऋभुभ्यो दूतमिव वाचमिष्य उपस्तिरे श्वैतरीं धेनुमीळे।
ये वातजूतास्तरणिभिरेवैः परि द्यां सद्यो अपसो बभूवुः १
यदारमक्रन्नृभवः पितृभ्यां परिविष्टी वेषणा दंसनाभिः।
आदिद् देवानामुप सख्यमायन् धीरासः पुष्टिमवहन् मनायै २
पुनर्ये चक्रुः पितरा युवाना सना यूपेव जरणा शयाना।
ते वाजो विभ्वाँ ऋभुरिन्द्रवन्तो मधुप्सरसो नोऽवन्तु यज्ञम् ३
यत् संवत्समृभवो गामरक्षन् यत् संवत्समृभवो मा अपिंशन्।
यत् संवत्समभरन् भासो अस्यास्ताभिः शमीभिरमृतत्वमाशुः ४
ज्येष्ठ आह चमसा द्वा करेति कनीयान् त्रीन् कृणवामेत्याह।
कनिष्ठ आह चतुरस्करेति त्वष्ट ऋभवस्तत् पनयद् वचो वः ५
सत्यमूचुर्नर एवा हि चक्रुरनु स्वधामृभवो जग्मुरेताम्।
विभ्राजमानांश्चमसाँ अहेवाऽवेनत् त्वष्टा चतुरो ददृश्वान् ६
द्वादश द्यून् यदगोह्यस्या ऽऽतिथ्ये रणन्नृभवः ससन्तः।
सुक्षेत्राकृण्वन्ननयन्त सिन्धून् धन्वातिष्ठन्नोषधीर्निम्नमापः ७
रथं ये चक्रुः सुवृतं नरेष्ठां ये धेनुं विश्वजुवं विश्वरूपाम्।
त आ तक्षन्त्वृभवो रयिं नः स्ववसः स्वपसः सुहस्ताः ८

अपो ह्येषामजुषन्त देवा अभि क्रत्वा मनसा दीध्यानाः।
वाजो देवानामभवत् सुकर्मेन्द्रस्य ऋभुक्षा वरुणस्य विभ्वा ९
ये हरी मेधयोक्था मदन्त इन्द्राय चक्रुः सुयुजा ये अश्वा।
ते रायस्पोषं द्रविणान्यस्मे धत्त ऋभवः क्षेमयन्तो न मित्रम् १०
इदाह्नः पीतिमुत वो मदं धुर्न ऋते श्रान्तस्य सख्याय देवाः।
ते नूनमस्मे ऋभवो वसूनि तृतीये अस्मिन् त्सवने दधात ११

(३४)

११ वामदेवो गौतम;। ऋभवः। त्रिष्टुप्।

ऋभुर्विभ्वा वाज इन्द्रो नो अच्छेमं यज्ञं रत्नधेयोप यात।
इदा हि वो धिषणा देव्यह्नामधात् पीतिं सं मदा अग्मता वः १
विदानासो जन्मनो वाजरत्ना उत ऋतुभिर्ऋभवो मादयध्वम्।
सं वो मदा अग्मत सं पुरंधिः सुवीरामस्मे रयिमेरयध्वम् २
अयं वो यज्ञ ऋभवोऽकारि यमा मनुष्वत् प्रदिवो दधिध्वे।
प्र वोऽच्छा जुजुषाणासो अस्थुरभूत विश्वे अग्रियोत वाजाः ३
अभूदु वो विधते रत्नधेयमिदा नरो दाशुषे मर्त्याय।
पिबत वाजा ऋभवो ददे वो महि तृतीयं सवनं मदाय ४
आ वाजा यातोप न ऋभुक्षा महो नरो द्रविणसो गृणानाः।
आ वः पीतयोऽभिपित्वे अह्नामिमा अस्तं नवस्व इव ग्मन् ५
आ नपातः शवसो यातनोपेमं यज्ञं नमसा हूयमानाः।
सजोषसः सूरयो यस्य च स्थ मध्वः पात रत्नधा इन्द्रवन्तः ६
सजोषा इन्द्र वरुणेन सोमं सजोषाः पाहि गिर्वणो मरुद्भिः।
अग्रेपाभिर्ऋतुपाभिः सजोषा ग्नास्पत्नीभी रत्नधाभिः सजोषाः ७
सजोषस आदित्यैर्मादयध्वं सजोषस ऋभवः पर्वतेभिः।
सजोषसो दैव्येना सवित्रा सजोषसः सिन्धुभी रत्नधेभिः ८

ये अश्विना ये पितरा य ऊती धेनुं ततक्षुर्ऋभवो ये अश्वा ।
ये अंसत्रा य ऋधग्रोदसी ये विभ्वो नरः स्वपत्यानि चक्रुः ९
ये गोमन्तं वाजवन्तं सुवीरं रयिं धत्थ वसुमन्तं पुरुक्षुम् ।
ते अग्रेपा ऋभवो मन्दसाना अस्मे धत्त ये च रातिं गृणन्ति १०
नापाभूत न वोऽतीतृषामाऽनिःशस्ता ऋभवो यज्ञे अस्मिन् ।
समिन्द्रेण मदथ सं मरुद्भिः सं राजभी रत्नधेयाय देवाः ११

(३५)

९ वामदेवो गौतमः । ऋभवः । त्रिष्टुप् ।

इहोप यात शवसो नपातः सौधन्वना ऋभवो माप भूत ।
अस्मिन् हि वः सवने रत्नधेयं गमन्त्विन्द्रमनु वो मदासः १
आगन्नृभूणामिह रत्नधेयमभूत् सोमस्य सुषुतस्य पीतिः ।
सुकृत्यया यत् स्वपस्यया चँ एकं विचक्र चमसं चतुर्धा २
व्यकृणोत चमसं चतुर्धा सखे वि शिक्षेत्यब्रवीत ।
अथैत वाजा अमृतस्य पन्थां गणं देवानामृभवः सुहस्ताः ३
किंमयः स्विच्चमस एष आस यं काव्येन चतुरो विचक्र ।
अथा सुनुध्वं सवनं मदाय पात ऋभवो मधुनः सोम्यस्य ४
शच्याकर्त पितरा युवाना शच्याकर्त चमसं देवपानम् ।
शच्या हरी धनुतरावतष्टेन्द्रवाहावृभवो वाजरत्नाः ५
यो वः सुनोत्यभिपित्वे अह्नां तीव्रं वाजासः सवनं मदाय ।
तस्मै रयिमृभवः सर्ववीरमा तक्षत वृषणो मन्दसानाः ६
प्रातः सुतमपिबो हर्यश्व माध्यंदिनं सवनं केवलं ते ।
समृभुभिः पिबस्व रत्नधेभिः सखीर्याँ इन्द्र चकृषे सुकृत्या ७
ये देवासो अभवता सुकृत्या श्येना इवेदधि दिवि निषेद ।
ते रत्नं धात शवसो नपातः सौधन्वना अभवतामृतासः ८
यत् तृतीयं सवनं रत्नधेयमकृणुध्वं स्वपस्या सुहस्ताः ।
तदृभवः परिषिक्तं व एतत् सं मदेभिरिन्द्रियेभिः पिबध्वम् ९

(३६)

९ वामदेवो गौतमः। ऋभवः। जगती, ९ त्रिष्टुप्।

अनश्वो जातो अनभीशुरुक्थ्योऽ रथस्त्रिचक्रः परि वर्तते रजः।
महत् तद् वो देव्यस्य प्रवाचनं द्यामृभवः पृथिवीं यच्च पुष्यथ १
रथं ये चक्रुः सुवृतं सुचेतसोऽविह्वरन्तं मनसस्परि ध्यया।
ताँ ऊ न्वस्य सवनस्य पीतय आ वो वाजा ऋभवो वेदयामसि २
तद् वो वाजा ऋभवः सुप्रवाचनं देवेषु विभ्वो अभवन्महित्वनम्।
जिव्री यत् सन्ता पितरा सनाजुरा पुनर्युवाना चरथाय तक्षथ ३
एकं वि चक्र चमसं चतुर्वयं निश्चर्मणो गामरिणीत धीतिभिः।
अथा देवेष्वमृतत्वमानश श्रुष्टी वाजा ऋभवस्तद् व उक्थ्यम् ४
ऋभुतो रयिः प्रथमश्रवस्तमो वाजश्रुतासो यमजीजनन् नरः।
विभ्वतष्टो विदथेषु प्रवाच्यो यं देवासोऽवथा स विचर्षणिः ५
स वाज्यर्वा स ऋषिर्वचस्यया स शूरो अस्ता पृतनासु दुष्टरः।
स रायस्पोषं स सुवीर्यं दधे यं वाजो विभ्वाँ ऋभवो यमाविषुः ६
श्रेष्ठं वः पेशो अधि धायि दर्शतं स्तोमो वाजा ऋभवस्तं जुजुष्टन।
धीरासो हि ष्ठा कवयो विपश्चितस्तान् व एना ब्रह्मणा वेदयामसि ७
यूयमस्मभ्यं धिषणाभ्यस्परि विद्वांसो विश्वा नर्याणि भोजना।
द्युमन्तं वाजं वृषशुष्ममुत्तममा नो रयिमृभवस्तक्षता वयः ८
इह प्रजामिह रयिं रराणा इह श्रवो वीरवत् तक्षता नः।
येन वयं चितयेमात्यन्यान् तं वाजं चित्रमृभवो ददा नः ९

(३७)

८ वामदेवो गौतमः। ऋभवः। त्रिष्टुप्, ५-८ अनुष्टुप्।

उप नो वाजा अध्वरमृभुक्षा देवा यात पथिभिर्देवयानैः।
यथा यज्ञं मनुषो विक्ष्वाऽसु दधिध्वे रण्वाः सुदिनेष्वह्नाम् १

ते वो हृदे मनसे सन्तु यज्ञा जुष्टासो अद्य घृतनिर्णिजो गुः।
प्र वः सुतासो हरयन्त पूर्णाः क्रत्वे दक्षाय हर्षयन्त पीताः २
त्र्युदायं देवहितं यथा वः स्तोमो वाजा ऋभुक्षणो ददे वः।
जुह्वे मनुष्वदुपरासु विक्षु युष्मे सचा बृहद्दिवेषु सोमम् ३
पीवोअश्वाः शुचद्रथा हि भूताऽयःशिप्रा वाजिनः सुनिष्काः।
इन्द्रस्य सूनो शवसो नपातो ऽनु वश्चेत्यग्रियं मदाय ४
ऋभुमृभुक्षणो रयिं वाजे वाजिन्तमं युजम्।
इन्द्रस्वन्तं हवामहे सदासातममश्विनम् ५
सेदृभवो यमवेथ यूयमिन्द्रश्च मर्त्यम्।
स धीभिरस्तु सनिता मेधसाता सो अर्वता ६
वि नो वाजा ऋभुक्षणः पथश्चितन यष्टवे।
अस्मभ्यं सूरयः स्तुता विश्वा आशास्तरीषणि ७
तं नो वाजा ऋभुक्षण इन्द्र नासत्या रयिम्।
समश्वं चर्षणिभ्य आ पुरु शस्त मघत्तये ८

सप्तमं मण्डलम्।

(४७)

४ मैत्रावरुणिर्वसिष्ठः। ऋभवः, ४ विश्वे देवा वा। त्रिष्टुप्।

ऋभुक्षणो वाजा मादयध्वमस्मे नरो मघवानः सुतस्य।
आ वोऽर्वाचः क्रतवो न यातां विभ्वो रथं नर्यं वर्तयन्तु १
ऋभुर्ऋभुभिरभि वः स्याम विभ्वो विभुभिः शवसा शवांसि।
वाजो अस्माँ अवतु वाजसाताविन्द्रेण युजा तरुषेम वृत्रम् २
ते चिद्धि पूर्वीरभि सन्ति शासा विश्वाँ अर्य उपरताति वन्वन्।
इन्द्रो विभ्वाँ ऋभुक्षा वाजो अर्यः शत्रोर्मिथत्या कृणवन् वि नृम्णम् ३
नू देवासो वरिवः कर्तना नो भूत नो विश्वेऽवसे सजोषाः।
समस्मे इषं वसवो ददीरन् यूयं पात स्वस्तिभिः सदा नः ४